PENGUIN

HISILA

HISILA YAMI is a Nepali politician and an architect. Born into a well-known Newar family in Kathmandu in 1959, she started her revolutionary life as a student activist in 1978. During the 1990 uprising against the Panchayat regime in Nepal, Yami was one of the most prominent women leaders. She has been arrested many times for her anti-monarchy stance. She graduated from the School of Planning and Architecture in New Delhi, India, in 1982 and completed her master's from Newcastle University, UK, in 1995. The same year, she became the president of the All Nepal Women's Association (Revolutionary). She also taught at the Institute of Engineering in Pulchowk, Kathmandu, for thirteen years.

Yami went underground in 1996 during the People's War (PW) in Nepal. She went on to become a politburo member of the CPN (Maoist), headed the Women's Department, was a member of the International Department and the secretary of the People's Power Consolidation Department in Rolpa during the PW.

In April 2007, she joined the interim government of Nepal as the minister of physical planning and works. She won the Constituent Assembly elections in March 2008 from Kathmandu's Constituency 7 and took over as the minister of tourism and civil aviation in April 2008 and the minister of land reform and management in August 2011.

She is married to a fellow architect and politician, Baburam Bhattarai, who went on to become the prime minister of Nepal (from August 2011 to March 2013). In 2015, Yami, Bhattarai and some other leaders abandoned the CPN (Maoist) to start the Naya Shakti Party, which later evolved into the Janata Samajwadi Party, Nepal.

Yami is a regular contributor to several publications in Nepal. She is also the author of *People's War and Women's Liberation in Nepal*.

ADVANCE PRAISE FOR THE BOOK

'A bold woman from an ethnic minority reflects on half a century of experiences. Yami's journey from an urban, apolitical upbringing to one at the forefront of Nepal's revolutionary politics, and at the centre of a rebellion whose violence claimed the lives of 17,000 Nepalis—a moment that decisively changed the course of politics, including the overthrowing the monarchy—is candid and rare'—Mallika Shakya, senior assistant professor, department of sociology, South Asian University

'Hisila's story is an absorbing narrative of a strong-willed woman breaking glass ceilings in not only a feudal, traditional Nepali society but also in the radical, communist organization of the Maoists in Nepal. The narrative is sprinkled with fascinating insights into the rise and transformation of the Maoists in the country—into their leadership characters, power and ideological struggles and their performance in democratic governance. A must-read for analysts, policymakers and discerning observers'—S.D. Muni, professor emeritus, School of International Studies, Jawaharlal Nehru University

'Combining the personal and political with remarkable candour and deep insights, Hisila Yami brings alive the story of Nepal's Maoist movement and its subsequent transformation into open politics. She weaves together the ethnic, class, caste, gender and regional dimensions of Nepal's underdevelopment to illustrate a society that was ready for change but also had to navigate older, entrenched structures of power. As an insider who participated in the movement, yet an outsider who came from a distinct background, Hisila Yami's life and book is both the story of political principles and its collusion with empirical realities. As a revolutionary leader and then a former minister in her own right, whose husband was a senior party figure who later became the prime minister, she is uniquely positioned to tell Nepal's story of war and peace. This is a must-read for all those interested in the fate of not just Nepal and South Asia but also the themes of oppression, political movements, power, gender, post-conflict transitions, politics of violence and inclusive democracy'—Prashant Jha, editor (views), *Hindustan Times*, and author of *Battles of the New Republic: A Contemporary History of Nepal* and *How the BJP Wins: Inside India's Greatest Election Machine*

'I have known Hisila Yami since the late-1980s, when she was multitasking as a teacher of architecture, an honorary official of the Nepal Engineers' Association, an energetic women's rights activist and an erudite canvasser of progressive politics. By the late-1990s, she had accepted a somewhat less prominent role than her Maoist ideologue partner, Baburam Bhattarai. The travails of a playful girl, from being a trendy college-goer in New Delhi, a dedicated rights activist in western Nepal and a fugitive insurgent to becoming the first lady at Baluwatar, make for an engaging read'—C.K. Lal, journalist and commentator

'This is an interesting and important autobiography, particularly because of the many roles the author has played and reflected upon—not only as a Maoist activist, minister and the wife of a prime minister but also as the youngest daughter of an elite Newar family, a feminist and a mother. The book deserves to be read by anyone with an interest in contemporary Nepal or in revolutionary movements'—John Whelpton, historian and the author of *A History of Nepal*

'Hisila Yami has played a critical role in shaping Nepali history for over four decades. This book offers a compelling personal account of her struggles and illuminates aspects of events and personalities that have so far escaped observers on the outside'—Aditya Adhikari, author of *The Bullet and the Ballot Box: The Story of Nepal's Maoist Revolution*

HISILA

FROM REVOLUTIONARY TO FIRST LADY

HISILA YAMI

PENGUIN BOOKS

An imprint of Penguin Random House

PENGUIN BOOKS

USA | Canada | UK | Ireland | Australia
New Zealand | India | South Africa | China

Penguin Books is part of the Penguin Random House group of companies
whose addresses can be found at global.penguinrandomhouse.com

Published by Penguin Random House India Pvt. Ltd
4th Floor, Capital Tower 1, MG Road,
Gurugram 122 002, Haryana, India

Penguin
Random House
India

First published in Penguin Books by Penguin Random House India 2021

10 9 8 7 6 5 4 3 2

The views and opinions expressed in this book are the author's own and the facts
are as reported by her which have been verified to the extent possible, and
the publishers are not in any way liable for the same.

ISBN 9780143427896

Typeset in Adobe Caslon Pro by Manipal Technologies Limited, Manipal
Printed at Replika Press Pvt. Ltd, India

www.penguin.co.in

MIX
Paper from
responsible sources
FSC® C016779

Contents

Preface   xi
List of Abbreviations   xvii

PART I: THE BEGINNING

1. 'Why Have an Aim in Life?'
   prelude to politicization   3
2. Black Flag, Dharnas, Toy Pistol Revolt
   first political steps   11
3. 'Why Do You Come Here?'
   falling in love   20
4. Victim of Underdevelopment
   motherhood and activism   29
5. People's Movement against the Panchayat Regime
   jail tales   37
6. Bout of Depression in the UK
   victim of my own study   46
7. 'Sorry, We Will Have to Leave This House!'
   from ballot to bullet   52

PART II: THE PEOPLE'S WAR

8. From Free Bird to Fugitive
    becoming a whole-timer   63
9. Relationships between Leaders
    diverse personalities   70
10. Centralization of Leadership
    my first experience of inner party struggle   77
11. 'I Will Fight with a Fuse Attached to My Heart'
    shift in inner party struggle   83
12. Development of Democracy in the Twenty-First Century
    a strategic leap   90
13. Solidarity, Sabotage and the South Block
    our relationship with India   96
14. 'Workers of All Countries, Unite!'
    international relations   103
15. Tears in Phuntiwang
    pain from one's own   109
16. Red Flag over Rolpa
    the making of a new world   115
17. Liberation or Death?
    gender issues   121
18. Love, Marriage and Children
    the morality question   131
19. Rape, Rebellion and Resistance
    tempering the steel   138
20. 'Are You a Newar or a Nepali?'
    the nationality question   143
21. The Oppressed of the Oppressed
    the Dalit question   152
22. A Twenty-First-Century Political Sati
    emergence of a stronger me   159
23. When I Saw the Siberian Birds
    triumph of republican agenda   170

24. *Dhai-Futte* Sena
    PLA narratives   178
25. Drums, Pen and Rifle
    the cultural front   188

Part III: A NEW BEGINNING

26. Maoists in Kathmandu
    wooing the middle class   197
27. How Monarchy Was Abolished Inch-by-Inch
    birth of a republic   205
28. Bungee-Jumping My Way to a Republican State
    being a minister   214
29. Fall of Prachanda
    taste of power   224
30. From Herder to Prime Minister
    at the helm of state affairs   233
31. The Cost of Being First Lady
    losing my identity   242
32. The Cost of Being a Middle-of-the-Roader
    electoral defeat   251
33. Prachanda and BRB
    two sides of a river   259
34. My Relationship with Prachanda
    innocence vs conspiracy   269
35. My Relationship with BRB
    complementary and contradictory   276
36. Manushi, Asmita and Astha
    bringing up a daughter   284
37. Army Integration and State Restructuring
    catch-22   293
38. Some Reflections
    will the oppressed rise?   303

Epilogue: New Beginning   311
Acknowledgements   317
Notes   319

Preface

On the afternoon of 25 April 2015, a massive earthquake measuring 7.8 on the Richter scale struck Nepal. Another earthquake of 7.3 magnitude occurred a fortnight later, on 12 May, around the same time. It razed to the ground my late father Dharma Ratna Yami's five-storeyed house in Bhurankhel, Kathmandu, where I was born. It was by no means an ordinary house. It was where great personalities such as B.R. Ambedkar[1] and Rahul Sankrityayan had visited my father who was an anti-Rana crusader, a poet, a social reformer, a writer and a deputy minister of forest (1951).

Looking at my late father's crumbling house and going through his old manuscripts, most of which were destroyed in the earthquake, I remembered the fate of the draft of my own book. One that I had been writing since December 2014. I did not want to take any chances, so I hurriedly emailed the first draft to my daughter, Manushi. At that time, she was studying in Jawaharlal Nehru University (JNU) in Delhi, India.

Writing this book was a journey in itself. Through this book I will tell the story of the Maoist People's War (PW) in Nepal, as the country transformed its feudal socio-economic structure to a capitalist one through a rich history of struggle. This narrative is one in which two accounts are intertwined, both public and personal, and the political and social.

I decided to write this book when I realized that I could share personal insights into the Maoist PW, which others did not have access to. I have also had the privilege of watching from close quarters the evolution of the strategy and the tactics of the PW, and the relations among the top leaders of the revolutionary movement. What compelled me further to write was the sudden demise of Comrade Diwakar (Post Bahadur Bogati), the general secretary of the Unified Communist Party of Nepal (Maoist)—UCPN (Maoist)—in 2014.[2] He was only sixty-two. By all standards, he looked quite healthy and fit, but he died of a cerebral stroke. I learnt from his wife that he had started collecting material for writing his memoir, and that was when the urgency of writing mine hit home. Baburam Bhattarai (BRB), a senior ideologue leader of the UCPN (Maoist), who also happens to be my husband, is now past sixty-six. And I am past sixty-one myself. I thought that I should not leave anything to chance. I apprehended that BRB, who is by nature an introvert, would probably never write an autobiography. He has been a significant part of more than forty years of my political journey.

Nepal, a small landlocked nation (1,47,181 square kilometres) and the oldest independent country with no history of colonial subjugation in the whole of South Asia, enjoys a strategic location between the two most populous and economically fast-growing Asian countries, India and China. Nepal has roughly 30 million people belonging to more than 100 castes and ethnic groups.[3] It is also one of the poorest countries in the world with an annual per capita income of about $1000, which works out to less than $3 per person per day.[4] This is also a country where the remittance inflow from Nepali migrant workers in foreign lands comprises more than half the annual budget.[5]

This book is about the complex and fruitful history of the communist movement in Nepal. Unlike the Jhapa rebellion, which took place in Jhapa district (adjoining India's Naxalbari) in eastern Nepal in 1971–75, as a follow-up to the Naxalite movement in India, the Maoist PW was not an outgrowth of any other movement within Asia.[6] The hallmark of the PW was that it spread throughout Nepal within a short period (1996–2006). Except Manang and Mustang districts, which lie in the trans-Himalayan region, the remaining seventy-three districts were in the grip of the PW.[7] At the peak of the war, the Maoist movement had everything: a 'base area', a strong and growing party, the People's Liberation Army (PLA), the United Revolutionary People's Council (URPC), fighting militia, production militia, small but growing industries, schools—almost everything except aeroplanes and helicopters! It was an all-out war challenging the Royal Nepalese Army (RNA), the judiciary and the royal government of Nepal. It was not a war for capturing resources but a war against vertical and horizontal inequality; it was a war seeking social justice, inclusive democracy and development.

During the PW, 16,719 people were killed on both sides, while 1327 disappeared and an estimated 50,000 were displaced.[8] It is estimated that more than two-thirds of those who were killed and disappeared belonged to the Maoist side. It would not be an exaggeration if one were to place the PW as the second most significant event in the history of the country after the unification of Nepal under King Prithvi Narayan Shah in the mid-eighteenth century. Internationally, too, Nepal's experience of war and peace has a special character. Unlike Russia and China, where the communist parties that launched revolutions gained absolute power after the fall of the old regime; and unlike Peru and Malaysia, where the communist parties lost to the ruling regime, in Nepal the revolution resulted in the Comprehensive Peace Agreement (CPA)[9] that sought to abolish the monarchy and draft a new Constitution through the Constituent Assembly (CA).

This is also a story of a unique, vibrant political party, which first used the ballot box to expose the futility of the monarchical parliamentary system. Then it took up arms to abolish the monarchy once and for all and negotiate peace. Thereafter, it returned to using the ballot box to institutionalize the gains made during the PW. It is the story of how class struggle has been intertwined with the fight against oppression based on gender, caste, regionalism and ethnicity.

It deals with personal struggle, inner-party struggle and class struggle. It also tells the story of my battle against oppression based on gender and ethnicity. It highlights struggle at both the national and international levels to arrive at a dynamic and creative application of Marxism.

Usually communist parties—particularly traditional communist parties—tend to discourage a personal account of history. However, I have decided to offer my personal experience of the various movements in which I was involved, backed by objective facts. I strongly feel that there should be space for a personal account in an objective world view, if it is to be holistic. After all, I was an architect by profession before I became a full-time party worker, and thus I have tried to maintain the correct proportion of content and form, and public and private life, in this book.

This book is also an account of my personal experience before, during and after the PW. It is an account of more than forty years of active life: initial experiences of being a part of the peaceful period of people's movements (1977–96), followed by ten years of the armed PW (1996–2006)[10] and, thereafter, the post-PW period (2006 onwards).

When I think back on my life, I realize that my urban upbringing in Kathmandu, my relatively upper-middle-class background, foreign education, oppressed gender, suppressed linguistic-ethnic and minority-religion background (I belong to the Buddhist Newar community) had made me feel alienated at some points and elated at others. BRB and I had a love marriage. He is a Hindu by religion and a hill Brahmin by caste. He was born into a middle-class peasant family in the Gorkha district. I hailed from Kathmandu Valley—once the centre of civilization in Nepal but later conquered by the rulers of Gorkha. Our marriage transformed both of us and made us more holistic as individuals.

I am particularly proud to have been a participant in a crucial juncture in Nepali history: the period that saw the end of the monarchy, which reigned for 240 years, and the dawn of a new federal democratic republic. Having been involved in the party's policymaking, and being the wife of its senior leader, I am aware of the risks of revealing inside perspectives on the dynamism of the inner struggles during and after the PW. It is a risk I have always been prepared to take.

The book deals with what it means to be a woman (in a feudal society), a mother (to a daughter), a wife (to a senior leader), a first lady (to a prime minister) and a leader in my own right (a politburo member). It is about being a victim of the political fallout within the party during the PW on the one hand, and being a minister during the post-PW period on the other. This is also an account of my personal journey from being a carefree apolitical woman to a committed Marxist politician/ revolutionary.

While writing this book, I considered myself doubly lucky because we, BRB and I, escaped unhurt in the earthquakes that rocked Nepal in 2015. When the first tremor was felt, we were in Gorkha, the epicentre of the earthquake.

At the time of the second quake, which was equally devastating, we were in Kathmandu.

It was the worst natural disaster to strike Nepal since the 1934 Nepal–Bihar earthquake.[11]

Politically, the two big shocks and the smaller aftershocks unwittingly resulted in breaking the impasse that had been holding back the promulgation of the Constitution through the CA after the peace process began in 2006. Amongst several other issues, the question of state restructuring had prevented the parties from arriving at an understanding for a long period. The two earthquakes created a psychological pressure on the major political parties to come to an agreement. It was as if an old clock, after having fallen to the ground, had started ticking again. But the journey from the PW to the peace process was more complex than I thought.

In June 2015, a sixteen-point agreement was signed between four major parties to arrive at a common understanding for finalizing the Constitution through the CA.[12] However, this triggered further dissatisfaction amongst the oppressed communities of the southern Terai region—the Madhesis,[13] Tharus and indigenous nationalities—who were not happy with the proposed federal structure.[14]

As I was writing this book, many important political events were taking place. The making of the Constitution and the opposition to the glaring lacunae in it kept us on our toes. Many a time I found myself an actor alongside others, going out in the streets to demonstrate, taking delegations to different legislative committees and party offices. Within the CA, BRB, as the chairperson of the Constitutional Political Dialogue and Consensus Committee (CPDCC), was fighting hard to make the Constitution more inclusive and secular. And within the party, we found ourselves struggling against tendencies to compromise on some of our core agendas.

In the end, this book also analyses how the Maoist movement, after having come to power, slowly disintegrated as it was unable to cope with the demands of the new phase of historical development—both political and economic. As a consequence, immediately after the promulgation of the Constitution on 20 September 2015,[15] we left the Maoist party. Later, we formed the Naya Shakti Party, Nepal,[16] which ultimately transformed into the People's Socialist Party, Nepal.

List of Abbreviations

ABNES	Akhil Bharat Nepali Ekta Samaj
AINSA	All India Nepalese Students' Association
AIPRF	All India People's Resistance Forum
AIPRM	All India People's Resistance Movement
ANWA (R)	All Nepal Women's Association (Revolutionary)
APF	Armed Police Force
BIPPA	Bilateral Investment Promotion and Protection Agreement
BRB	Baburam Bhattarai
BS	Bikram Sambat
CA	Constituent Assembly
CC	Central Committee
CCM	Central Committee Member
CCOMPOSA	Coordination Committee of Maoist Parties and Organizations of South Asia
CPA	Comprehensive Peace Agreement
CPDCC	Constitutional Political Dialogue and Consensus Committee

CPI (Maoist)	Communist Party of India (Maoist)
CPI (ML) PW	Communist Party of India (Marxist–Leninist) People's War
CPN (Bidrohi Masal)	Communist Party of Nepal (Bidrohi Masal)
CPN (Maoist)	Communist Party of Nepal (Maoist)
CPN (Masal)	Communist Party of Nepal (Masal)
CPN (Mashal)	Communist Party of Nepal (Mashal)
CPN (ML)	Communist Party of Nepal (Marxist–Leninist)
CPN (UML)	Communist Party of Nepal (Unified Marxist -Leninist)
CPN (Unity Centre)	Communist Party of Nepal (Unity Centre)
DSP	Deputy Superintendent of Police
DU	Delhi University
FPTP	First-Past-The-Post
HQ	Headquarters
IIT	Indian Institute of Technology
IGP	Inspector General of Police
IoE	Institute of Engineering
JNU	Jawaharlal Nehru University
LSR	Lady Shri Ram
LTTE	Liberation Tigers of Tamil Eelam
MCC	Maoist Communist Centre
MISA	Maintenance of Internal Security Act
CWD	Centre for Women and Development
HURON	Human Rights Organization of Nepal
MLM	Marxism–Leninism–Maoism

MNLF	Magar National Liberation Front
MPRF	Madhesi People's Right Forum
NA	Nepali Army
NC	Nepali Congress
NRN	Non-Resident Nepalese
NS	Naya Shakti
NSA	Nepalese Students' Association
OB	Overseas Bureau
PBM	Politburo Member
PCP	Peruvian Communist Party
PLA	People's Liberation Army
PM	Prime Minister
PMO	Prime Minister's Office
PR	Proportional Representation
PW	People's War
RIM	Revolutionary International Movement
RNA	Royal Nepalese Army
SJMN	Samyukta Jana Morcha Nepal
SLC	School-Leaving Certificate
SPA	School of Planning and Architecture
SPA	Seven-Party Alliance
STF	Special Task Force
TRC	Truth and Reconciliation Commission
TU	Tribhuvan University
UCPN (Maoist)	Unified Communist Party of Nepal (Maoist)
ULF	United Left Front
UML	Unified Marxist–Leninist

UNMIN   United Nations Mission in Nepal
UNPM   United National People's Movement
URPC   United Revolutionary People's Council
WPRM   World People's Resistance Movement

PART I

The Beginning

1

'Why Have an Aim in Life?'

prelude to politicization

I was eighteen years old when my future husband, BRB, asked me this question: 'What is your aim in life?' I had just finished a game of tennis and was standing in front of the tennis court at New Delhi's School of Planning and Architecture (SPA) hostel. BRB, then twenty-three, had come to SPA for a master's degree in architecture. He had completed a BArch (bachelor of architecture) degree from Chandigarh. I was then a second-year student of BArch at SPA. Apart from studies, I was enjoying several other pursuits: I was learning classical music at Mandi House, the centre of art and culture in Delhi, and transcendental meditation in Defence Colony. I remember having replied spontaneously: 'Why have an aim in life? Let life flow freely.' This was the level of my apolitical thinking.

Being in the heart of Delhi during the Emergency (1975–77) imposed by Indira Gandhi, we hardly felt its pangs as our elite college kept its distance from politics. We used to entertain ourselves with dances and special dinners on weekends. I was blissfully unaware that, under the Maintenance of Internal Security Act (MISA), many political activists were being hunted down.[1] I had vaguely heard about the forceful sterilizations ordered by Sanjay Gandhi during that period. My peers and I were concerned, but only to a certain degree, when there was a drive to evict squatter settlements in an attempt to beautify Delhi.

During that time, I recollect the launch of a new fizzy drink called Double Seven (77), meant to commemorate the end of the Emergency in 1977.[2] It was an Indian soft drink launched by the Janata Party in place of Coca-Cola, which we missed a lot. The Janata Party had come to power after the Congress, under the leadership of Indira Gandhi, lost the election. I remember my friends making fun of Prime Minister Morarji Desai for drinking his own urine as a form of medical therapy.[3] They used to call it 'Morarji Cola!'

Although my parents, Dharma Ratna Yami and Heera Devi Yami, were politically active in Nepal, I had little knowledge of politics. Being the youngest of seven children, I had had a pampered upbringing. Even when I lost my mother at the age of ten, I was never made to feel her absence because my sisters and brother took good care of me. Amongst them, Timila Yami, my second-eldest sister, stood out as she was the one who got me admitted to Central School (Kendriya Vidyalaya) on the Indian Institute of Technology (IIT) campus in Kanpur, which is where she was studying electrical engineering. At that time, I was twelve years old and joined the seventh grade. The year was 1971. Since I was a minor, it was with great difficulty that she got permission to put me up in the IIT girls' hostel. All the girls there treated me like their little sister, possessively telling me to eat this and not that. They taught me the art of simple living. Indeed, I saw established scientists and engineers clad in simple kurta-suruwal and slippers. This was in great contrast to what I had seen in Kathmandu, where most of the people were overdressed. Alongside studies, I participated in sports, cultural activities and debates in school. During those days, I was bubbling with energy—a jack of all trades and a master of none.

I remember stumbling upon a magazine called *Manushi* while pursuing BArch in Delhi around 1979. It was an English feminist magazine edited by Madhu Kishwar and Ruth Vanita.[4] Soon, I started attending their meetings. I think gender awareness seeped into my being at the IIT Kanpur girls' hostel, where I saw many strong, intelligent women compete with men. Girls were allowed to visit the boys' hostel and vice versa. The atmosphere on the campus was quite egalitarian. This was in contrast to the rest of Uttar Pradesh, which had a predominantly patriarchal setting. Maybe this was why I was drawn to *Manushi*. I wrote my first feminist article and letter for this magazine.

Influenced by *Manushi*, I wrote my first English poem:

Inside the Four Walls

Inside the four walls you will hear
Cracking of fire splinters
Scrubbing of utensils, floors
Crying, wailing of hungry babies
Followed by hushing.
Inside the four walls you will hear
Thuds, jerks, beatings
And growling of male voice
A faint voice pleading
Moaning, sighing and dying.
Who knows what goes on inside the four walls!
Inside the wall of a 'secure home' she is to fall.
. . . except those martyrs unheard and unsung.
Pleading from societal graves their daughters to waken![5]

Even though the politics of gender began to make sense to me, I was not yet politically sensitive. I was not even aware of the reason behind the India–Pakistan war of 1971. All I knew was that when the siren sounded, we had to make sure all lights were switched off and the entire area was pitch-black. This was to prevent Pakistani warplanes from spotting us.

I remember listening to a speech by Indira Gandhi in 1975. Her helicopter had landed on the grounds of IIT Kanpur amid great anticipation. Around the same time, I had overheard some students in the IIT hostel whispering about the presence of *laal bhaiyas* which, I later learnt, meant Naxalites. I had heard them talking about Mao Zedong and the Naxalite movement. The lower clerical staff and radical students fondly remembered the leftist professor A.P. Shukla who used to fight for their rights on campus. He used to say that IIT was a white elephant, where students from all over India came to study for a government-subsidized fee but after graduation went off to serve the cause of American imperialism. I was told that Professor Shukla had been imprisoned and tortured during the Emergency.[6]

Every summer, we used to go back home to Kathmandu. I remember asking my father one day in 1972, when I was thirteen years old: 'Father, who do you like, Indira Gandhi or Mao Zedong?' Instead of answering my question, he said, 'Do not ask such questions.' That put an end to my political inquiry for the time being. Looking back, I realized that none of us was introduced to politics during his lifetime. At that time, King Birendra ruled Nepal with absolute power but under the disguise of a party-less Panchayat system.[7] Perhaps my father's loyalties towards the monarch prevented him from answering my question.

After successfully taking the higher secondary exam in Kanpur, I joined SPA in 1976. From the close-knit, spacious, green campus of IIT Kanpur I had come to the hub of bureaucracy, Delhi. The Delhi Development Authority building at one end and the Delhi Police HQ at the other dwarfed the SPA hostel, with the Indraprastha thermal power station across the ring road. There were no residential buildings nearby. At night, we were by ourselves with no neighbours except the empty, tall buildings with chowkidars guarding them. There were two big clusters of squatter settlements a few kilometres from our hostel.

It was as if I had come from a village to a high-flying city. I felt lost in the concrete jungle. Walking from the hostel to the college was unsafe, especially at night, with men on cycles or scooters riding past and trying to touch us. I remember an incident where a young man accosted an Odia student from SPA as she walked along the ring road to get to our institute one night. He assumed she was a prostitute walking on the highway, looking for a client. He pulled her, but she managed to free herself and make her way back to the institute. Similarly, a Nepali friend who had come to visit me was pulled away as we were walking together in Old Delhi. Apparently, there were many Nepali sex workers in a nearby red-light area, and the man had thought she was one of them.

In those days, SPA was much ahead of its time. I remember my friends making fun of me because I was still drinking milk while they were drinking coffee and smoking cigarettes, and sometimes even marijuana! The college had on its roll students like Arundhati Roy who later went on to win the Booker Prize in 1997. Cyrus Jhabvala, a gifted Parsi, was the head of the architecture department. Jhabvala was jovial and unconventional. On holidays, he came to the studio in shorts to guide the students on their projects, sharing jokes and cigarettes with them. I later found out that he was married to Ruth Prawer Jhabvala, a Booker Prize-winning novelist and two-time Academy Award-winning screenwriter. Among my classmates, Arundhati Roy stood out the most as she was unconventional and particularly snappy with male chauvinists.

SPA was apolitical to the extent that once, when the Yamuna was flooded and breached its banks just across from our hostel, its students stayed put, while students from Delhi University (DU) and Jawaharlal Nehru University (JNU) came out to help the squatters who lived along the riverbank.

Our hostel in Indraprastha Estate was unique in the sense that male and female students shared a mess, living room and a common sports room. The atmosphere of SPA, particularly that of my class, has been well depicted in Roy's 1989 National Film Award-winning TV film *In Which Annie Gives It Those Ones*.

The renowned painter Jatin Das taught us the theory of art. His was a powerful and inspiring voice. The bold strokes of his paintings matched his teaching technique. In short, SPA was one of the best architecture schools in India where we had the privilege of listening to lectures by stalwarts such as R. Buckminster Fuller.

BRB, who came to SPA in 1977, was pursuing a master's degree in town and country planning. My first impression of him was that he looked too simple to fit into the urbane and elitist SPA crowd. He was lean and thin, and wore a bright orange jacket, which made him look all the more unsophisticated and out of place. Unlike most of the other students, he was serious and introverted. He did not smoke or drink; he had a clean-shaven face and sported neatly combed hair. He looked more like an ascetic than an eccentric, which was how most of the artists and architects in our college could be described.

However, gradually, he started getting noticed. He was president of the All India Nepalese Students' Association (AINSA), coordinating with all Nepali students studying in India. He got many visitors and scores of letters. Sometimes his letters would number more than those of the entire hostel! And his mess bill used to be one of the highest because he had so many visitors. I could not help but take note of his serious, dignified nature and his consistent reading habit. I was surprised to find that he read all sorts of magazines, from news magazines to those on films, and newspapers in our common room. Despite his brilliant academic record, he never wore a smug look and always down-to-earth.

When a Nepali student introduced me to BRB, he immediately asked me, 'Are you Dharma Ratna Yami's daughter?' I was surprised that he knew my father. Then he went on to talk about my father's political background. He had read about my father in 1971, in a rare book titled *Ma Nepali Congress ko Ek Sadharan Sevak Hun* (*I am an ordinary servant of the Nepali Congress*), written by Bharat Shamsher Rana and published in 2025 Bikram Sambat (BS), or 1968.[8] He told me how my father and mother had fought against the Rana regime[9] and been arrested many times, and that the Ranas had confiscated my father's property. He later told me how my father had come to India during the anti-Rana period and tried to mediate between two warring Nepali Congress (NC) leaders, Bishweshwar Prasad Koirala (B.P. Koirala) and Dilli Raman Regmi, to come together to fight against the Ranas. At that time, Nepal was in the grip of 104 years of oligarchic Rana rule.[10]

I was both pleasantly surprised and embarrassed to realize that he knew my father's political achievements better than I did.

Before I met BRB in Delhi, my concern for my country was social, not political. On the IIT campus, I used to see Nepali maids working in professors' houses and feel uncomfortable when invited to their houses for dinner. In most hostels, the cooks and helpers were from Nepal. Similarly, in most office buildings I would see Nepali guards. In the highly polluted industrial city of Kanpur, I saw Nepali workers slogging in the grimmest conditions, working for a measly pay in dhabas and factories. Many of them lived in squatter settlements. I used to hate how Indian people called Nepali workers *bahadur* and *kanchha*. These were derogatory terms for the poor Nepalis in India.

In Delhi, too, I was disturbed to see Nepali workers living in squatter settlements, which looked like little rat houses amidst towering high-rises. I was infuriated to see Nepali women in brothels.

Frankly, I got to know about the real Nepal only in India; so cut off was I from my country at the young age of twelve. We took a plane from Kathmandu to Patna, from where we travelled to Kanpur by train. I hardly knew life beyond the Kathmandu Valley. This was generally true for most Newars. The valley being the centre of all political, economic, cultural and educational activities, the Newar community did not need to travel beyond it. I, therefore, had no idea about the vast rural sector. My Nepali language skills were weak; I would either speak Nepal Bhasa (language of Newars) or English. I learnt much later that many poor Nepalis who came to work in India hardly knew Kathmandu, as they had barely any economic or other connection with it.

Seeing the plight of some of the Nepali workers in India, I had a social awakening, which was to be transformed into a political awakening.

2

Black Flag, Dharnas, Toy Pistol Revolt

first political steps

It was not that I had absolutely no political intuition when I came to Delhi. I had some patriotic feelings for my country. I had just not found the right environment to express it. I had some notional opinion against the monarchy in Nepal. My naive consciousness told me to reject monarchy on two strong bases even before I became politically active. My association with the secular, republic and multiparty parliamentary system in India at an early age made me question the monolithic, tradition-based authority of the monarch in Nepal. I could not digest the fact that they were above the law. Secondly, being gender-conscious, I could not understand why only men were entitled to the throne. I started questioning why my only brother was given the privilege of staying in a hostel and studying in an English-medium school. I felt it was unfair that we, the six sisters, were sent to a government school. I also found myself questioning why he became the automatic heir to the huge house, along with the acres of land, that belonged to my father. In short, I started seeing sons as mini monarchs in every household in Nepal, and daughters and wives as mini proletariats. Just as I saw an average prince suddenly becoming a powerful king, I saw many mundane men turning macho after marriage. Sadly, I also saw many talented, smart and educated girls fade into oblivion after they got married.

Before I met BRB, I had already formed a negative opinion of the monarchy in Nepal. In Delhi, the Embassy of Nepal in Mandi House represented a symbol of that monarchy. Demonstrations against the Panchayat system became bigger and more frequent in front of the embassy as the democratic and republican forces became more and more active.

Though BRB did not belong to a political family, he had many Nepali Congress (NC) sympathizers among his relatives. When the king banned political parties and introduced the autocratic Panchayat system, one of his uncles had to go underground. He later landed up at his house in Belbas village, Gorkha. BRB used to read his anti-monarchy scribblings. He was also witness to a massive manhunt of anti-monarchical forces. His uncle miraculously escaped from his house when the police and army came to arrest him. BRB, being scientific-minded and logical, had rejected the monarchy that derived power from the belief that kings were reincarnations of Lord Vishnu. All he knew was that Nepal had to become a republic. Beyond that, he had neither any affiliation to the NC nor to the communist parties.

It was while studying architecture in Chandigarh (1972–77) that BRB was gradually drawn towards politics. The worldwide craze for Che Guevara among the youths in the 1970s and the plight of Nepali workers in India had ignited a sense of revolt and social responsibility in BRB. This led him to student activism and culminated in the formation of AINSA in 1977. At the first conference of AINSA, held in Chandigarh, he was elected its president.

After completing BArch, BRB had come to the Indian capital to learn more about politics and philosophy, as it was the hub of political activity. The Nepalese Students' Association (NSA), Delhi chapter, was dominated by English-speaking, self-financed students from urban and rich backgrounds. They had easy access to the Embassy of Nepal, where they were often invited to dinner parties and events. However, there was another big group of Nepali students studying Sanskrit and staying in various Hindu temples in Delhi. They were given free lodging and education. Generally from poor rural backgrounds, these students did not speak English. There was yet another group of poor students who worked menial jobs. They were not easily given membership to the NSA, nor were they invited to the embassy for any programmes. BRB was very popular with these excluded students because he used to speak up for them and encouraged their membership to the NSA. He also fought to get them access to the Embassy of Nepal, often accompanying them there to voice their demands. The group of elite Nepali students did not like BRB for this reason. I remember one of our friends, Bal Krishna Man Singh,[1] used to threaten them saying, '*lourole hirkaunchhu* (I will thrash them with batons)'. He had come to Delhi to study chartered accountancy and to work. Like many students, he had to support his mother and sisters back in Nepal. He became the president of the NSA, Delhi, in 1980, which would not have been possible had it remained an elite students' association.

One political incident changed the course for AINSA. It was in January 1978, when BRB issued a statement asking for the release and treatment of the ailing B.P. Koirala.[2] A former prime minister and NC supremo, Koirala had been living in exile after the coup by King Mahendra in 1960.[3] In 1976, when he was returning from India to Nepal under the *Melmilap Neeti* (reconciliation policy), he was arrested and denied permission to get treatment for cancer. Later, he was not only released but the Nepali government decided to finance the entire cost of his health expenditure. At that time, nobody in Nepal dared to question the king's decision to imprison him. After BRB's statement on Koirala, a counter-statement was issued by the then NSA president, Delhi, Prabhat Ghimire, who was a supporter of the royals.[4] It was done on the instigation of the Nepali ambassador, as BRB had started campaigning boldly against the monarchy and Panchayat system. It was embarrassing for us because Ghimire was the presidential candidate we had supported against Bhairaja Pandey, who was the NC's choice. The Embassy of Nepal went out of its way to campaign for BRB's removal as AINSA president. This proved counterproductive as AINSA, which had been politically neutral so far, developed a more anti-monarchy stand. AINSA later became a common platform to expose the ills under an autocratic monarchy and to support the democratic movement in Nepal. By then, we had grown sympathetic to the communist ideology. During those days, major leftist forces saw the royalists as being more nationalist and progressive than the NC.

In my opinion, this incident became the turning point for BRB to plunge into full-fledged party politics.

It was during this time that BRB took me to meet the charismatic leader B.P. Koirala in Delhi's South Extension. Koirala, who had been following all these events, was happy to talk to BRB and discussed the latest political scenario both in Nepal and India. He was suffering from oral cancer and his voice was weak; he looked frail, but his brilliance and enthusiasm shone through.

Soon, I started becoming active in AINSA, which had become a popular platform for all banned political parties of Nepal. I remember having attended the second national convention of AINSA in Delhi in 1977, where BRB was elected the president and I was elected the cultural secretary.

In this capacity, I met Durga Subedi, who was implicated in the June 1973 hijacking of a Royal Nepal Airlines plane carrying Nepal Rastra Bank money to Kathmandu.[5] He told us the inside story of the hijacking and the wrangling that took place within the NC while distributing the money seized. The NC's men were hounding him because he had left the party and was critical of its reconciliatory policy towards the monarchy. Among renowned personalities who used to attend our conferences were Rishikesh

Shah, a scholar and former foreign minister of Nepal. He was very fond of BRB and often said he wished he had a son like him. He used to tell us about all the conspiracies that used to go on within the royal palace.

BRB and I used to go to Kathmandu regularly to collect articles and get advertisements for *Janamanas*, the mouthpiece of the AINSA. In the course of our work, we used to meet political figures and they would often fondly recollect meeting my father. I especially remember Siddhi Charan Shrestha, the renowned poet, who used to call us to his place often. He was affectionate towards BRB and would often dig out his old revolutionary songs and make us listen to them. Because I was a local Newar and the daughter of Dharma Ratna Yami, we had easy access to politicians. I realized that my father's political background was such that he could relate to all schools of thought and was known to all political figures, from communists to NC members to royalists. Arun Sayami,[6] who at one point became the general secretary of the AINSA, also helped us with collecting advertisements and articles. His father, Dhuswan Sayami, was once the cultural attaché to India and also a great literary figure. Mahesh Maskey, a public health expert, was another active member who rose to become the president of AINSA and later Nepal's ambassador to China.

I began as AINSA's cultural secretary and was then elected treasurer (1979) before becoming the general secretary in 1981–82. It was AINSA that introduced me to most of the Nepali and Indian political leaders. AINSA was quickly gaining momentum as a popular platform for debate on political movements in Nepal. Students from all over Nepal, as well as from India, would eagerly wait for the annual AINSA conference, where they would get the latest information on politics in Nepal. This was because it gave student activists, intellectuals and political leaders (who were underground in Nepal) a space to meet without the fear of persecution, a platform to vent their opposition to the monarchical Panchayat system and to propagate their ideological and political stands. For the Indian intellectuals and politicians, the conference gave them an opportunity to sympathize with and support the democratic movement in Nepal.

AINSA provided a space for veteran leaders like Mohan Bikram Singh, Nirmal Lama, Tulsi Lal Amatya, Rishikesh Shah, Pradeep Giri, Durga Subedi and others to lend their support to a patriotic and democratic movement in Nepal. From India, eminent people such as V.M. Tarkunde, Swami Agnivesh, Shamsul Islam, Professor S.D. Muni, Professor Manoranjan Mohanty, Kuldip Nayar and others used to visit and deliver speeches in support of democracy in Nepal.

During those days, M.B. Singh was the most talked-about underground leader who headed the radical left party called the Communist Party of Nepal (Masal)—CPN (Masal), or just Masal for short. At that time, the Communist Party of Nepal (Marxist–Leninist), CPN (ML), also had its organizational presence in India. I remember being very curious about one of its main leaders, Chandra Prakash Mainali, better known as C.P. Mainali, who was said to be a brilliant student before setting out to lead the Jhapa uprising.

In 1979, an event took place that left me embarrassed, but at the same time it put me more firmly on a political path. King Birendra was on a trip to Delhi and was visiting Raj Ghat, a memorial dedicated to Mahatma Gandhi. We had decided to show black flags and throw pamphlets at the king during his tour, condemning the Panchayat system and asking for democracy and a republican state. Just when the king's car arrived, my instinct told me to run away from the scene, leaving BRB behind. But he, unlike me, remained unfazed and managed to throw a handful of pamphlets at the king's car. He was immediately whisked away to a nearby police station and let off the next day.

He had passed his political test, and I had failed mine. Feeling embarrassed, I started devoting more time to political activities by participating in street dharnas (sit-in protests) and processions. During those days, the streets of Delhi used to witness demonstrations against the shah of Iran. I remember how the storming of the Embassy of the United States by the public in Iran made big news in Delhi. We also used to join demonstrations in support of the Palestine Liberation Organization, alongside students from JNU and DU. Similarly, we used to frequent India Gate, where dharnas used to take place almost every day.

On 11 November 1980, we got a call from someone saying that the Delhi Police had arrested three students from the Embassy of Nepal—Puroshottam Pokharel, Harihar Adhikari and Narayan Subedi, all students of Sanskrit and members of our organization. They had gone to meet Bedananda Jha, the then Nepali ambassador to India, to put forward the demand for establishment of democracy in Nepal. They had also demanded that a Nepal House be set up in Delhi as a temporary shelter for Nepali visitors, just like in Benaras (Varanasi). They had carried a toy pistol, kerosene and a knife in their bags. When Jha refused to relent, one of them threatened him with the toy pistol. They were soon overpowered by the embassy staff and handed over to the Delhi Police. We had a tough time getting them out. Our connections with Indian politicians and human rights activists, particularly from the People's Union for Civil Liberties (PUCL) and People's Union for Democratic Rights (PUDR), helped us get them released and have the case dismissed. That was our first brush with a small, naive revolt.

After this event, Jha called me to his office. He said, 'Your father was a good friend of mine. Why do you indulge in anti-monarchical activities? You have come here to study, not to do politics. I will help you if you will help me.' He was visibly upset with me. I replied, 'I do not know you, but I do know that Nepal needs democracy.' That was the level of change I had undergone in my political journey. Later on, I came to know that Jha, a leader of the Nepal Terai Congress, had become a cabinet minister under the Panchayat regime. And he was indeed my father's friend.

From an apolitical student I had been transformed into a leftist student. We soon started getting involved in the Akhil Bharat Nepali Ekta Samaj (ABNES), an organization of workers in India that served as a front for the underground CPN (Masal) headed by M.B. Singh. Raju Nepali, an active member of the Masal, was working as a domestic helper in the house of a member of the Planning Commission of India. He introduced BRB and me to M.B. Singh. BRB was at first a radical social democrat by persuasion. In 1980, he became a member of the Masal. ABNES helped instil in us an understanding of class politics. We would go to squatter settlements to politicize and organize Nepali workers. BRB contracted jaundice several times while living and working in such unhygienic conditions. He would often recollect how he had to go to an open defecation corner with a stick in his hand to ward off the pigs that would scurry around for fresh stool.

I soon realized that the people close to M.B. Singh had started looking at me critically. One day, Raju Nepali objected to my singing and dancing to apolitical ethnic songs such as '*Chyangba hoi chyangba! Damfule aja ke bhanchha? Jaon kata jaon . . .* (Hey lad! What does the tambourine say? It says let us go somewhere . . .)' After that, I stopped singing and dancing to such songs. I found my space in Nishant Natya Manch, a progressive street-play troupe run by Shamsul Islam and his wife, Neelima Sharma. We often had artists from the National School of Drama in Mandi House participating in our cultural programmes. I was now singing inspirational songs such as '*Tu zinda hai, toh zindagi ki jeet mein yakin kar . . .* (If you are alive, believe in the victory of life . . .)'

In 1981, Nishant Natya Manch, in collaboration with Bedana Sanskritik Pariwar, a progressive cultural troupe from Nepal, performed at the Nepal Academy Hall in Kathmandu. They performed a street play called *Khaldo* (Ditch). It was a political play, showing the futility of elections within the Panchayat system. I was told that this was possibly Nepal's introduction to the concept of street plays.

In Delhi, my association with BRB helped me expand my outlook, as I went from simply being a freethinking gender-conscious woman to a politically awakened one. It was in 1981 that I finally became a member of the Communist Party of Nepal (Fourth Convention).

While in India, we enjoyed the goodwill of all the anti-monarchical parties of Nepal operating in India. We also formed relationships with leaders of different Indian political parties of like Chandra Shekhar, Karan Singh, K.C. Pant, Sharad Yadav, George Fernandes and others.

In a way, Delhi became a good grooming ground for our political awakening. And we exploited it to the hilt!

3

'Why Do You Come Here?'

falling in love

BRB completed his masters from SPA in 1979 with flying colours. I was amazed at how he did it. His hands were full with political commitments when the final date for the submission of his thesis approached. During those days, there were many demonstrations against the monarchical Panchayat system, both in Nepal and in India, which finally led to a referendum between the multiparty and reformed one-party systems in 1980. I saw him working on his thesis for 110 hours at a stretch from Friday evening till Wednesday morning. He would take a break to eat but not to sleep. The topic for his postgraduate research was 'Regional Development of Nepal: A Study of Gandaki Growth Axis', and he graduated with top marks. Bijit Ghosh, the head of department of town and country planning, was so impressed with BRB's performance that he introduced him to Professor Moonis Raza, the founder chairman of JNU's Centre for the Study of Regional Development and also the rector of the university, as a political activist and brilliant student. Prof. Raza immediately invited BRB to join JNU.

BRB joined JNU for his PhD in regional planning. Through AINSA, he already knew a number of students at both JNU and

DU, besides civil society intellectuals and professors. So he was very comfortable in his new university.

BRB, who had come to Delhi with the idea of immersing himself in academics and books, was, in many ways, satisfied when he joined JNU. In fact, he got locked inside libraries twice while studying till late—at JNU and at Nepal's APROSC (Agricultural Projects Services Centre) library. So focused was he on his books!

His departure from SPA meant that it became a less political place, particularly for me. I visited his hostel in JNU often in connection with students' activities. One day, when I was paying him a visit, he suddenly asked me, 'Why do you come here?' I was completely taken aback by the question, failing to see any reason behind it. He read my expression and asked if I had received his letter. I told him that I hadn't. Then, with some hesitation, he told me the contents of the letter that had already been sent to my SPA address. In it, he had written about his aim in life: he wanted to lead a life dedicated to the service of his country and its people. But he had fallen in love with me! And that was tormenting him. He was torn between marriage and the dedication to his dream. He was scared that marriage might burden him. So, in that letter, he had asked me not to come and meet him! At the same time, he was confused because he had read *Hints for Self-Culture* by Lala Har Dayal, which explained why idealists must marry.

I was shocked to hear that. I had no idea that he thought of me in that way. Soon, he began talking to me about his life, his aim and the uncertainties that plagued him. He toyed with the idea of marriage and how life might change. When he proposed to me later, I said I would think about it. I had received proposals before, but not like this. There was an Indian classmate with whom I used to bicker constantly, till one day he sent me a note in a book, confessing that he had fallen in love with me. There were two students from Sikkim studying in SPA who wanted to marry my sister Kayo and me, respectively. In fact, the one who had fallen for me nearly bashed BRB's face when he came to know of our relationship.

BRB came to drop me back to SPA the day he proposed. On the way, I thought to myself: Why not get married to him? He was a devoted, genuine, democratic and open-minded man. He was good in studies, too. After all, my parents had also married for love back in 1945. And it was based on political commitment.

That very day, I gave him my consent. I felt the butterflies in my stomach. I remember asking myself: Now that I would be sharing my life with him, probably forever, was I prepared? I used to call him Baburam *dai* (elder brother) until then. What would I call him henceforth?

We kept our relationship a secret. It was easy because our love was born more out of a rational understanding than impulsive feelings. We experienced the heady rush of love just like any other young couple, but we never showed it overtly. We spent a lot of time together but behind the veil of political and student activities; nobody guessed that we were a couple. We could not hide it for too long though.

One day in 1981, I got a call from a law student, Sushil Pant, now a senior advocate in Nepal. He informed me that BRB had met with an accident and had been hospitalized at All India Institute of Medical Sciences (AIIMS). I reached there to find him in an unconscious state with a bloated face and swollen, closed eyes. There was blood everywhere. BRB regained consciousness after forty-eight hours. I took him straight to our guest room, which was just below the girls' hostel rooms in SPA, and nursed him day and night. I think it was around then that people from ABNES started wondering about our relationship. Similarly, people at the Embassy of Nepal were watching our activities closely. At that time, he was the adviser of AINSA and I was the general secretary. The annual conference was nearing. So, before people started politicizing our relationship, we decided to get married.

We applied for a court marriage. However, since we were Nepali citizens, we had to go through a long procedure. We were told to have a legislative member as a witness to our marriage in order to get fast-track approval. Our lawyer further suggested that we give it a traditional touch. So we arranged for Swami Agnivesh, a *bandhuwa mazdoor* (bonded labourer) activist and a member of the legislative assembly, Haryana, to perform our marriage ceremony on 29 March 1981. Prof. Shamsul Islam's house was fixed as the venue. I borrowed my friend's cotton sari to dress up for the ceremony, but BRB came in his usual attire.

I remember Swami Agnivesh, who passed away in September 2020, gave a wonderful interpretation of fire as the destroyer of evil and creator of life, and spoke of its transformational power to change one element to the other. It was a small gathering of about twenty-five; we spent around Rs 150 in Indian currency on the ceremony, and our wedding feast consisted of simple tea and *samosas*. April Fool's Day was approaching; those not invited thought our marriage was an April fool joke! We sent our marriage declaration letter to our well-wishers, in which we pledged to fulfil our roles as agents of progressive transformation of human society:

**Marriage declaration of Baburam Bhattarai
and Hisila Yami**

On this occasion of publicly declaring our mental, physical
and emotional attachment to each other (which has been
traditionally termed as 'marriage'), we pledge by our free
conscience to exercise the human capabilities inherent in
us with utmost rationality, and to fulfil our roles as agents
of progressive transformation of human society to higher
social formations with utmost sincerity. We unequivocally
renounce all forms of exploitative mechanisms of religion,
communalism, casteism, superstition, etc., introduced in
human relations by persons in positions of power in different
periods of human history and on the contrary are committed
to live in conjugal life free of any sexual discrimination
and marked by absolute freedom of thought and action of
both the partners. We have entered into this special human
relationship by our own free volition at a state of our full
conscientiousness and pledge to maintain it so long as it fulfils
our mutual aspirations and contributes to the realization
of our higher selves. With effect from this day, we declare
ourselves as man and wife.

Hisila Yami   Baburam Bhattarai
Date: 29.03.1981

People had reason to doubt our marriage; ours was such an odd
match! He was serious, shy and an introvert, while I was an
extrovert, easy-going and talkative. Unlike in SPA, where falling
in love was something to display, our relationship in JNU was a
discreet and serious one. Before our marriage, I often visited BRB
in his Poorvanchal Hostel room, sometimes even spending the

night there. I continued this even after our marriage. I remember how I once came to meet him all dressed up in a red sari and light make-up. But he only gave me a stone-cold, silent look! That was my first and last attempt to impress him.

One day, the hostel warden asked me who I was and why I had been frequenting BRB's room. BRB boldly replied that I was his wife. The poor fellow felt embarrassed and left without saying a word. Bad timing on his part! We were already married by then.

Once, when we were attending a demonstration, a policeman accompanying us teased us: 'Bhattaraiji, Yamiji, you did not even invite us to your wedding. Go on protesting! Some day you will become ministers and prime ministers of your country and we might have to escort you here!' Hari Charan Shrestha had once said that BRB could be the prime minister of Nepal some day. He was the editor of a bulletin that used to be published by the Embassy of Nepal, New Delhi. Little did we know this would actually come true!

Soon, we got a room in the married scholars' hostel in JNU. There I met a student who, upon hearing my name, asked if I knew Dharma Ratna Yami. His name was Urmilesh Singh and he was pursuing his MPhil on Rahul Sankrityayan's[1] literature. He told me that Sankrityayan had written a short biography of my father in Hindi. It was only after reading the book that I realized the depth of my father's multiple talents and learnt about his political life and sufferings under the Rana regime. I realized he was a poet and writer, a scholar in Buddhism and a great social reformer. This revelation made me feel proud of my background and made me all the more responsible towards my country.

I later asked BRB what made him want to marry me. He said he was impressed by my innocence, curiosity and independent mindset. Ours was an inter-caste marriage, which is often risky in Nepal. It is worth mentioning how people close to us reacted when I revealed our relationship to them. Before our marriage, Parvati, BRB's younger sister, had visited us in Delhi. She had said outrightly that BRB's parents would not accept the match because he was a Brahmin, while I was a Newar. Similarly, when I told my sister Timila about BRB, she warned me that he might already have a wife in his village. I was obviously nervous when I went to his village for the first time in 1980, the year before we got married. To my great relief, I found out that he was not already married!

His parents, too, were not that conservative. When they heard that we had got married in Delhi, I was told they were, in fact, relieved. This was because BRB had been getting proposals for marriage since the age of twelve, but he had been refusing every single one of them! BRB told me that one family of seven daughters had even brought proposals from each of the girls, from the eldest to the youngest! When BRB did not respond, the father started spreading rumours that BRB was 'not physically fit' for marriage. Naturally, his parents were happy to see him married at last. They were even more relieved when we had a daughter.

The trip to my new house in Belbas village in Gorkha was full of surprises. Before marriage, I had asked BRB all sorts of questions about his village life. For instance, I wanted to know if there was electricity in his house and if one could reach it by rickshaw. We had to hitch a ride to reach a tarred road recently constructed by China. From there, we had to walk for three hours to reach his house. The narrow and slippery road—barely six inches wide—that cut through rice plantations saw me lose my footing several times. Upon reaching his house, I saw that they had built a temporary toilet with a jute-covered door. There was no electricity anywhere. The only luxury I enjoyed was the continuous flow of fresh water in the public *dhunge dhara* (stone water tap). Sheltered in a shed below our bedroom were buffaloes, cows and goats. I loved feeding them.

I remember having lied to my mother-in-law about my period, fearing I would be ostracized. Unlike in our Newar community, Brahmins at that time did not allow a menstruating girl to sleep in the bedroom or eat with the rest of the family. I had confided in Parvati about this and she had supported me. I was unaware of the feudal atmosphere that prevailed in Gorkha. Once, BRB's aunt took my example and said she would get her daughter married just like me. I was happy to hear that. But, to our great surprise, she got her under-age daughter married to an already married, much older military man. They had planned a secret wedding in Kathmandu. We decided to break it up; BRB swooped into the marriage hall, rescued the bride and lodged her in my maternal house in Bhurungkhel, Kathmandu. Later, despite our opposition, their marriage was consummated. This incident taught me to be watchful of conspiratorial moves that seemed to go in tandem with feudalism. It unsettled me because I was not used to it.

In Gorkha, BRB introduced me to his school friends who were mostly farmers after dropping out from school. It was only then that I realized the importance of education in rural areas. Education seems to be the only way to uplift one's status from poor to rich, from rural to urban, from farming to white-collar jobs. He showed me the *choutari* (a platform shaded by a tree) where he got his basic education from an ex-military man, Bhakta Bahadur Bhujel. BRB also took me to Amar Jyoti High School run by Christian missionaries in Luitel, from where he passed his school leaving certificate (SLC) examination, scoring the highest marks in all of Nepal. He was the first student from a rural area, outside Kathmandu Valley, to have topped the national board exams.

Reaching the school meant a three-hour journey through dense woods between Belbas and Luitel. BRB said he often used to spot wild beasts on the way! He showed me the place where he, along with his sister, brother and cousins, made *chhapro*, a temporary hut covered with leaves, in which they used to cook, study and sleep. Every weekend, they would go back to their village to get food for the whole week.

He had joined Amar Jyoti school in Class 3. He showed so much promise that within six months of joining, he was promoted to Class 4. Another six months later, he was promoted to Class 5. He took me to meet his favourite schoolteacher, Eleanor Elkins, a Scottish–American missionary teacher from the USA who was then in her forties. She lived alone in a hut within the school compound. I found her to be simple, sweet and dedicated to her job. (We met her again in 2011 in the USA, when BRB, then the prime minister of Nepal, went to New York to attend a UN meeting.) She played an enormous role in shaping BRB's mind. Even in the absence of electricity, she used to make him listen to the BBC news on a transistor.

It was sheer hard work and a focused mind that brought BRB from his village to Kathmandu and from Kathmandu to Delhi.

Unlike me, who was keenly observing BRB's village and family, BRB rarely showed any interest in the personal lives of my relatives, my community or my upbringing. I remember having fought with him once after he refused to attend a social gathering of our Newar community. I often wondered, 'Have I married a blank wall?'

4

Victim of Underdevelopment

motherhood and activism

After working in a private architecture consultancy firm for a year in Delhi, I came back to Nepal to join the Institute of Engineering (IoE) in Pulchowk in 1983. BRB remained in Delhi to complete his PhD thesis. I was twenty-three, and I was teaching students, some of who were as old as me. I loved teaching.

Gradually, I started taking an active part in political, cultural and gender issues. At the time of my arrival in Nepal, the movement against the monarchical Panchayat system was slowly building up. The anti-monarchy student agitations of 1979 had resulted in a referendum between the multiparty and reformed one-party (Panchayat) systems in 1980. Although the result was 'in favour' of the partyless system, the government merely instituted minor reforms in the Panchayat system. Not satisfied with this, the NC started the satyagraha movement in 1984.[1] However, they had to abandon it when the Nepal Janabadi Morcha led by Ram Raja Prasad Singh carried out bombings in Kathmandu in protest against the monarchy in 1985.[2] Ram Raja Prasad Singh was a fierce republican who entered public life after he was arrested for his political beliefs. In the Rashtriya Panchayat election of 1971, he had won in a constituency reserved for graduates with bachelor degrees. Yet, not only was he disallowed from taking the oath, but he was also imprisoned for his beliefs. Slowly, united fronts were building up against the Panchayat system.

For a short while, I ran my own architectural consultancy venture called Vastuk Consultants. I also worked on gender issues at the Centre for Women and Development (CWD), a Kathmandu-based NGO. I got elected as the treasurer in the Nepal Engineers' Association. I was also active in the Nepal Professors' Association. I even joined a journalism class run by the press council, but I did not complete the course. I was mostly out on the streets demonstrating for political rights, women's rights and indigenous nationalities (*Adivasi Janajati*) rights. In fact, for me, teaching came second to my political commitments. So engaged was I in these activities that I even went to cast my vote in the Nepal Professors' Association elections at IoE, just one day after my first child was born in 1985.

Many times, I found myself amidst students of IoE during street demonstrations against the government. Once, after I had demonstrated in a five-star hotel against Nepal's first beauty pageant, which it was hosting, my architecture students asked me why I had opposed the beauty contest when the subject I taught was based on aesthetics. I told them that we were not against beauty contests as such but against the commercialization and commodification of the bodies of women. For the government, I was a big headache. They sent their emissaries to put pressure on my dean and the campus chief to take action against me. However, they could find no legal fault with me as I was taking classes regularly. Luckily, the days I was taken into custody happened to be holidays. The only punishment I got at IoE was that I was not allowed to have a permanent job until much later. I taught on a contract basis since the time I joined in 1983.

It is worth recollecting that ABNES conducted raids on red-light areas in India and sent the rescued girls back to Nepal.

Before they were sent back to their villages in Nepal, I often sheltered them in Kathmandu. We would then expose the racket to the press. Sometimes the girls' parents would not come forward to accept them. In such circumstances, I would keep them in my maternal house before finding suitable homes for them. I used to interview them and try to understand what kept the human flesh trade going. There was one interesting case where five girls who worked as backstage dancers in Kathmandu were lured to go to Delhi. They were promised that their dark complexion would be lightened so that they could then leading roles as beautiful heroines. Before they landed in the jaws of prostitution, they were rescued and brought back to Kathmandu. After many years, I met one of them who had married an army man. I was happy to see her well-settled. Another had married a local stationery shop owner. But she was suffering from cervical cancer and could not bear a child. When she learnt about her illness, she tried to get her husband remarried. I heard later that cancer had claimed her. Her story reminded me of *Pakeezah*, a Hindi movie directed by Kamal Amrohi, in which the plight of a nautch girl was well depicted. It brought tears to my eyes.

While I was teaching at IoE, I also travelled to different parts of the country while being engaged with CWD. In order to study the spread of acquired immunodeficiency syndrome (AIDS) among sex workers, I went to Banke and Bardiya districts populated by Baadis, who are considered to belong to the lower strata among Dalits. Traditionally, they used to be dancers and entertainers for feudal lords, but later they turned to prostitution. In this community, parents prepare their daughters to take on prostitution, while sons are taught to make *madals* (traditional drum) and act as pimps for their sisters.[3] I went to collect blood samples from sex workers in Gagangunj, a red-light area in Nepalgunj, in 1988. I did the same in Banghusari village in Bardiya district.[4] To our great relief, none of the women Baadis whose blood samples we had drawn had been infected by the human immunodeficiency virus (HIV).

It was during this period that I got to know about the plight of
the Tharus. They were oppressed by hill upper castes, and it was
widely perceived that rich businessmen and bureaucrats sexually
exploited Tharu women.

In BRB's absence, I kept myself busy doing all sorts of work
besides teaching.

I was already twenty-five years old and married for four years;
BRB was yet to complete his PhD thesis. We decided to have
a child and hoped it would be a girl. I went to Delhi soon after.
Our work in India and Nepal had made us gender-sensitive. We
almost took it for granted that our child would be a girl and
named her Manushi even before the birth. We borrowed the
name from the feminist magazine *Manushi*. In Sanskrit, the word
is close to 'Manasi', which means 'of the mind or intellect'. The
more politically aware I became, the more my gender-sensitivity
grew. I drew inspiration from my mother who not only fought
against the Rana regime but also bore immense difficulties in
bringing up her seven children. She was one of the founding
members of the underground Nepal Mahila Sangh, which was
at the forefront of the anti-Rana movement.[5] BRB, too, was
sensitive and sympathetic to the women's cause. His mother,
who took the lead in running their household, influenced him
deeply. We were aware of how underdeveloped our country was
with regard to women's issues. They had to work twice as hard
as men, yet they were underpaid and undervalued. And they were
sold like cattle in brothels.

I was very excited about my first child. I read up all I could
about the birth process, child psychology and parenting. I kept
myself happy, healthy and busy, knowing all these factors would
have a positive effect on the child's cognitive power. I remember
getting BRB's photo blown-up and staring at it, wishing my child
to look like him. I had read in a magazine that staring at a photo
of the person you love and thinking about him has an effect on the
unborn child. I wanted my child to be like him.

When the child was born in February 1985, it was a boy. He looked exactly like BRB: serene and serious, he gave me a deep and penetrating look. But he had jaundice and within fourteen hours of his birth, he was declared dead. I remember frantically asking for a paediatrician, but there was not a single one on duty that day. Thapathali's Prasuti Griha was the only maternity hospital in Nepal and they could not afford a single resident paediatrician! I had never imagined that I too would fall victim to the underdevelopment of Nepal: right in the heart of Kathmandu! I had taken all the necessary precautions, including bilirubin tests to detect jaundice. And yet I had lost my child! I felt like I had lost a part of my body, my soul, which I had carefully nurtured for the first time. I had been so optimistic.

In the preface to his PhD thesis, 'The Nature of Underdevelopment and Regional Structure of Nepal', BRB paid tribute to the child he had not even been able to lay his eyes on as a victim of Nepal's underdevelopment. I came to know later that Nepal's maternal and child mortality rates are among the highest in the world.[6] My sisters took great care of me, fearing that I would fall prey to depression. To make matters worse, BRB was not with me.

When I became pregnant again, BRB had still not finished his PhD. He sent me a book, *The Daughters of Karl Marx: Family Correspondence 1866–1898*, addressed to our unborn child and me. This time, I wanted my unborn child to not only be a daughter but also to look like me. I had a huge mirror in front of my bed where I looked at my own face every day. To my great surprise, I did give birth to a daughter. And she looked just like me. I eagerly named her Manushi. I again remembered the magazine that said that the image internalized during pregnancy has an effect on the child's appearance. For me, this seemed to have worked twice over.

BRB and I were determined to have only one child. During those days, having a single child—a daughter at that—was considered culturally unacceptable. Communist leaders, too, would try for a son, even if it meant having more than two children. I strongly believed that bringing up a child involved science and art. I was particularly careful to ensure that Manushi, being an only child, did not become a spoilt brat. I started reading books and magazines on how to bring up a single child. We made sure we were unified in handling Manushi, encouraging her to be independent and inquisitive. We made sure we acted in unison when we had to teach her that there was a lesson to be drawn from any mistake she made.

When BRB came back to Nepal after completing his thesis in 1986, he continued his political activities. He became the editor of a weekly paper called *Prishthabhumi*. In those days, editors were looked upon as *berojgaar*, or unemployed. I remember how editors of other papers used to make fun of him saying that a highly capable person like him was now engaged in editing. That same year the police, as a pre-emptive measure to avoid disturbance during the silver jubilee celebrations of the king's autocratic rule in the name of Panchayat regime, arrested him. This was his first experience of police custody in Nepal.

It was King Mahendra, the heir of Tribhuvan Bir Bikram Shah, who had introduced the Panchayat regime after dissolving the Parliament and suspending the Constitution in December 1960.[7] Alleging that the parliament system was alien to the culture of Nepal, he espoused the reformed one-party Panchayat regime based on Hindu religion, hill Hindu culture and the Nepali language. He dismissed the democratically elected government of B.P. Koirala and banned all political parties. The Panchayat system was to last for thirty long years.

During the Panchayat system era, we opened a progressive bookshop in a corner of Asan, which acted as a centre of contact for expanding our party activities in Kathmandu. The year was 1987. It reminded me of my own father's soap shop in 1940, which was situated close to where we had taken our bookshop. The soap shop used to be known as the anti-Rana broadcasting centre.

We also started running a monthly magazine called *Jhilko* (spark) where, through analytical articles, we used to have regular interactions with intellectuals. This way we increased the intellectual base for our party. For a while, BRB also joined a civil rights group called Human Rights Organization of Nepal (HURON), headed by Rishikesh Shah. HURON was one of the first human rights bodies to be formed in the country in 1988. This organization played a role in protecting fundamental rights to some extent during the Panchayat era. The front also helped him do legal work while being part of an underground party led by M.B. Singh. However, this was not to last long. He was again taken into police custody for protesting against the expulsion of Nepalis from Meghalaya (India) in 1987.

By this time, BRB had started becoming sceptical of CPN (Masal)'s leadership and its commitment towards a democratic revolution. He concluded that Masal, under M.B. Singh, had fallen victim to dogmatic opportunism. This meant that in theory one would uphold the revolutionary doctrine in the name of purity, while in practice one would take the opportunistic route and never prepare for a revolutionary upheaval. By claiming that both the monarchy and Indian expansionism were simultaneously the 'main enemies' of revolution, it was avoiding taking any concrete steps against either. BRB was clear that the primary task of the Nepali revolution was to do away with the 'internal enemy', namely the monarchy. He was disappointed that the call for Constituent Assembly (CA) elections was shelved. Instead, the banner of ultranationalism was raised time and again to accommodate the interests of the monarchy. He was for the creative application of Marxism, where the struggle between different political lines would result in a correct synthesis of opinions. In short, BRB was questioning the Stalinist model of party functioning, which was monolithic, bureaucratic and discouraged internal debates.

As BRB raised these questions, M.B. Singh, the general secretary of the party, started spearheading a campaign against him, calling him a careerist, opportunist and rightist. M.B. Singh was also not interested in aligning with other parties, while BRB strongly favoured an alliance with anti-monarchy forces to make Nepal a republic.

Slowly, the people's movement was gearing up to end monarchy.

For me, this was the beginning of a great exposure—both personally and politically. I was undergoing the experience of motherhood in an underdeveloped feudal country, which was on the verge of a momentous political upheaval amidst sharp ideological debates.

5

People's Movement against the Panchayat Regime

jail tales

While in Delhi, we were active on the streets; we organized seminars and built united fronts against the Panchayat system. However, in Nepal I had to work under the very nose of the Panchayat regime. I had to be careful. All party activities were banned. Press was censored. The so-called guided democracy was, in essence, absolute rule under the monarchy that was declared to be above the Constitution. It was commonly believed that family members of the king would go unpunished when they allegedly committed crimes such as rape and rampage and hit-and-run incidents that killed or injured pedestrians. Political parties used to operate through mass fronts of students, women, intellectuals and professors.[1] Activists were repeatedly arrested when they voiced the need for democracy.

BRB's arrival in Kathmandu in 1986 added further momentum to the movement against the monarchy. I made use of the political momentum, too.

Every year, on the occasion of International Women's Day, 8 March, we would organize programmes to attack the Panchayat system indirectly. Dissidence against the Panchayat regime started rolling in slowly. BRB was heading a united front called Samyukta Rashtriya Janaandolan, or the United National People's Movement (UNPM), which consisted of several communist parties and groups committed to an elected CA and a people's republic. This was established in February 1990. Similarly, under the leadership of Sahana Pradhan, the United Left Front (ULF), committed to a Westminster-style parliamentary system, was formed the same year by unifying many shades of moderate communist parties. Meanwhile, in 1988–89, India had imposed an economic blockade on Nepal, making life in a landlocked country difficult. News of arrests, harassment and shooting incidents against supporters of a multiparty system came in from different parts of Nepal. While the UNPM was launching a movement against the monarchy, the ULF aligned with the NC to create a movement against the Panchayat regime for a constitutional monarchy.

In February 1990, at Pokhara, a girls' hostel in Prithvi Narayan Campus was raided. Women celebrating the release of Nelson Mandela were dragged out, thrashed and molested by the police. The same month, in Jaduguwa village in Dhanusha district, five people, including three women, were shot dead when they protested against the arrest of a political activist. There was a spate of arrests in various districts as people organized demonstrations in support of democracy. This accelerated the movement in various urban centres of Nepal.

Celebration of 8 March became quite challenging in 1990. Women leaders with varied political affiliations came together to celebrate International Women's Day at Padma Kanya Multiple Campus in Kathmandu. The leaders and attendees had tied black bands on their arms to protest against the atrocities in Pokhara and Jaduguwa. We spoke against the Panchayat system and pledged to fight for democracy. Within seconds, a police van arrived. Five leaders, including myself, were arrested. This was my first experience in police custody. I remember Timila telling me how my own mother was taken into custody along with her month-old daughter in 1948. And at that time, living conditions in lock-ups were so bad that one had to eat, sleep and shit in the same crowded room. We, too, were kept in a small, dirty room with scanty ventilation and light, in a place swarming with lice and bugs. Luckily the bathrooms, though common and filthy, were separate from our room.

I was released the next day, but arrested again days later, along with about 700 intellectuals. This was on 20 March when the Professional Solidarity Group, under the leadership of co-chairpersons Mathura Shrestha and Devendra Raj Pandey, had organized a seminar on 'The Role of Intellectuals in the Present Context of Nepal' at Tribhuvan University (TU).[2] I remember Mina Poudel, general secretary of the Nepal Nursing Association, had boldly spoken against the monarchy, which created quite a sensation inside the hall. Soon enough, we were all bundled into waiting trucks and taken into custody.

While the police released most of the participants, I, along with Kalyani Shah and Mina Poudel, was taken to Hanuman Dhoka police station, where we spent the night. There we met a woman named Alpana (not her real name) who had been rescued from a red-light area in Bombay. Mina Poudel claimed that Alpana could be the first HIV-positive woman in Nepal. From there we were sent to the women's prison. Just like us, nine men, including Mathura Shrestha, Devendra Raj Pandey, Narhari Acharya and Kapil Shrestha, were taken to the men's prison, Bhadragol Jail in Kathmandu. The women's prison was situated near this jail. That was my first experience of being in a jail. It reminded me of the time back in 1942 when my father had been arrested. He had been sentenced to eighteen years and all his property was confiscated.

I met Sahana Pradhan, Uma Regmi and Manju Thapa, all of whom had been arrested before me. Sahana Pradhan was not only a 'woman' leader but also a political leader in her own right. She was the wife of Pushpa Lal Shrestha, the founder-leader of the

Communist Party of Nepal (CPN). She had been a friend to my mother during the anti-Rana period. Surprisingly, Sahana Didi did not talk much about politics with us; perhaps she saw us as too young and unprepared. However, she taught me how to knit and cook. I was really bad at such things. At Central School in IIT Kanpur, I had refused to learn knitting and sewing, which was reserved for girls, and had instead taken electrical training, which was largely meant for boys.

While in jail, I knitted a cardigan for my daughter under Sahana Didi's guidance. That was the first and last time I ever used knitting needles! Uma Regmi was a lecturer and a NC leader. Mina Poudel and I used to get along very well. We once fought for the rights of a young woman who was severely anaemic and had fallen ill. She cried the whole night, while we kept insisting that the prison warden bring a doctor to tend to her. She died the next day, and only after that did the doctor come. We fought with the prison officers for their callousness. We later found out that she was the kept woman of a high-level police officer who had abandoned her and left her in jail after alleging that she was a lunatic.

I used to frequent other cells in the prison to find out about the backgrounds of the other inmates. There I met drug traffickers and women who had killed their husbands or their children or carried out abortions.[3] I was particularly interested in meeting women traffickers. I was familiar with the modus operandi of traffickers from my experience of working with rescued girls in Delhi. I had heard their stories and was interested to know what drove these women traffickers to sell other women. To my surprise, I found that most of them were victims of trafficking themselves before they, too, became traffickers. I particularly remember one such woman with a little girl, her daughter, aged about three. One day, I was telling the child a story with a river in it, when she asked me what a river was. I realized then that she had been born in prison and had never seen a river in her life.

The mentally disabled were designated to a separate cell. Most of them were chained, and those who were not were in a miserable state. Not knowing what they were doing, they would sometimes smile and laugh at us and sometimes torment us. When we went to the common toilet—the door was always open—they would burst in, throwing stones at us or pulling our hair. They would use filthy language, sometimes even spitting at us. Some would be giving speeches, while some would be dancing naked.

Water was a scarce commodity, so the place from where we used to draw water was always the scene of fierce fights. It was an overcrowded place, with every cell packed beyond capacity. There used to be only one television set for the entire jail: we could never watch it as non-political inmates monopolized it. We had access to limited information and newspapers.

When I was in prison, Manushi was four years old, and my stepmother was taking care of her.[4] BRB had gone underground. I had requested our jailer to let Manushi in when she came to meet me. Children beyond a certain age were not allowed inside the prison. Luckily, I got permission to see her for a few minutes. I proudly took her to all the places to make her familiar with my prison life. It saddened me to see so many children hanging around the prison gate to meet their mothers.

We would often hear the shouts of protesters taking the people's movement forward. We used to crane our necks to catch a glimpse of them, but the prison walls were too high. Once our friends from the men's prison sent us cooked meat. We were delighted to find a letter in a plastic bag concealed within the meat. Through the letter, we came to know of the latest events. We were always annoyed that only the men got visitors and information while we were left to fend for ourselves.

We had heard about the historic Nepal bandh (general strike) called by the UNPM on 6 April 1990. BRB was directing the movement from a clandestine destination. The masses swept the main roads in Kathmandu that day. The crowd marched towards the palace, resulting in a mass shooting.[5] One protester climbed atop the statue of late King Mahendra to smash it and was shot dead on the spot. In that incident, many were killed and many injured, while many disappeared.

The growing movement within Kathmandu Valley and outside forced King Birendra to negotiate with the agitators. However, the protesting groups themselves were politically divided. The UNPM had demanded an election to a CA, whereas the NC and ULF had only demanded the dissolution of the Panchayat system and legalization of the banned political parties. Thus, the NC and the ULF went to negotiate with the king. On 8 April 1990, the king removed the ban on political parties. On 16 April 1990, the Panchayat system was dissolved and a multiparty system under a constitutional monarchy was put in place. We were released after eighteen days, at a time when the curfew was on.[6] A new Constitution was drafted in November 1990 through a Constitution Recommendation Commission headed by the former chief justice, Biswanath Upadhyaya. The commission consisted of representatives of the king and members of the NC and the ULF.[7] While the NC and the ULF were hobnobbing with the king, BRB, heading the UNPM, declared that the agreement reached was a betrayal of the movement. The UNPM vowed to continue its struggle for a CA. We were on the streets once again, to expose the NC and the ULF's deceptive alliance with the monarchy and the futilities of a compromised parliamentary system.

By then, dozens of people had been martyred in the people's movement.

Interestingly, in 1990, I was declared 'Woman of the Year' and Krishna Prasad Bhattarai from the NC was declared 'Man of the Year' by the magazine *Antarashtriya Manch*. Ironically, however, while Krishna Prasad Bhattarai became the interim prime minister, I was once again taken into police custody on 23 August 1990. I was arrested for allegedly being involved in pelting stones at the queen in public. It was *Teej*, the Hindu festival where women fast for their husband's long life, and the queen had gone to the Pashupatinath temple complex to pray. The incident had taken place after we had left the spot.

Even after the first people's movement, I continued to be active on the women's front. We registered an NGO called Prerana Mahila Pariwar to work on gender issues. We launched various programmes such as publishing monthly poetry leaflets and books, and celebrating Teej with a progressive outlook. I was also the founder member of Nepal's Women Security Pressure Group, a united front of women from various parties, NGOs and INGOs (international NGOs). It was a pressure group to fight for women's rights and security.

Even when we were actively involved in the first people's movement, an internal struggle was brewing between BRB and M.B. Singh with regard to the political line, organizational handling and programmes. BRB finally left Masal in 1990, along with his team, to form a new party named Communist Party of Nepal (Bidrohi Masal), headed by Haribol Gajurel. CPN (Bidrohi Masal) and other parties came together to form a new party, the Communist Party of Nepal (Unity Centre), the same year. Prachanda became its general secretary.

At the time, there was utter confusion within the CPN (Unity Centre) on how to handle the new political situation, especially the impending parliamentary election of 1991. While Prachanda was all for fielding independent candidates, BRB advocated forming a united front under which candidates would be fielded. It was decided to register Samyukta Jana Morcha Nepal (SJMN) as the new party with the Election Commission. From then on, the SJMN became an open front of the underground CPN (Unity Centre). The purpose was to use the election as a front for the struggle to expose the futilities of a ritualistic parliamentary system and to prepare the ground for a new democratic revolution.

The NC won overwhelmingly in the May 1991 national election. An NC government was formed under Prime Minister

Girija Prasad Koirala (the youngest brother of B.P. Koirala). The Communist Party of Nepal (Unified Marxist–Leninist), or the UML, stood second. The SJMN won nine seats, coming in third. The NC is one of the oldest parties, which spearheaded the anti-Rana movement. Originally established with socialism and democracy as its ideals, it has over the years come to represent and draw support predominantly from the feudal and elite class.[8] The UML consists predominantly of leaders who participated in the Naxalite-inspired 1971 Jhapa uprising.[9] However, over time it has made a complete surrender to parliamentarism and broadly enjoys the support of the middle class.

Our party was satisfied with the result because, unlike the UML, it was not in our plans to make a complete submission to the standards of liberal democracy and constitutional monarchy. Instead, we had decided to use the Parliament to expose its duplicity and prepare for the new democratic revolution. The party even participated in the local election of 1992 and won significant numbers in the local bodies at district, village and municipality levels. All these parliamentary achievements were going to be used for organizing the masses for the impending revolution.

With the end of the Panchayat system, I succeeded in becoming a permanent lecturer of architecture at IoE. After the promulgation of the multiparty system, BRB and I were invited to give a talk at the Center for South Asia, University of Wisconsin-Madison, in 1990. Our trip to the USA was initiated and planned by Stephen Mikesell, an American anthropologist. It was a month-long trip beginning in Chicago, covering Wisconsin, Cleveland and Ithaca, and ending in Washington DC. The scale of American farming, infrastructure and skyscrapers impressed me.

In Wisconsin, and in Ithaca, we spoke on the people's movement in Nepal. I focused on the role of women in making the movement a success, while BRB concentrated on the politics and economy of the country and the unfinished agenda of the movement. The social science department of the university was known to lean towards the left.

Even before embarking on our trip to the USA, I was curious about the LGBT community. It was a coincidence that the woman who was my guide at the University of Wisconsin-Madison revealed that she was a lesbian. In those days, lesbians and gays were not very safe in the USA. It was interesting that they had their own bookshop catering exclusively to the LGBT community. I also found it shocking that women carried whistles to the library to guard themselves against rape.

Being architects, we went to see buildings by Frank Lloyd Wright, one of the greatest American architects, in Chicago. To our great surprise, we came to know that his first apprentice, noted architect and engineer William W. Peters, had married Joseph Stalin's only daughter, Svetlana Alliluyeva, in 1970.[10]

Our first-hand exposure to the economy and society of the USA further strengthened our belief in the need for completing the democratic revolution in Nepal.

6

Bout of Depression in the UK

victim of my own study[1]

After becoming a permanent staff member at IoE, I was selected to pursue a master's degree in housing at Newcastle University in the United Kingdom in 1993. I was excited to know more about the country where the Industrial Revolution began, where Adam Smith was born and where Karl Marx took political refuge. I was also greatly interested in their fierce, Conservative Prime Minister Margaret Thatcher, the 'Iron lady'. She was a controversial woman, also nicknamed 'milk snatcher' because she removed free milk at school during her tenure as PM.[2] However, by the time I went there, John Major was leading the Conservative government.

At the time of my arrival, two major incidents were making headlines. One was the closure of the Swan Hunter shipyard in Wallsend. Swan Hunter was once the largest shipbuilding company in the world. Its closure had brought gloom to the city as hundreds of workers were laid-off. Another incident was the chilling murder of a two-year-old boy, James Patrick Bulger, in Liverpool in February 1993. He was abducted, tortured and murdered in the most gruesome manner by two ten-year-old boys. He went missing from a shopping centre before his mutilated body was discovered near a railway line. I found this incident particularly disturbing because I had my seven-year-old daughter with me. What scared me the most were the mothers I saw carrying their children strapped with leashes around their bodies, like dogs. I could never do that to Manushi. But every time I went to shopping malls or the metro railway station, I would shiver at the thought of what had happened to James Bulger and hold Manushi close.

Initially, I found it difficult to adjust to my new life in Newcastle. From such a busy political life in Nepal, I suddenly found myself leading a sedentary, academic life. The married scholars' hostel was completely occupied. I was told to look for a private room or house on rent. I couldn't get a place on rent because I had a daughter, so I had to stay illegally in the girls' hostel of my university. Every time Manushi laughed or talked loudly, I had to hush her saying that the warden would come. One day, she burst into tears and said that she wanted to go back to Nepal. I was so desperate that I had to find some incentive for her to stay. I told her that we needed the money she was getting as child benefit (around £49 a month) in order to complete the house we were building at Koteshwor in Kathmandu. I had left the house unfinished. It was ironic that the topic of my MArch thesis was gender issues in housing in Nepal, and I couldn't get housing in Newcastle because I had a daughter. I became a case study in my own thesis. I became a victim of my own study.[3] It was only after a few troublesome months that I finally found accommodation in council housing.

The weather was miserable! I was used to sunshine throughout the year, except during the monsoon, but here it seemed to be the other way round. I had been warned that the weather in the UK could result in depression among Asians, but I did not know it was waiting to happen to me. In my case, however, there were multiple factors responsible for my impending condition.

Meanwhile, Manushi faced racial discrimination in a school that I had admitted her to. She would come to me complaining that the other children had thrown her hairband away. Her friend from Sudan got even worse treatment. I would tell Manushi that the only way to retaliate was by scoring better marks. It was a relief to find that the teachers liked her because she was disciplined and good in studies, too.

That particular school, although close to our residence, did not have a day-care centre. As a result, after she finished school, I had to take her to class with me at the university. I would tell her to draw sketches of my classmates who had come from different countries. I had a difficult time concentrating with her around. There was a lot of pressure piling up on me. My appetite was waning, I had sleepless nights and I would cry for the smallest of things. Soon, I realized that I was suffering from depression. My doctor suggested that I go back to Nepal. Also, my relationship with one of my closest friends in the university was getting worse. I tried to talk to her about my depression, but she would avoid talking to me just when I needed her the most.

Gradually, my depression lifted as my problems started getting sorted out one by one. Manushi got admitted to a new school that had many Asian students and a play centre. There was no more racial harassment. Manushi liked it there. I found a marked increase in her activity and creativity when I put her in the play centre. Every time I went to pick her up, I walked around appreciating every nook and corner of the school. It had won an award in an architecture contest.

I was able to work through the problems I faced in the university with the help of a classmate who was rather good with his studies. To my great relief, he later confessed to me that he, too, had experienced depression. I read many books on overcoming depression and thought of how poor women in remote villages in Nepal struggled to eke out a living. I wondered how they would have coped with depression with neither the knowledge nor a conducive environment. I spoke to BRB on the phone and confided in him about my state. I asked him whether I should come back to Nepal. BRB, always the cool cat, told me to do whatever made me comfortable. That was so very assuring to hear.

Frankly, I was out of touch with what was happening in Nepal at the time. I was later told that BRB, along with the other parties, had been spearheading an agitation against the NC government to inquire into the deaths of Madan Bhandari and Jibaraj Ashrit in the Dasdhunga case. They were both leaders of the CPN (UML).[4] BRB was even taken to jail for leading the agitation in the same case in 1993. Despite all that was happening in his life, he was unfazed and told me to take my decision calmly. Had he reminded me that I, being the brave 'woman of the year', should soldier on through my depression, I would have felt even more nervous. Had he told me to come back to Nepal, I would have lost confidence in myself. His response of letting me decide for myself further strengthened my respect for his democratic way of handling the crisis.

Finally, when I came out of depression, I asked my closest friend why she had been avoiding me earlier. To my great surprise, she revealed that she, too, had been undergoing depression around the same time.

I remember writing a letter to BRB, stating that I was two steps ahead of him: firstly, I went through depression; and secondly, I came out of it successfully. I was, however, concerned about how I appeared to Manushi. She had seen me as a strong leader in Nepal. And here, she was seeing me in such a pathetic and weak state. I was thankful that she handled the situation so well, silently and patiently watching me without ever complaining.

Around this time, my friend Jivraj Pokharel, who was a fellow lecturer at IoE and also studying in the UK, sent Ganesh Thapa, a young Nepali engineer from Bajura (a remote far-western district) to share accommodation with me. Ganesh taught me yoga, which helped me immensely in keeping my mind and body fit. He was a devout Hare Krishna follower. I was now keen to keep myself mentally and physically fit, knowing my temperament. I was aware that I would have to face life in jail once I went back to Nepal. I also attended a self-defence course, which helped me later during the days I was underground.

One incident particularly enlightened me. One of my English neighbours, who belonged to the working class, lost her cool when she heard the news on the radio that the UK government was sending funds amounting to £100 million to Africa. 'Why should Africa get so much money when in the UK they are becoming poorer and facing unemployment?' she complained. I explained to her that a large percentage of the grant money that Third-World nations received came back to the rich countries through the bourgeoisie of their country who came to work there as experts. She was surprised to hear that.

I was impressed by the welfare system in the UK. Having decided that BRB and I wanted no more than one child, I had long wanted to get laparoscopic sterilization done, but it had not been possible in Nepal. Back home, I had asked my enlightened 'gender-friendly' doctor to do a sterilization by laparoscopy on me, but to my surprise, she had refused, saying a single child could bring uncertainty into my married life. In contrast, I was impressed by the sensitivity shown by the doctors at Freeman Hospital, which was located nearby. They brought in an Asian doctor to speak to me, to make sure I wanted to go ahead with the procedure. When they were sure that I was mentally prepared, they performed the operation. It made me feel like I had control over my body. I felt liberated and thankful!

I loved visiting the municipality library where I used to get access to a variety of resources and information. In the UK, libraries seem to be the hub of all activities, serving as a centre for art exhibitions and tourism information, and a place for discussion. The library had various sections catering to almost all age groups and languages. I was surprised to find separate bookshelves for Bengali and Malayalam books. The section for the elderly had books in large fonts, which were easy on the eye. I was particularly impressed by the children's section, with its many colourful, illustrated and creative books. They made for relaxing and creative bedtime reading for my daughter and me. In the library, I also found the classic texts of communism, which I read with great interest.

I took every opportunity to participate in political meetings. I attended the 'Save Gonzalo' international meet in Dusseldorf, Germany, in 1993, where BRB was also invited. Com. Gonzalo, or Abimael Guzman, was the chairman of the Communist Party of Peru, or the Peruvian Communist Party (PCP), more commonly known as the Shining Path.[5] He had been arrested while leading an armed struggle in Peru. We met Gonzalo's father-in-law and mother-in-law in Germany. In London, I often visited the shadow offices of the Revolutionary International Movement (RIM), which was propagating the revolution in Peru. I also attended a week-long course on Marxism run by the Socialist Workers Party, a Trotskyist party. I visited the London office of the *Morning Star*, one of the few progressive newspapers in the UK, and made it a point to drop in at the office of the Communist Party of Great Britain, where I met veteran communist leaders. I even visited the tomb of Karl Marx in Highgate Cemetery, London. I also took the train to visit the site from where the Chartist Movement had started in Newcastle.

I regularly attended meetings held in the home of a professor of Durham University, where women professors from both Newcastle and Durham universities met to discuss the latest developments in feminism. I also used to have discussions with one of my teachers, Peter Kellett, on the nationality question.

I could have never imagined that I would become a more committed communist in capitalist UK! BRB noticed positive changes in Manushi and me when we went back to Nepal. He said I had become more knowledgeable in Marxist literature, while Manushi had become more creative and intelligent.

The credit goes to all the facilities we got in the UK and the struggles that we were able to overcome.

7

'Sorry, We Will Have to Leave This House!'

from ballot to bullet

I jumped right back into political activities as soon as I returned to Nepal in 1995. The party engaged me mostly in open activities. However, I was working discreetly at the district level. By then, many changes had taken place in the political arena. Once again, the country was seething with discontent. The NC, headed by G.P. Koirala, had advocated a neo-liberal economic policy, selling government-run factories to private companies.[1] It privatized many public enterprises such as Hetauda Textile Factory, Bansbari Leather and Shoe Factory, Harisiddhi Bricks and Tiles Factory and the Bhaktapur Brick Factory. It also downsized the bureaucracy without creating alternative jobs. The moves created a deep sense of frustration amongst the civil servants and factory workers alike. This made it easier for the SJMN to expose the fallacies of the existing parliamentary system.

At the international level, our party was engaged with the political developments in Peru, where the PCP was escalating its attack on the Alberto Fujimori-led government, a puppet of American imperialism.[2] Our party was studying PCP literature as the model on which we would develop the PW in Nepal. The arrest of PCP chairman Com. Gonzalo in September 1992 had shocked the revolutionaries of the world, particularly those in Nepal. Our party launched a movement for his release. We had managed to mobilize human rights activists such as Padma Ratna Tuladhar and others. We had even tried to facilitate Padma Ratna's visit to Peru for this (although it did not materialize). We got an opportunity to stage a rally once again when Hillary Clinton, then the first lady of the USA, visited Kathmandu in April 1995. I was taken into police custody for waving a black flag at the rally we organized during Clinton's visit. We were at the airport premises to protest against the detention of Com. Gonzalo, since the USA was supporting the dictatorial President Fujimori at the time.

It was even more exciting for me as I had already attended the 'Save Gonzalo' international meet in Germany in 1993.

After coming back from the UK, the first task given to me by the SJMN was to stand as the presidential candidate for its women's wing, the All Nepal Women's Association, in 1995 in Chitwan. The same national convention chose me to become the president under the new name, the All Nepal Women's Association (Revolutionary), ANWA (R). My mother, Heera Devi, had been the founding member of the women's association of Nepal, which was formed clandestinely during the Rana regime. This was the first time I was elected to the top executive post on the women's front.

Meanwhile, dissatisfaction with the G.P. Koirala government heightened with the civil servants' strike, the Tanakpur Barrage agreement, which was perceived as being favourable for India, and the rise in prices of essential commodities. Internal bickering within the NC made things worse. There was a rumour that a no-confidence vote would be tabled against the government, hence G.P. Koirala dissolved the Parliament in August 1994. A mid-term election was called in November 1994, in which the NC lost. The CPN (UML) became the largest party in Parliament, but without a majority. A minority UML government was formed, with Man Mohan Adhikari as the prime minister. This time, the

SJMN boycotted the election on the grounds that a traditional parliamentary system had not yielded any good for the ordinary citizens.[3]

It wasn't too long before the UML government started showing signs of social fascism. We were the only force fighting against this. They were particularly harsh towards us as they considered us extremists. Once again, I was taken into police custody for being part of *Bhitta Kanda*, or the Wall Episode (1995), a confrontation between the UML students and our party workers over the use of a wall that belonged to the Nepal Electricity Authority for writing political slogans. BRB came to meet me while I was in custody, proudly displaying the imprint of shoes on his shirt. He had been roughed up by a group of UML youths, and someone had hit him on his chest with shoes. I was told later that he had just managed to escape before someone tried to attack him with a kukri (a traditional knife). It was the SJMN leaders and cadres who had saved him.

In May 1995, the opposition parties moved a no-confidence motion against the UML government.[4] Prime Minister Man Mohan Adhikari resigned and recommended the dissolution of the Parliament. However, the Supreme Court, which had approved the dissolution of Parliament in 1994, tabled by G.P. Koirala, rejected Adhikari's move.[5] The Parliament was revived in September 1995 under the leadership of Sher Bahadur Deuba from the NC, with the support of smaller parties. All these events discredited the parliamentary system among the masses.

All the while, supporters of the SJMN were targeted by the state for boycotting the election and organizing people's resistance in many parts of the country. The first target was Rolpa, where the boycott of the election had been the most widespread.[6] It became the major site of the police's oppressive crackdown, known as Operation Romeo, against the SJMN in 1995. The onslaught was also the result of a series of violent confrontations between the NC and the SJMN cadres, in which the police had openly sided with the NC, resulting in the escalation of violence. Our party had sent Pampha Bhusal and me to Rolpa in November to observe the abuse of human rights during the operation.[7] Jhakku Subedi (elected president of Rolpa's District Development Committee from our party) picked us up in a police van arranged by the DSP of Rolpa district. On the way to Gam village, I saw children throwing stones at the police van. This was the first time I witnessed the antagonism of the people towards the police in the district.

Pampha and I met men and women in prison, who claimed to have been tortured by the police. Many young people, students, teachers and farmers claimed that they had been falsely implicated in the court of law, and were on the run. Women were allegedly whipped with stinging nettle (sishnu) on their private parts, which caused severe burning and pain. They told us they had been molested, raped and tortured. There had also been regular clashes between the communists and the NC in village melas. The police force always seemed to side with the NC.

This helped in making Rolpa the bastion of our revolution.

In 1994, the first national conference of the CPN (Unity Centre) was held, in which a detailed plan to wage the PW was prepared. In February 1995, I was invited to attend the third extended meeting of the party in Chitwan, where a decision to break away from its previous peaceful and legal struggle was taken. In short, it was a preparatory meeting for launching the PW. At that meeting, the party's name was changed from CPN (Unity Centre) to Communist Party of Nepal (Maoist), CPN (Maoist). The term 'Maoist' was incorporated to herald the revolutionary line, as opposed to CPN (Unity Centre), which was associated with reformism and the parliamentary line. We chalked out a politico–military policy, outlining the strategy and tactics of the PW.

We used slogans such as 'Everything is an illusion except political power' and 'Political power flows through the barrel of the gun'. By then, Nirmal Lama and his followers, like

Narayankaji Shrestha, had separated from the party. They were against the PW; they were for an urban insurrection, yet insisted on taking part in the parliamentary exercise. After this group left, there was unanimity about the need to launch an armed revolution even though there was difference of opinion regarding the modality. Prachanda and BRB insisted on taking a big leap into advancing the PW, while Kiran (Mohan Vaidya), one of the senior-most leaders of the Maoist party, opted for a 'wait and watch' policy.

Once again, police atrocities had started taking place. In January 1996, an incident occurred in Kubinde village of Sindhupalchowk district in central Nepal, where the police had gone to arrest a left-leaning teacher. The people in the village chased them away, resulting in the disappearance and death of a policeman who fell into a river. This resulted in the arrest of about a hundred villagers. Among them, about 70 per cent were women. The culmination of all these incidents became the catalyst for the initiation of the PW in Nepal. Things were moving rapidly. Incidents of physical assault on known goons were sporadically reported from different parts of Nepal. Later, I found out that our party had planned them as a test before waging the PW. All cultural shows were also gearing to prepare for the PW. I particularly remember the song *Krantikari Nepal lai mukta banai deu . . . niskana jhatta niska, banduk bokera niska!* (Revolutionaries, liberate Nepal . . . come out and come out soon with guns)', sung by Dhruba Gyawali who was said to be martyred during the PW. Talk of the PW had been in the air for quite some time. But we did not know when it would actually begin. M.B. Singh, the general secretary of Masal, had been talking of waging an armed revolution since the 1950s, but he had done nothing concrete to help it materialize.[8]

I had been arrested five times on various charges during this preparatory phase of the PW. While I was active in Kathmandu Valley, preparation for the PW was afoot in the rural areas. According to Bhakta Bahadur Shah, a Maoist central committee leader and former member of the CA, who belonged to the royal lineage of the Jajarkot king and had been in the militant wing throughout the PW, the voluntary defence group was formed first. The second layer was the defence force and the third was the combat force. Being the senior-most in the hierarchy, the secretary of the district party guided the combat force.

Amidst all this, I was adding a new storey to my house, which I had built in 1990. I had managed to save some money from Manushi's child benefit and my scholarship allowance in the UK and spent it all on the construction work. During this time, BRB was away on a month-long political tour. From one corner of the country to the other, he attended rallies creating the right atmosphere for the political storm that would soon sweep the country. It culminated in Kathmandu in December 1995, with the declaration that the PW would be launched. It is interesting to note that the strategy of initiating an armed struggle had been formulated almost four years earlier in the Unity Convention of the party held in Chitwan between November and December 1991. Taking part in the parliamentary election and boycotting the polls were all part of the preparation for the PW. Similarly, forming the SJMN as an open, united front and keeping the mother party underground were also tactics put in place with the same aim.

On 4 February 1996, the SJMN, led by BRB, marched to the prime minister's office to give a forty-point memorandum[9] to Prime Minister Deuba. The demands—put forward with an ultimatum of fifteen days—aimed to safeguard nationalism, democracy and the livelihood of the people.

I remember when, on behalf of the women's front, we held a press conference in Kathmandu to announce our activities; the journalists asked me why the word 'revolutionary' had been added to the name (earlier it was known as All Nepalese Women's Association). I said it was because we were revolutionaries. At that time, little did they know that it had been added in preparation for the PW.

When BRB returned from the tour, I showed off the new addition to our house. Instead of being impressed, he declared, 'Sorry, we will have to leave this house!' At first I thought he was joking. But then he told me the entire plan, and that he was leaving soon for the PW. He left on 11 February 1996, telling me to follow him soon. I told my sister Kayo about the plan of waging an underground war. I told Manushi, too; she was only ten years old. She was used to watching us being arrested and leaving Kathmandu for our party activities, and so she was not too surprised. I left Kathmandu early on the morning of 13 February 1996, leaving Manushi with my sister. I was also leaving my thirteen years of teaching job at IoE.

That very morning, posters started appearing in several places with the slogan: 'Let us march ahead along the path of People's War to establish a new democratic state demolishing the counter-revolutionary state!' Then came a barrage of attacks (*janakarwahi*) on nearly 600 police posts, banks and moneylenders from the eastern to the western parts of the country, concentrated in and around Rolpa, Rukum, Gorkha, Kavre and Sindhuli districts. In Kathmandu, a bomb was hurled at the Pepsi cola factory to signify our attack on multinational companies, which symbolized American imperialism. In Gorkha, the state-owned Agriculture Development Bank in Chyangli village was attacked. It symbolized an attack on a modern extortionist institution, the bank. In Kavre, a landlord's house was raided, and property and loan documents were destroyed. This was a warning to all the feudal forces. Police posts were attacked in Rolpa, Rukum and Sindhuli.

I carefully dressed in a sari and put on some make-up. Apart from my single attempt to impress BRB during college days, I had never done this before. Now I needed to conceal my identity for my journey from Kathmandu to Pokhara. Narayan Dahal, a party worker, guided me to where BRB was staying—a professor's house in Pokhara. BRB, I found, was down with a viral fever. His enthusiasm, however, did not ebb. I discussed the paper with BRB, which I was to present at a seminar on the nationality question, organized by the All India People's Resistance Forum (AIPRF) in Delhi. The next day, I left for Bhairahawa (present-day Siddharthanagar), my passage to Delhi.

Looking back, I realized that I was burning all the bridges to my past, to my secure and normal life, as I crossed the border.

PART II

THE PEOPLE'S WAR

8

From Free Bird to Fugitive

becoming a whole-timer

I was relieved once I crossed the border and entered India without getting caught by the police. It was very different from the time I had come here as a student. I was now a serious whole-timer of the revolutionary party. It meant that I would work full-time only for the party. I wore a sari, but had a tough time walking in it, as it was not easy matching that attire to my sprightly gait. I had put on light make-up as well and, because I was not used to it, I kept smudging my eyeliner and misplacing my bindi as I tried to wipe the sweat off my face. I kept my head covered with the pallu of my sari, as my hair was still short. I also started using different names in different cities. I found it safer, less suspicious to use names of goddesses. I would introduce myself as Durga, Saraswati, Parvati. The PW had turned not only the state of Nepal but also my life upside down. I felt my personality changing. I felt more responsible: from being a free bird I had become a fugitive, an underground party worker.

On reaching Delhi, I presented a paper on the 'Nationality Question in Nepal'.[1] The AIPRF had organized an international seminar titled 'Symphony of Freedom: Papers on the Nationality Question'. It was a front organization for the underground party, the Communist Party of India (Marxist–Leninist) People's War (CPI [ML] PW). This was my first introduction to the CPI (ML) PW. It was a grand forum attended by many foreign delegates. For the first time, I got an in-depth understanding of the various national movements around the world, including the ones in India. Thereafter, I went to attend meetings of the World People's Resistance Movement (WPRM), an anti-imperialist mass front of the RIM, in Chennai, Mumbai and Calcutta.

By the time I came back to Delhi in 1996, many events had taken place in Nepal. I recall reading in the papers that the then home minister had declared that the Maoist movement would not last more than three months.[2] The government machinery was frantically looking for BRB because he was one of the few well-known faces of the movement. They had no clue about the identity of Prachanda, the general secretary of the CPN (Maoist). There was even a popular rumour that Prachanda was the king in disguise. One section even thought that it was a movement supported by the monarchy against the parliamentary forces. Some speculated that Prachanda was actually BRB in disguise. Those who were arrested stated that they knew BRB as their leader and had never met Prachanda. This further deepened the mystery surrounding Prachanda, even as he was coordinating events using the phone line from my sister Kayo's house until it became too dangerous. He nearly got caught when he tried to move out of Kathmandu in March 1996. A spy had tracked him to a bus leaving the valley, but he remained undetected when his wife, Sita Dahal, strategically rested her head on his shoulder to make it seem like they were just another ordinary couple.

The plans made in the third extended meeting of the party (1995, Chitwan) were being executed one after another. Prachanda had studied Nepal's military history in great detail. He made plans following the policy of arming the masses. Accordingly, the fighting group, defence group and volunteer group were devised. The party made it compulsory to induct at least two women in each of these groups. As the PW advanced, a special task force (STF) was formed by putting together the best fighters from different villages and districts.

BRB's deep knowledge of the regional structure of Nepal, gathered through his PhD thesis, helped in chalking out zones in the country based on strategic importance. The middle hill regions from east to west were the backbone of the PW. The country was divided into three zones—eastern region, middle region and western region based on the north–south flow of the rivers Kosi, Gandaki and Karnali. The eastern region was put under the command of Com. Chandra Prakash Gajurel (C.P. Gajurel 'Gaurav'), the middle region under BRB and the western region under Com. Ram Bahadur Thapa 'Badal'. Prachanda was in charge of the movement in Nepal as a whole. Thus, they formed the core team. When the PW started, there were altogether nineteen central committee (CC) members, which included only one woman, Com. Pampha Bhusal 'Bidhyut'.

In the politburo meeting held in Syangja in Nepal (April 1996), it was concluded that we had achieved more than what we had planned in the first initiation period.

Soon, women led by ANWA (R) started to demonstrate against state repression. Encouraged by this, students from the All Nepal National Independent Students' Union (Revolutionary) started taking to the streets, too.

As operating within the country became increasingly dangerous, the top Maoist leadership team decided to shift to India. They used Siliguri in West Bengal and Patna in Bihar as the base for the eastern region. Similarly, Gorakhpur in Uttar Pradesh served as a base for the middle region, as Lucknow did for the western region. Meanwhile, the government launched the brutal Kilo Sera II military operation in May 1998, which made movement difficult.[3] Forced to operate only during the night, most of the Maoist leaders had turned pale due to the lack of sunlight.

So far, I had been moving around relatively freely in India. My real underground life began when BRB came to Gorakhpur, from where he was running the middle region. He was the party in-charge for that region. BRB was being sought both within the country and outside. I had to be indoors most of the time. Being accustomed to an active life, it was difficult to adjust to underground life in the beginning. BRB, on the other hand, adjusted quickly because he was a voracious reader and content with a secluded life. Yoga, which I had started practising in the UK, helped a lot. It helped me keep myself calm. BRB used to keep crossing the border, which was highly risky. Once, in 1998, he came back from Nepal with a fractured hand. Luckily, Dr Buddhi B. Thapa, who had been an active member of AINSA while studying in Ranchi, India, had treated him clandestinely in Pokhara.

To disguise myself, I started growing my hair. I also took to wearing spectacles, even though I did not need them, to alter my appearance. With my saris, bangles, necklaces, earrings and bindis, I looked like a typical housewife. Even my sister-in-law, Durga, could not recognize me when she came to visit.

I got a chance to visit some villages in the Gorkha district in June 1998. It was my first visit to one of the PW-affected districts as a full-time worker in disguise. I was surprised to find that the party had, within a short span of time, reached high mountains and remote areas where the Dalits and members of the Adivasi *Janajati* (indigenous nationalities) community lived. Before the PW started, our party's presence used to be concentrated in urban centres, and was limited to Brahmins, Chhetris and men. Now, it had reached the rural poor and women, too. I grew emotional when I saw the first exclusive women's militant squad, which had been given the duty to look after my safety. I was very touched when my mother-in-law came all the way to meet me with a bottle of milk at night. I safely returned to Gorakhpur after my trip to Gorkha.

After staying in Gorakhpur briefly, I was assigned as a member of the central headquarters (HQ) under Prachanda in Ghaziabad, Uttar Pradesh. I had to rent a room near the HQ, where Prachanda and his family stayed. I had to look after his books and logistics, and arrange meetings for him. BRB would come and visit the HQ off and on, as did other leaders. Prachanda and BRB used to have long discussions on the development of the PW within Nepal. I also used to overhear them discussing leadership issues within the party.

Being at the HQ meant that many informal meetings used to take place in my quarters. It was there that I gradually began to understand the different personalities and inclinations of the various leaders. BRB and Prachanda were interacting quite well. However, I felt that the same was not true of Kiran and BRB. Before the PW, I knew Prachanda only formally. He used to come to our house in Koteshwor, cycling all the way from Lalitpur to meet BRB. Being an underground leader, he looked too simple and young to be noticed before the PW started. But once I went underground, I started noticing his personality. He was an extrovert and loved meeting people; he could give political lectures to cadres hour after hour. He had a magnetic quality, enhanced by his powerful oratory skills, which drew everyone's attention to him.

Unlike Prachanda, his wife, Sita, was an introvert and not very sociable. In the beginning, she was not too popular with the cadres, especially with the HQ staff. People said she exuded a feudal arrogance. In fact, CC member Dandapani Neupane, who was later 'disappeared' by the old state, accused her of behaving like a queen during a meeting. He was later made to take back his words. Those loyal to Prachanda would ask me to convey these thoughts to her so that she could change her behaviour. But when I tried to do so, she retorted by telling me that I had failed to protect her image. She used to be moody during her stay in Ghaziabad. I noticed that whenever Prachanda came to my flat to refer to books (all books belonging to the party were stacked in my flat), she used to insist on leaving the flat as soon as possible. The more I tried to show my concern towards her, the more she rebuked me. Later, Prachanda told me that she did not like my presence in their flat. I was shocked, and from then on spoke to her only if needed.

To be fair, I think one needs to know Sita's background. She was only fifteen years old when she married Prachanda, who was of the same age. In fact, she was six months older than him. In the next few years, she gave birth to three daughters and a son. She had no formal education. Her parents were financially better off than Prachanda's. Prachanda was hard-working and educated, and Sita's parents thought that one day he might become a teacher with a permanent source of income. But he turned out to be a fugitive revolutionary leader. Considering his rising popularity, it was but natural that she felt isolated and insecure about her husband. She would insist that her son, Prakash, be around his father to protect him at all times.

Both BRB and I enjoyed watching good movies. Sometimes we took risks to see them. One such film was *Maachis*, directed by Gulzar, based on the Khalistan movement in Punjab, India. It depicts the struggle of young men who left their homes in Punjab to move to Himachal Pradesh in order to train as guerrilla fighters. The film struck a chord as it reminded me of Kathmandu. The song '*Chhod aaye hum woh galiyan* (We've left behind those lanes)' took me back to the streets down which I used to cycle with Manushi, back in Kathmandu. It made me think of my daughter and my sisters, whom I had left behind. The movie reflected my own situation in a way. It brought tears to my eyes.

Soon after I watched it, I got a chance to visit Kathmandu in 1997. It was risky, as I was well known there. I stayed away from my relatives' homes; I didn't even let Manushi know, as that would jeopardize my visit. By now I was used to my sari, long hair and spectacles. I would even limp while walking on the road so that people wouldn't recognize me. Sometimes, I would wear the Tibetan *bakhu*.

One morning, I was interrogated by policemen at the Sonauli border post while returning to Gorakhpur. I was overdressed and had a lot of make-up on, which led the policemen to think I was being trafficked! I told the policemen I was a teacher visiting my husband who was doing his PhD in IIT Kanpur. I thanked them for the dedication they showed to prevent Nepali women from being trafficked, and they were happy to let me go my way.

Since the very beginning, my journey as a whole-timer was in many ways different from most of my fellow comrades. While most of them participated in the PW physically in different parts of Nepal, I did so through the international department, the HQ and the overseas bureau in India. How was I to know that while they would be involved predominantly in a class struggle against the reactionary state, I would be partaking in an ideological war within the party itself? The debates that take place within the communist party on differing ideological and strategic questions, or positions, are commonly encapsulated as 'two-line struggle' or inner party struggle.[4]

In order to comprehend the inner party struggles, it is important to be familiar with the top leaders and the relationships between them. I was lucky that I was given work in the HQ during the first few months of the PW. It was the hub of the most important meetings, where unity, contradiction, transformation (and sometimes conspiracies) took place among the main leaders.

9

Relationships between Leaders

diverse personalities

During a war, the relationships between leaders matter the most. And for a communist party at war, it matters all the more. This is because the monolithic nature of communist-party functioning makes the relationship between leaders sensitive and complex. In the international arena, Stalin's relationship with other leaders, including Lenin, within the party was one such controversial example. It is to be remembered that in the 1930s, all the members of Lenin's politburo, except Stalin, were killed in a political purge.[1]

In Nepal, the main leaders who started and concluded the Maoist PW were Prachanda (Pushpa Kamal Dahal), Kiran (Mohan Vaidya), Laldhwoj (Baburam Bhattarai), Badal (Ram Bahadur Thapa) and Diwakar (Post Bahadur Bogati).[2] Since I was constantly in touch with them while working at the HQ, I could study their personalities closely.

When analysing leaders and their relationships with each other, we have to bear in mind that Nepal is predominantly a rural country with a subsistence agriculture economy. This brings with it a feudal mindset and a petty bourgeois tendency, which is compounded by the fact that the country is landlocked, with difficult, hilly terrain. So, the dominant character of most of the Nepali communist leaders would be petty bourgeois despite their commitment to Marxism–Leninism–Maoism (MLM).

It is equally important to know the history of the communist party, and also which branch each leader came from. The Communist Party of Nepal (CPN) was formed in 1949 in Calcutta, India.[3] Pushpa Lal Shrestha, the founding general secretary, was one of the crusaders who fought against the Ranas, hand in hand with the NC.[4] His elder brother, Ganga Lal Shrestha, had been hanged by the autocratic regime in 1941 for his anti-Rana activities. He was a member of the clandestine Nepal Praja Parishad.

Pushpa Lal Shrestha was soon overthrown from his position of leadership in the communist party, which he had formed. Within the undivided party, there were known to be two lines or factions of political thinking. One was the Pushpa Lal line that laid emphasis on the democratic question; he was for aligning with the NC in order to fight against the monarchy.[5] The second was known as the Rayamajhi line, headed by Keshar Jung. Rayamajhi. He was a medical doctor by profession but belonged to the landlord class. His line emphasized nationalism; he wanted to align with the king to fight against Indian expansionism. He, too, became general secretary of the communist party and later openly allied with the king. Thus, the genesis of what came to be known as the two-line struggle in the communist movement in Nepal can be traced to these two leaders. In the communist party, such a two-line struggle is looked upon as a tension between two tendencies and ideologies, one is forward-looking with an eye on the future and the other harks back to past glories.

Prachanda's name, which in Nepali means 'fierce one', in my opinion, does not match his character. Politically, he may look fierce, being the leader of a Maoist movement, but in person he is flexible. Born in a Hindu Brahmin family, his real name Pushpa Kamal, means 'lotus flower' in Nepali. Coincidently, the lotus fits his nature, too, as he is soft and has a magnetic character. One of his biggest strengths is his dynamism, coupled with his ability to take swift decisions. His lesser-known pseudonym is 'Biswas', meaning trust.

The son of a hard-working farmer who had settled in Chitwan in search of greener pastures, Pushpa Kamal Dahal 'Prachanda' saw his father being humiliated by rich Newar merchants and internalized a hatred for the upper classes at a young age. He wanted to join the Nepali Army (NA) but was rejected and decided to become a schoolteacher instead. He even worked briefly on a USAID (United States Agency for International Development) project after graduating from the Institute of Agriculture and Animal Science in Chitwan district.[6] He finally took the plunge into full-time politics in 1981. At thirty-five, he had already become the general secretary of one faction of the splintered communist party, known as 'Mashal', and remains at the top-most executive post in the unified party from 1990 till today.

However, he could easily be won over by adulation and get vindictive when criticized. He mastered the numbers game and the power game. His followers in the party were often power-hungry. Many criticize him for being an opportunist.

He sounded like a dogmatist but was a pragmatist in action. He was centrist and, to retain power, he kept shifting between BRB, who was more aligned to the Pushpa Lal line, and Kiran, who leaned towards the Rayamajhi line.

I used to get along with him quite well in the beginning. However, with the intensification of the inner party struggle, I began to see his essence and found him to be quite the conspirator. He preached like a revolutionary but was unreliable.

The second leader was Kiran, which literally means 'ray' in Nepali. However, the name he was given defies his character. Unlike the rays, he is devoid of colour and is too serious. Politically, he was more theoretical than practical. He was born in a Hindu Brahmin family. He had obtained a master's degree in Sanskrit and was well versed in philosophy, literature and literary criticism. I often saw him fiddling with his hair when confronted with disputes, or when he had to make a big decision. It is said that he often fumbled when faced with challenges. He was the senior-most whole-timer politician in the party. He was known more as an ideologue of classical Marxism than a politician. His real name is Mohan Vaidya. Some say his surname 'Vaidya' befits him because it refers to an Ayurvedic healer or a traditional medicine practitioner, and the line of Marxism he followed was traditional, too. This earned him the nickname Marxist Vaidya. He was often criticized as a dogmatist leader who was good at defining classical Marxism but could not apply it to address existing realities and future challenges. However, he was known as a principled and honest leader. Being senior-most, he had a fatherly image in the party. Since he was not very outgoing, we had a very formal relationship.

Kiran was the general secretary of CPN (Mashal) before it became CPN (Unity Centre). But Prachanda replaced him after the 'Sector *kanda*' of 1986. The 'Sector kanda' was an attack on various police posts in Kathmandu to thwart the Panchayat election. The attack was a failure and many leaders and cadres were arrested and tortured. Prachanda, in fact, has often referred to Kiran as his political guru.

There had been a constant tussle between Kiran and BRB on the question of political lines, but it never boiled down to a personal struggle. While Kiran advocated dogmatic Marxism, BRB was for creative Marxism. And Prachanda had been taking advantage of the struggle between the two by swinging from one line to the other, making sure he got the numbers to stay in power.

I had a high regard for Kiran's principled stance on classical Marxism but found him impractical. Whenever I needed books on the subject, I would borrow them from him. His wife, Sushma, was uneducated, but after the PW she made bold attempts to complete matriculation. They have three daughters.

The third leader in the party was BRB. He was known as Laldhwoj in the party, which in Nepali means 'red flag'. Ironically, despite bearing the most revolutionary name, the allegation of being bourgeois was often levelled against him because of his excellent performance in academics and his PhD degree. This was especially circulated during the PW where the uneducated cadres were in majority. BRB, too, was born into a Brahmin family. He is known for practising Marxism according to the demands of the time. Hence, he is also known as 'Marxist Doctor'.

His political line looked at the monarchy, and not Indian expansionism, as the main opponent of revolution in Nepal, making him an easy target for the Rayamajhi line supporters within the party. His higher education in India and his political activities there had made him easy prey for those who wanted to portray him as pro-India. BRB was an idealist when it came to questions of organization and power. His lack of focus in organizational matters had not only left him powerless often, but also brought suffering upon his followers. His critique of the party's monolithic tendency was looked upon as support for Trotsky. He was strictly against using organization as power to suppress dissidents. His followers were generally those who gave weightage to ideological supremacy. Right from 1980, when he joined the communist party, he had been struggling against the negative aspect of the Stalinist schooling, which advocated a predominantly monolithic thinking and style. As a result, he found himself up against M.B. Singh, Kiran and Prachanda's ideological positions.

While most of the leaders had been vacillating on whether to give primacy to the democratic question or the national question, BRB had steadfastly sided with the former.

The fourth leader was Ram Bahadur Thapa. He was called Badal, which means 'cloud' in Nepali. He is the only leader among the five to belong to the Adivasi Janajati community. He is a Magar; Magars comprise the largest oppressed indigenous ethnic community in Nepal. The name 'Badal' befits him, but

only as a cloud that produces a rumble without any rain. Badal
is philosophical when he describes contradiction, dialectics and
relativity, but when it comes to inner party struggle, he often fails
to firmly assert his political stance.

He had gone to study agronomy in Moscow but left his
studies halfway to start a revolution in Nepal. Being a janajati
leader, he was assumed to be the military commander of the
PLA, although that was not true. Having a janajati leader of his
stature in the party created a positive vibe among the janajati
masses, especially in Rukum and Rolpa. Badal talked a lot about
dialectical methodology, but in practice he was quite dogmatic in
his approach. Badal's father was a mercenary soldier, a *lahure*, who
served in the Indian Army. His wife, Barsha, was educated. They
have a son and a daughter. Badal had a brief setback in his political
career—he was demoted from a being politburo member to an
ordinary party member when he was found to be having extramarital
relations with a junior unmarried woman leader in 1997.[7]

The fifth leader was Diwakar. He passed away in 2014 after a
cerebral stroke. His name means 'the sun' in Nepali. His real name
was Post Bahadur Bogati; he came from a Chhetri family. Unlike
his name, he was like the moon, cool and composed. Throughout,
he had been a supporter of Prachanda. He always sided with the
main line passed by the majority. Post Bahadur Bogati fit the
image of an ideal communist. He belonged to a poor peasant
family and had to drop out of school after Class 8. He had gone
to India to earn money, as any impoverished farmer would do in
those days. He played a cushioning role for Prachanda. Because of
his proletariat background and his simple lifestyle, he was looked
upon favourably by most of the cadres. He was perceived as a
unifying figure within the party.

I had a good equation with him. I respected his humble
background, his modesty and his love and concern for the party.
When he passed away suddenly in 2014, I experienced a deep
sense of grief and loss. He was something of an extrovert, and

married Ram Maya, who was later a nominated member of the legislature-Parliament. The couple had two daughters and a son who was martyred during the PW.

I felt a great need to see a woman leader coming up. I looked forward to seeing Pampha Bhusal, the only female CC member when the PW started, as one of the top leaders. She was unmarried and belonged to the Brahmin caste. I was the senior-most leader after her. After the PW started, we were the only two women to reach politburo positions in the party. Unfortunately, she was demoted from being a CC member to an ordinary party member when it was discovered that she was having an extramarital affair with Badal.[8] Her ideological position matched Kiran's, which did not become mainstream during the PW.

As for myself, I became the victim of vilification. I was considered more bourgeois than BRB because I was from Kathmandu and belonged to the Newar community. I was not only educated but also asserted my opinion freely. Above all, I became an easy target because I was the wife of BRB, against whom the inner party struggle was directed during and after the PW.

The impression most leaders had of me was that, at best, I was modern, smart and amusing; and, at worst, a bit out of place, too frank and an embarrassment to BRB.

10

Centralization of Leadership

my first experience of inner party struggle

As military action accelerated in Nepal, I began to notice a strain in the relationship between Prachanda and BRB. Those close to Prachanda felt that he should be given full credit for the success. Prachanda would not raise the issue directly, but we knew he did so indirectly through his trusted cadres. He had the knack of appearing friendly to his opponents and instigating his aides to attack them.

As a cult started developing around Prachanda, BRB observed the negative side of the Stalinist tendency growing within the party, namely the bureaucratic centralization of leadership.[1] In fact, difference of opinion had always been perceived as a breach of the party's discipline and command. Even presenting a critical political comment on the leadership met with the same fate. BRB had always been critical of the undemocratic tendency that had roots in the Stalinist school of thought, which most leaders in the communist movement in Nepal used to follow. For this, M.B. Singh had accused him of following the Trotskyist line before he left the Masal.

BRB wrote a timely article on Marx, published in the weekly paper *Jana Ahwan*, titled 'Karl Marx Bata Siknuparne Kehi

Mahatwopurna Gunharu (Some of the important qualities to be learnt from Karl Marx)'. In it, he referred to Marx's answers to the twenty questions that his daughter Jenny had asked him.[2] BRB's piece was in fact a veiled attack on the narcissism and slave mentality that was growing within the party.

Citing 'simplicity' as the most coveted quality according to Marx, BRB was indirectly lashing out at those who were promoting pomposity and arrogance within the party.[3] Similarly, citing 'arrogance and hypocrisy' as the most hated quality in Marx's book, he tried to expose the personality cult that was developing within the party. Referring to 'submission' and 'servility' as the most hateful characteristics, he was trying to tell the cadres to oppose these tendencies that were seeping slowly into the Maoist movement. When asked what satisfied him the most, Marx had answered, 'to fight'. BRB interpreted this to mean that the cadres needed to find satisfaction in fighting to right wrongs within the party, too, and not only outside. The work he sought to do the most, Marx said, was 'book-worming'. This reply meant that reading theoretical works was as important as waging the PW. It is important to note that among the party cadres there used to be debates over the supremacy of 'book philosophy' versus 'life philosophy', with the former looked upon as a bourgeois tendency. It was an indirect hit against BRB. Those with degrees and intellectual capabilities were looked at with suspicion, and the dogmatists clumped them together into BRB's camp even before they knew him in person.

Lastly, while talking about Marx's motto of 'doubt everything', BRB was attacking the party's dogmatic, monolithic tendency. His article hit the nail on the head and stoked controversy, polarizing the cadres into those who liked it and those who did not. Those who appreciated the article were stamped as BRB supporters even if they had never met him. Even some of those who had been on Prachanda's side were not spared when they praised the article.

BRB stuck to his opinion about the centralization of power within the party, insisting that leadership should be organically established in proportion to the advancement of the PW.

Prachanda did not like it, and in this, he was strongly backed by Kiran.[4] Being a pro-Stalinist, Kiran was in favour of centralizing power and leadership around Prachanda.

This became particularly clear in the CC meeting held in June 1999 in Gurgaon, Haryana, during which a document relating to the centralization and establishment of leadership was presented. When BRB expressed his scepticism, he had to face heavy criticism because he emphasized on the need to focus more on policy and programme, and its execution, rather than on the establishment of a person as a leader. He was in favour of voluntary centralism. It was not enough to be 'red' aka revolutionary, it was equally important to be critical. In short, he tirelessly questioned the modus operandi of democratic centralism, where the question of managing different and dissident views was thwarted in the name of imposing centralism. He was for the creative application of Marxism where supremacy of ideology could prevail through interaction between different ideas and voluntary centralism could come in place of bureaucratic centralism. Being part of the HQ team, I noticed that many people were not talking to BRB and to those who sided with him. I felt like an odd woman out.

Within a few days, the fourth extended meeting of the party was held in August–September 1998 in Faridabad, Haryana. I was invited to participate in it as a regional bureau member. This meeting was important for me because it was my first encounter with the bitter inner struggle within the party. It was a war within the war! Sometime before this, BRB had given me a book to read, *Stalin: A Political Biography* by Isaac Deutscher. It gave me a rational perspective on Stalin and the question of centralization of leadership in the communist movement.

In the fourth extended meeting, two main agendas were raised. One was regarding the establishment of base areas in

Nepal. The other was the centralization of leadership within the party. While there was unanimity on launching base areas, there was serious debate on the centralization of leadership. Prachanda was for centralization of leadership on all three fronts—the party, the united front and the army. Kiran supported him, but BRB objected to it.

BRB was against the establishment of one leader in all the three instruments of revolution. It is important to note that up until then, Prachanda was the leader of the party and BRB was the chairperson of the SJMN, or the united front. Although there was no formal post given to anyone, there was a general rumour that Badal was the head of the party's armed wing (which he was not).

BRB's opposition was interpreted within the party as a manifestation of his desire to become the leader himself. Prachanda and his supporters went to the extent of saying that BRB, who had never stood second in class, could not tolerate playing second fiddle in the party. However, past history contradicted that charge. For instance, in the fifth national congress of the then Masal party, held in Ayodhya in 1984, even when the cadres proposed BRB as a CC member, he had declined humbly, saying that the time was not ripe for that. Again, in 1991, when CPN (Bidrohi Masal) was formed, BRB had declined to take the position of general secretary that was offered to him. He instead proposed that Haribol Gajurel take the post.

He was accused of being bourgeois, rightist and reformist because of his critique of Stalin. His criticism of centralization was also wrongly construed as opposition to the formation of the base area. BRB, on the other hand, challenged the party leaders to come up with a political justification for the centralization of leadership. His main concern was that the party should not repeat Stalin's mistakes. By centralizing all power and authority in one individual, inner party democracy could be muzzled and the party could be converted into a huge bureaucratic machine as had happened in Stalin's Russia. I later learnt that the idea of establishing Prachanda as the main leader had been hotly debated at a meeting held in Gorkha in 1995, before the PW started. It was Badal (otherwise very close to Prachanda), along with some others, who had vehemently opposed it. Kiran, however, went out of his way to support Prachanda.

One may wonder why centralization of leadership became so important for Prachanda. Before the PW started, the masses did not know of the underground party CPN (Maoist), nor did they know of its leader, Prachanda. The SJMN, which was BRB's brainchild, functioned as the front of the underground party and carried out most of its open activities. After the 1990 people's movement, it was BRB who had insisted on registering the open united front under the name of SJMN, to participate in the election while keeping the CPN (Unity Centre) underground.

The question of centralization was in limbo at the time. Prachanda raised it again at a meeting in Lucknow in 1998. Since then, Prachanda had meticulously planned to raise this issue through his confidants in the fourth extended meeting. Of all Prachanda's followers, Ishwori Prasad Dahal, a CC member, better known as 'Asare Kaka', was particularly harsh towards BRB. I remember him openly rebuking BRB, saying, 'These bourgeois careerists should be squeezed like lemons and thrown!'[5] By then, Kiran and Alok had become allies, defending Prachanda. Alok, whose real name was Yan Prasad Gautam, often went out of his way to establish Prachanda and attacked BRB relentlessly.[6]

Centralization of leadership became a recurring issue throughout the PW.

While at the third extended meeting Prachanda and BRB were in agreement during their decision to wage the PW, the fourth one saw increased mistrust between them. Prachanda's followers started using his photograph on all party material and made it mandatory to refer to his 'quotes' in all meetings and literature. This alienated BRB further from Prachanda because

BRB had developed a strong conviction over the years that a new communist party should make a clean break with Stalin's monolithic and bureaucratic organizational model.

It was Com. Suresh Wagle 'Basu' who came up with some practical advice to bridge the growing distance between the two leaders, Prachanda and BRB, in a CC meeting held in Ropar, India, in 2000.[7] He said Prachanda should help BRB establish his image within the party and BRB, in return, should help Prachanda establish his status outside the party. Sadly, Suresh Wagle was martyred within a month of that meeting.

It was a sound and practical piece of advice because Prachanda had a strong base within the party, while BRB had a hold on the public. This plan was approved by the CC. It prepared the ground for internal unity and rectification.

This was my first-hand exposure to inner party struggle. It made me a bit nervous. But I also began to see how the main leaders thought.

11

'I Will Fight with a Fuse Attached to My Heart'

shift in inner party struggle

After the fourth extended meeting, I was transferred from Prachanda's HQ to be jointly in charge of Haryana, which came under the Delhi region. Our party had divided India into six units: Delhi, Bombay, Madras, Calcutta, Lucknow and Punjab. I was entrusted with organizing Nepali workers in Haryana. It was the first time that I was engaged in fieldwork and organizational activities as opposed to departmental, theoretical and logistical work. Over time, I observed that the relationship between Prachanda and Kiran was getting colder. In fact, on one occasion in Kalimpong, they had such a loud and aggressive debate that we were scared the police might turn up! Kiran was insisting that Prachanda take tough action against BRB on charges of slander, as he had formed his own clique against the party. This was never proved. At that time, almost everyone who belonged to the erstwhile Masal group (led by Kiran) was pressuring Prachanda to take action against BRB.

After the bitter experience of the inner party struggle in the fourth extended meeting, I started taking a keen interest in reading theoretical material.[1] I remember reading the book *The Communist Movement: From Comintern to Cominform*,[2] which BRB had borrowed for me from the JNU library. I photocopied it and gave it to Prachanda. At the time, I was staying in Mangolpuri, a crowded, relocated squatter settlement then outside Delhi. The settlement reminded me of the urban poor evicted from the heart of Delhi during the Emergency period. Merely shifting urban squatters from the centre of the city to the outskirts meant that the resettled squatters came back to their original spaces. After all, that is where they were employed, after selling their new plots to land dealers.

I used to live alone in one of the flats there. I had told everyone I was from Darjeeling. BRB used to visit me sometimes, so the people there began to wonder if I was a kept woman. My landlord even asked me once if that was the case. I went numb and could not answer! Later on, I thought that was an intelligent guess, so I said yes! That saved me from further inquiries.

In a small public garden in Mangolpuri, BRB and Prachanda used to discuss *The Communist Movement*. The book deals with the question of democratic centralism and Stalin's mistakes in handling contradiction within the party. It also dwells upon the dialectical relation between the international and national communist movements. It actually laid the foundation for the second national conference document of our own party. It also helped Prachanda come to terms with the new modality of party organization, which BRB had been trying to explain over the years.

The second national conference was held in Bathinda, Punjab, in February 2001.

The hallmark of this conference was that it took a leap in the ideological field: 'Correctness or otherwise of the ideological and political line decides everything. If it is correct, everything is gained, but if it is wrong, everything is lost.'[3] It adopted the document titled 'Great Leap Forward: An Inevitable Need of History'. This document contained the synthesized political, organizational and military strategy based on all the experiences gained in the five years of the PW. Amidst heavy debate, this synthesis was summed up as the 'Prachanda Path', which was to be the guiding principle of the party. The big question posed was, how do you develop a new strategy of revolution in the twenty-first century?

Accordingly, two groundbreaking modifications to the tactics of the protracted people's war were introduced.

First, the party recognized that the success of the standard Maoist method of encirclement of the cities from the countryside and the eventual capture of the national capital was becoming more and more difficult. Concentration of all political and economic power, particularly military power, in Kathmandu meant that the 'capture' of the city would likely fail even if the Maoists controlled all of the countryside. Therefore, it was proposed that a Leninist-style 'urban insurrection' needed to be 'fused' with the Maoist-style protracted people's war. This meant that the party needed to stimulate a mass uprising in the national capital. With this realization, the party initially focused more on campaigns that would get them political attention and publicity in the city. By 2005, the emphasis shifted to military raids figuratively phrased as 'climb on the back and strike at the head'—the 'head' referred to the district headquarters and the national capital, the 'back' referred to the areas surrounding the cities.[4]

Second, the party leadership decided to put more effort into developing contacts and dialogues with leaders of the parliamentary parties. This meant that alongside an armed revolution, simultaneous attempts for peace negotiations were to be carried out. The second national conference announced its main political slogan as: 'Consolidate and expand base areas and local state power! Advance towards the creation of central people's government.' The party outlined some specific schemes: to utilize the contradictions within the enemy camp and target assault on the main enemy; continue the policy of being open for negotiations with different forces, including the reactionary government; focus on issue-based tactical alliance against the main enemy; the slogan of this tactical initiative was to be 'Form an interim government through a conference of all political parties and organizations! Guarantee the formation of a people's Constitution under the leadership of the interim government!' A further extension of the party's programme included the demand for an election for a CA.[5]

These steps signified major political departures for the party: from an initial exclusive reliance on armed/military struggle in the hinterlands to its fusion with an urban mass movement; from sole reliance on war to incorporation of peace talks and demand for CA elections.

These shifts in political and tactical approach were in essence a reflection of significant ideological departures that the party was undergoing during this period. Until the second national conference, the Stalinist influence was heavy within the party's leadership. This conference addressed the necessity to learn from the mistakes of the international communist movement, particularly Stalin's. While Stalin played a crucial role in fighting against fascism and defending the communist movement across the world, when it came to handling internal party affairs, debates and decision-making, he had made serious mistakes. The party recognized that Stalin's treatment of the communist party as a monolithic unit devoid of internal differences and debate was problematic. Therefore, it was considered more appropriate to take a cue from Mao's understanding of dialectics. For Mao, inner party struggle (or the two-line struggle) was the lifeline of the party.[6] According to him, as long as different classes exist in society, different parties would exist, and as long as a political party exists in society, inner struggles/debates would persist. He had asserted that the struggle and unity between opposing tendencies was the correct 'dialectical' method of arriving at the correct decision/conclusion. In short, negation of internal differences and ideological debates in the name of practising 'democratic centralism' would throttle the development of Marxism. He also felt that it was not enough to make the party a 'vanguard' organization; it needed to infuse voluntary and spontaneous participation of the people, too.

The Maoist party in Nepal, by arriving at this ideological clarity during the second national conference, had essentially hit out against dogmatic and sectarian tendencies within the party leadership. BRB was visibly pleased and optimistic about these shifts. However, for Com. Kiran, these changes were very hard to accept and internalize. The Stalinist influence was relatively stronger and deeper when it came to Kiran and his supporters. I remember Kiran venting furiously during the conference, 'I will fight this battle with a fuse attached to my heart!' I had never seen him so angry and emotional before. Throughout this conference, I noticed that Prachanda stayed aloof from Kiran, which surprised me because he used to consider Kiran his political guru.

I couldn't help but feel sorry for Kiran.

If one were to recall the genesis of inner party struggle in Nepal's communist movement, it was Pushpa Lal's insistence on a 'democratic' alliance against the monarchy versus Rayamajhi's 'nationalist' alignment with the Panchayat regime and the king to oppose the 'bourgeois' political parties. It exposed the first visible cracks within Nepal's communists. This debate had been haunting the communists ever since it surfaced in the second congress of the Unified Communist Party in 1957, and later resurfaced inside the Maoist party as well. Simply put, the 'nationalism vs. democracy' debate revealed the dilemma among the party leaders regarding their political strategy of identifying the 'chief enemy' or 'chief contradiction' in existing society in order to utilize the divisions within the 'enemy class'. The faction led by BRB gave greater priority to a 'democratic' struggle to topple the autocratic monarchy. The more orthodox view led by Kiran insisted on accomplishing a 'nationalist' alliance with the monarchy against Indian expansionism and imperialism, and their domestic stooges—the parliamentary parties.

It was obvious that Kiran would be upset with the second national conference's decision to fuse the orthodox protracted people's war with urban insurrection and to simultaneously reach out to parliamentary parties for peace talks and CA elections. He considered the idea of forming an interim government through an all-party conference and the creation of a new Constitution through an elected Constituent Assembly as an ideological deviation and a thoroughly 'revisionist' shift in the party's political strategy.

Kiran was also not very happy with the naming of the party's guiding principle as 'Prachanda Path'. He preferred the name 'Prachanda Thought'. To ensure that this did not deify any person, the conference's political document clearly spelt out that 'Prachanda Path' represented an advanced set of ideas based on 'collective leadership'. Henceforth, Prachanda was to become the 'chairman'—a new post created in place of general secretary of the CPN (Maoist). This conference also prepared the groundwork for the formalization of the armed force into a formal military structure—the PLA. Additionally, it created the base for launching a central people's government in the form of the United Revolutionary People's Council (URPC), which was to be headed by BRB.

So, while in the fourth extended meeting Kiran and his faction had triumphed, in the second national conference it was BRB's ideological and political line that prevailed. This was the turning point, which brought the party to peace negotiation.

This conference was important to our line as it finally endorsed BRB's ideological and political line with overwhelming support. In this conference, a total of four women were inducted into the CC. So far, Pampha Bhusal had been the only female CC member, but she too was demoted because of an extramarital affair. Now I was inducted along with her and two other women—Jaipuri Gharti and Rekha Sharma. The political document approved by this meeting made a significant reference to the role of women in accelerating the PW.

I was overwhelmed to reach this position after so many years of overground and underground work. Belonging to an oppressed linguistic community myself, I was also happy when the party decided to fuse the national liberation movement with the proletariat movement.

12

Development of Democracy in the Twenty-First Century

a strategic leap

After the historic second national conference in February 2001, a major incident took place in the summer of the same year, which altered the course of Nepali history as well as the trajectory of the Maoist movement in a significant way. On 1 June 2001, the entire royal family, including the king and nine others, were massacred inside the palace.[1] It was widely circulated that Crown Prince Dipendra had killed his own family because of his parent's refusal to allow him to marry the woman he loved. This was the official version, but many did not buy it. Subsequently, the deceased king's brother, Gyanendra Shah, who was suspected to have played a role in the royal massacre, ascended the throne. It is worth recollecting that Gyanendra Shah, the second grandson of King Tribhuvan, was declared king at the age of three (in 1950) by Mohan Shumsher Jung Bahadur Rana (the last PM of the Rana regime) when King Tribhuvan went into exile in India.

This incident further stimulated the Maoists to focus on the tools and infrastructure needed to build their base areas in order to quickly realize their aim of capturing the central state power.

As a follow-up to the second national conference, I attended the first national conference of the PLA at Kureli, Rolpa, in September 2001. For this, the combat force, the defence force and the volunteer forces were transformed into regular PLA formations such as sections and platoons, signifying a qualitative leap in the structure of the army. This resulted in the formation of the military headquarters, of which Com. Prachanda was declared chief commander.

The next day, at the same spot, the first national conference of the URPC was held. In this conference, the common minimum policy and programme of the URPC was ratified. I was excited by this development as the URPC consisted of representatives from the CPN (Maoist), the PLA, various class and mass organizations, the local people's committees and prominent personalities. The URPC was formed to function as the embryo of the future central government. Its main objective was to institutionalize the new democratic people's republic in the country. BRB was the chief of the URPC.

Interestingly, both these events took place even as the first round of peace talks was going on with the government in Kathmandu. These two events had long-term strategic importance. They helped consolidate and expand base areas through many successful military raids, and they expanded the reach of the URPC to new areas.

In June 2003, I was called to attend the CC meeting at Dumla in Rolpa. BRB had already left for Kathmandu to prepare for a second peace talk in February. Before the dialogue for initiation of peace could happen, BRB was in favour of aligning with all the political parties against the monarchy to strengthen the democratic republic agenda. Knowing BRB's intentions, the king refused to meet him, even though he was the head of the peace negotiation team. In August the same year, when the peace-dialogue was in progress, the Royal Nepalese Army (RNA) executed seventeen unarmed Maoists in Doramba, thus ending the ceasefire and peace talk.[2]

I was travelling to Rolpa via Balrampur in India. A woman comrade was supposed to help me reach my destination in Dumla. Unfortunately, she lost the way and we kept going around in circles. Finally, we reached a spot that was clearly used for defecating and realized that we were close to human habitation. We found a hut from where we got directions. Minutes later, we spotted a *goral*, a deer-like animal, in a river that had run dry. She cornered it and killed it by throwing stones at it. Carrying the kill, we looked for a hut to rest at night, but we couldn't find one. Then the sound of dogs barking led us to more huts. It was already dark, and we took shelter in a hut in which an old man lived. The man saw the dead goral but refused to believe that a woman could have killed it. He kept insisting that the animal must have been sick. We hid our anger at his underestimation of our capabilities and shared the meat, carrying the rest of it to eat later.

The closer we got to Rolpa, the better the communication system seemed to get. There were communication posts at regular intervals where we could rest, eat and read the latest magazines and newspapers. Our local comrades guided us from each post like in a relay race, where after crossing each post our guides would also change. The party had collected food for us from the masses.

People in Rolpa were surprised at how nimbly I could climb mountains. They had thought that I would find it difficult to trek as I came from Kathmandu. I told them that I was called 'mountain goat' in India, a nickname I had earned from some foreign students when the Indian Council for Cultural Relations took us to Kashmir. The secret was that I was a good sportswoman. I had been told by one of the foreign students that when you have to walk continuously on a steep incline, you should look at the ankle of the trekker ahead of you. I used this technique when I had to climb high mountains in Rolpa. Sometimes I used to get dizzy looking at the continuous waves of mountains that we had to traverse.

Upon reaching Dumla, I attended the CC meeting where the historic document 'Development of Democracy in the 21st Century' was approved. As mentioned earlier, the discussions at the second national conference had already prepared the ground for formulating this crucial document.

The document was historic in the sense that it was not only a critical evaluation of the dogmatic communist movement, but it also introduced a restructure of party functioning so as to have space for democratic exercise. The document began with a quote by Lenin: 'Marxism is not a lifeless dogma, nor a completed, ready-made immutable doctrine, but a living guide to action.'[3] It was an attack on the dogmatist way of thinking, which emphasized the monolithic tendency in all aspects of life. The Kiran faction did not like the document. What surprised me was that even RIM[4] did not appreciate it; they considered it to be a sort of reformism as it weakened the concept of 'dictatorship of the proletariat'. This document helped our party to break away from the Stalinist line.

The essence of the document was that a party and a people's state needed to be under the constant scrutiny of the masses. This was because it had been observed that a party and a people's state considered to be proletarian, revolutionary, democratic or socialist at a particular time, place and condition turned out to be counter-revolutionary at another time, place and condition.

It was thus concluded that the masses should have the right to participate in the socialist competition through free and democratic exercises. They should have the right to check impending counter-revolutions through control and supervision of, and intervention into, state matters. Similarly, they should have the power to recall elected leaders if they betrayed the masses. However, it was also spelt out that free democratic or socialist competition could take place only within the limits of an anti-feudal and anti-imperialist state. It had been observed that communists were good at destroying the old reactionary state, but when it came to making a new progressive state, they had often fallen into counter-revolution. Thus, the people had the right to form a new revolutionary party to counter the old one.[5]

Shortly after the ratification of this document, the URPC held elections in all the villages in Rolpa, Rukum and Salyan districts. In most of the villages, candidates officially endorsed by the Maoist party won. In Rolpa, one Maoist candidate lost in Oat village, while in Rukum, out of forty-three villages, Maoist candidates lost only in the villages of Purtim Kanda, Kotjahari and Rugha. In Rolpa, Santosh Budha Magar was elected as the head of the district people's government. In the state organizations, 40 per cent quota was reserved for women and a 20 per cent quota for the Dalits in the ward, village and district people's government. We often found that party committees were more powerful than the people's government. This was not a healthy trend as the function of the party is to make policies, not to intervene in day-to-day matters of local governance.

I was excited when the document 'Development of Democracy in the 21st Century' was approved unanimously because this would have far-reaching consequences in the communist movement across the world in general and Nepal in particular. The question of striking the right balance between democracy and centralism had always hounded me. BRB and I often thought about how the communist movement would be sustainable, particularly when the party came to power. We were concerned that communists often could not handle leadership effectively, especially when it came to choosing and replacing leaders and running the state. In short, we wondered why a counter-revolution often followed a revolution.

One book that gave us clarity on the subject was *Crisis of Socialism: Notes in Defence of a Commitment* (2006), written by Randhir Singh. He had been a professor of political science at Delhi University, and also happened to be the father of one of my classmates from SPA, Priyaleen Singh. In the book, he dwelled in great detail on handling democracy within a party. We bought several copies and circulated them as reference material among party leaders in Nepal. Just as *The Communist Movement* helped in formulating the historic document of the second national conference, *Crisis of Socialism* helped in shaping 'Development of Democracy in the 21st Century'.

After attending this historic CC meeting at Dumla, BRB and I returned to India. We watched a movie called *Munna Bhai M.B.B.S.* in the theatre. Interestingly, we found a parallel between the thrust of our political stance in Dumla and the movie's message. In the movie, the bureaucracy within the medical system was artfully exposed. A fake doctor, Munna Bhai, was shown winning the hearts of patients through simple, warm gestures and egalitarian behaviour. On the other hand, the bureaucratic real doctor, the principal of a medical college, was cleverly portrayed as the bad guy for his anti-mass approach. We told our friends not to miss the movie.

Our honeymoon with Prachanda soon came to an end when leaders such as Com. Kiran and Com. Gaurav were arrested in India. Gaurav was the first to be arrested (August–September 2003) in Chennai, followed by the arrest of Ram Karki, Matrika Yadav, Upendra Yadav, Bamdev Chhetri and Suresh Ale Magar (January–February 2004) in Delhi. Prachanda had a narrow escape. Kiran was arrested in April–May 2004 from a hospital in Siliguri, where he had gone for an eye operation. Eleven CC members were apprehended in Patna in May–June 2004.

The arrest of our party leaders in India brought another twist in our party's inner struggle. The democracy vs. nationalism debate made a sour entry once again.

13

Solidarity, Sabotage and the South Block

our relationship with India

Communism and Maoism came to Nepal through India—Calcutta, to be precise—and not directly from China.[1] The first Communist Party of Nepal was established not in Nepal but in Calcutta in 1949. So was the Nepali Congress Party. The Naxalite movement in India directly influenced the Jhapa uprising in eastern Nepal. Nepal's people's movements, too, drew inspiration from events in India. Most Nepali politicians had, at some point, either studied or lived in India. Moreover, during India's freedom struggle, some Nepali politicians had not only participated in the movement for Independence but also been arrested for it.[2]

During the anti-Rana period, Benaras and Calcutta were bases for Nepali leaders on the run in India.[3] My father, too, had visited Calcutta, Benaras, Patna and Delhi during the anti-Rana movement. It is not surprising that there is a sister organization of almost every major Nepali party functioning in India.[4] The open border with India, coupled with a largely similar culture, has facilitated cross-political activities in both countries. It so happens that the most densely populated states in India—Uttar Pradesh and Bihar—border the densely populated Terai region of Nepal.

After the Treaty of Sugauli was signed between Nepal and British India in 1816, the former took on the status of a semi-feudal and semi-colonial country.[5] Because of the slow industrialization, compounded by low productivity and dependence on agriculture for subsistence, unemployment was rampant. For most of the villagers in the remote parts, Kathmandu, the capital city of Nepal, held no charm. Instead, urban centres in India mattered more as they provided employment, and even education. Also, many cities in India are more accessible than Kathmandu from some villages in Nepal.

On the flip side, the overwhelming influence of India in almost all arenas prompted most leaders, particularly the leaders of the communist movement in Nepal, to be critical of its role in Nepal. The open border between Nepal and India has been looked upon as a safety valve for maintaining status quo in Nepal.[6]

However, for those longing for democratic changes in Nepal, India has been a 'model', 'help' and 'safe haven'.

Considering the mass migration of Nepali workers to India, the CPN (Maoist) had already envisaged the strategic advantage of using the neighbouring country as a rear base. The Overseas Bureau (OB) had already divided India into six regions, with Delhi, Bombay, Madras, Calcutta, Lucknow and Chandigarh as the central points of operation. When the party's HQ was shifted to India, the importance of the OB grew even more. The main leaders of the PW were staying in different parts of India, where politburo and CC meetings of the party used to take place clandestinely. Through the ABNES, the mass organization front of the party in India, the OB used to make arrangements for logistical support. This is why ABNES was banned by the Indian government in December 1998.[7] Family members of Nepalis working in India were of great help as they not only provided logistical support to the Maoists but also, in some cases, joined the PW in Nepal.

Since BRB and many other leaders like Raju Nepali, Bamdev Chhetri, T.B. Pathak and Moti Rijal had studied or/and worked there, we used our contacts to mobilize Indian politicians, students, civil rights activists, cultural groups, intellectuals, journalists and sympathizers in favour of the PW. Some of them were Gautam Navlakha (then associated with the *Economic and Political Weekly*), Anand Swaroop Verma (editor of *Samkaleen Teesri Duniya*), Professor Randhir Singh (Delhi University, retired; passed away in 2016) and Professor S.D. Muni (JNU, now retired). We used India, particularly Delhi, as a centre to mobilize the masses to support the PW through demonstrations, seminars, interactions and cultural programmes. The most memorable programme was a grand mass rally organized in Delhi on 15 February 2004, in support of democracy and establishment of a republic in Nepal. One of the notable speakers was Prof. Muni who spoke about the fallacy of the Indian government's policy on Nepal. We regularly organized such events to launch our activities at the South Asian level through our International Department. It became a base to expand our international contacts.

Human rights activists like Padma Ratna Tuladhar, Daman Nath Dhungana and Devendra Raj Pandey came to India to meet with us and to facilitate peace dialogues between the Maoists and Nepal government.

Having been in India before the PW started, I saw great changes in the functioning of the OB. Before the PW, the bureau used to engage itself with the rescue of those cheated by human traffickers and would look into the welfare of Nepali workers in India. During the PW, the OB used to operate in various states in India for propaganda, for sheltering and hospitalizing injured and sick combatants, for logistical supply, for establishing Asian and international contacts, and for garnering support for the PW. The presence of Nepali workers across India made the country fertile ground for giving them political training, organizing them and recruiting them as fighters in Nepal.

We used to assert that we had the power to cause disruption in sensitive places in India if it played tough on our leaders working there. We could have very well pulled it off as there were Nepali people working as security men, cooks and caretakers in the homes and offices of important politicians, bureaucrats and businessmen. Let's take the example of Raju Nepali. The eldest of seven children, Raju came to Delhi from Arghakhanchi district in Nepal to work in a hotel, earning Rs 100 per month. He then went on to work as a night guard, earning Rs 500 per month. After that, he worked as a cook in the house of a senior Planning Commission member. Raju's servant quarters were used as a meeting place for many fugitive communist party leaders like M.B. Singh, Nirmal Lama and C.P. Gajurel 'Gaurav'. He was entrusted by M.B. Singh to contact BRB and bring him into the Masal party fold. He was also given the job of launching ABNES.

One day, Rishikesh Shah, an ex-minister of Nepal, came to meet Raju at his servant quarters. Raju had arranged for him to meet M.B. Singh. The house owner, who happened to open the gate, was pleasantly surprised to see Rishikesh Shah at his door and asked him the reason for his visit. Shah replied that he had been given this address to meet Raju Nepali. It was then that Raju's employer realized how important his servant was for Nepal. Later, Raju Nepali went on to become the central adviser of the Maoist party. He not only participated in the PW but his wife was martyred during the movement. It was he who introduced BRB to M.B. Singh. No wonder BRB calls him his organizational guru.

Bamdev Chhetri was another Nepali worker who came to India in search of a job and education at the age of seventeen. Born to a hill Brahmin family in the Gulmi district of western Nepal, he was the eldest of seven children. His father had to sell his land so that he could study up to Class 10. He ended up in the JNU canteen, working as a waiter, when he met Professor Parimal Kumar Das. Prof. Das found Chhetri to be a promising young man and employed him in his house. While working there, he

completed his schooling till the twelfth standard. He attended
night classes and eventually won a scholarship and completed a
master's in economics. He then started working at the JNU central
library as a section officer. In 1998, he left his job to become a
party whole-timer. He was one of the important links between the
party and Indian politicians, intellectuals and civil liberty groups.
No wonder he was one of the few Nepalis who were arrested and
sent back to Nepal during the PW. He later rose to become a
politburo member in the party.

Being familiar with Delhi beforehand was a great advantage
for me as an underground cadre. In Delhi, we changed our shelter
several times. I was particularly surprised to find myself in an
underground shelter in Rohini Enclave in 2001, a settlement I
had visited in 1979 as a student of architecture. At that time, it
had been in its rudimentary form. Little did I know that I would
be staying in the same settlement as a fugitive some day!

The OB played an important role in collecting funds for
launching the PW. Each party member contributed his or her
month's salary once in a year, which was collected and sent to
the HQ. Such periodic collections played an important role in
sustaining the PW in the beginning.

A campaign named *Sagarmatha Dekhi Sagar Abhiyan* (from
Mount Everest to the sea) was launched to spread the message of
the PW and to organize the Nepali workers employed in India.

Party workers in India often took the huge risk of transporting
injured PLA or cadre members from Nepal to India and back.
T.B. Pathak, one of the important leaders of the OB, told me of
one such incident. Two injured PLA comrades were being sent
from Nepal to India for treatment. The accompanying comrades
had booked the two injured comrades in separate compartments
of a train. However, one of the injured comrades, a female
PLA member, died in the train before reaching Jalandhar, their
destination. Fearing that he would be recognized, the person
accompanying the body disembarked at Jalandhar, where Pathak

was supposed to receive them. The train reached its terminal station, Amritsar, with the body on board. It was a challenge to search for and bring the comrade's body out of the train. However, at last, they located it and brought it to a safe place in the cover of darkness. The cremation, too, was fraught with risk.

Pathak represented a typical migrant worker in India. He was the youngest of seven children and came from a poor family in Gulmi. At the age of sixteen, he came to Delhi to study further and used to stay in his elder brother's rented room. At eighteen, he joined the Indian Army in Gorakhpur in 1967 and participated in the 1971 war between India and Pakistan.[8] He left the army in 1976 to join Indian Overseas Bank in Jalandhar as a clerk. He quit in 2005 to become a whole-time worker in the party. His family, particularly his wife, were supportive of the PW. He later became a CC member in the party.

Using our contacts, we sent Indian doctors who were sympathetic to the PW to various regions of Nepal. These left-leaning Indian doctors not only treated the injured combatants but also trained the health team in Nepal. They were impressed to see how health assistants were conducting major operations—mostly in cowsheds—successfully. We did not have a single MBBS-degree holder in our health team. As the Indian doctors secretly treated the injured in the border areas, they marvelled at their fast recovery and zest for life.

The Indian Nepali community in Jalpaiguri, Dooars and Darjeeling in West Bengal played an important role in supporting the PW. Some were even martyred for the cause in Nepal. They were brought within the party fold through AINSA and ABNES. Organizing them was not very difficult since they belonged to an oppressed nationality and were often exploited by tea estate owners in West Bengal. I particularly remember a Dalit Indian Nepali woman who was pursuing a PhD at the University of North Bengal. After she joined AINSA, she tore up her certificates and plunged into the PW in Nepal. She later got married to a Maoist

cadre from Dailekh district in Nepal. She was nominated as a
legislative member in 2007. I have been told that she went back to
Siliguri after the PW to complete her PhD.

There was also a teacher and a member of the Communist
Party of India (Marxist), CPM, who had joined ABNES along
with other CPM cadres. There was such a close relationship
between the Indian Nepali community and our party that Kiran
and Prachanda even got their daughters married to students in
Siliguri. Our organization in Siliguri hosted many CC meetings,
including international ones. During the state of emergency in
Nepal (2001), many Indian Nepali party workers and leaders were
imprisoned in India, and many had to flee their homes when the
Indian security forces came after them. Today, they feel isolated,
as the focus of all activities has shifted to Nepal.

According to Pathak, who continues to work in the OB, nearly
seventy Nepali workers and students from India were martyred
in the PW. The bureau had sent approximately three brigades of
workers from various parts of India to fight in Nepal.

However, there was a great sense of fear and anxiety within the
party when a string of arrests of Nepali Maoist leaders from various
parts of India started taking place. King Gyanendra tactfully used
the 2001 World Trade Centre attack in New York to brand the
Maoist PW as 'terrorism', both at home and at an international
level. The arrests began with that of C.P. Gajurel 'Gaurav', who
was working as a party representative of RIM, in south India, just
as he was about to board a flight to London.[9]

All these incidents corroborate our claim that the royalist
canard to link the PW with the Indian government is total
hogwash. Our relation with India was with its people, not the
state.

14

'Workers of All Countries, Unite!'

international relations

The party had already gauged the importance of India as a launching pad to expand its international relations. This was especially true of the Revolutionary International Movement (RIM), which had opened a South Asian outpost in India, where Com. C.P. Gajurel 'Gaurav', a standing committee member of the CPN (Maoist), was working along with staff members from Nepal and Bangladesh.[1]

The RIM was founded in London in 1984, with the aim of making it a centre for all Maoist forces in the world. By 2004, it comprised fourteen communist parties from twelve countries. Some of the parties from South Asia were the Communist Party of Nepal (Maoist), the Communist Party of India (Marxist–Leninist), the Maoist Communist Centre (MCC), the Ceylon Communist Party (Maoist), the Communist Party of Bangladesh (Marxist–Leninist), the Purba Banglar Sarbahara Party and the Communist (Maoist) Party of Afghanistan. Outside South Asia, there were the Peruvian Communist Party, the Revolutionary Communist Party, USA; the Communist Party of Iran (Marxist–Leninist–Maoist); and the Maoist Communist Party (Turkey/north Kurdistan).[2]

BRB had been working in the international department even before the PW started. His involvement in international activities became more pronounced during the PW. I, too, joined the department as soon as I became a whole-timer. Communists are, by nature, internationalists. The famous cry 'Proletarians have nothing to lose but their chains. They have a world to win. Workers of all countries, unite!' reflects it. My personal experience tells me that the closer you are to revolution, the more attached you become to the international communist movement.

Once the PW was launched, international relations with different communist parties began to expand. BRB, as head of the international department, was responsible for publishing regular issues of *The Worker*, the English mouthpiece of the CPN (Maoist). It was published right from the start of the PW till its very last year. I, too, started working for the magazine. My job was to collect material and get the Nepali articles translated into English. *Janadesh*, a weekly Nepali newspaper of the CPN (Maoist) reprinted in India, kept me abreast of the latest news. I regularly contributed articles in *Janadesh* and *The Worker* on gender, Dalits and other burning issues. *A World to Win*, the mouthpiece of the RIM, used to be printed from Delhi and covered developments in revolutionary movements across the world. This magazine offered updates on Nepal's PW for readers in different parts of the world. At the South Asian level, the World People's Resistance Movement (WPRM) was formed in India under the aegis of the RIM.[3] It was an anti-imperialist and anti-feudal forum that mobilized forces in India in support of Maoist movements within South Asia. They helped us form an organization called All South Asian Lawyers and Human Rights Activists in Nepal, which looked into litigation and human rights issues in South Asia and also the propaganda of the PW. Li Onesto, an American journalist, went to the base areas in western and central Nepal to report on the PW in 1999.[4] She was a Maoist sympathizer and a correspondent for the *Revolutionary Worker* newspaper; she helped in internationalizing the PW in Nepal through her book *Dispatches from the People's War in Nepal,* based on her journey to the base area.

At the regional level, we formed the Coordination Committee of Maoist Parties and Organizations of South Asia (CCOMPOSA) on 1 July 2001. This was set up in line with our party's concept of building a platform to bring together all the revolutionary movements in the region and to exchange experience and ideology. One of the aims of this group was to build a strong anti-imperialist resistance movement. The CPN (Maoist) from Nepal, the Ceylon Communist Party (Maoist) from Sri Lanka, the Purba Banglar Sarbahara Party (Central Committee), the Purba Banglar Sarbahara Party (Maoist Punargathan Kendra) and the Bangladesh Samyabadi Party (Marxbadi–Leninbadi) from Bangladesh, the Communist Party of India (Marxist–Leninist) People's War (CPI [ML] PW), MCC, Revolutionary Communist Centre of India (Marxist–Leninist–Maoist) and Revolutionary Communist Centre of India (Maoist) from India constituted the CCOMPOSA.[5] The first meeting of CCOMPOSA took place in Siliguri. The media reported with alarm that a 'compact revolutionary zone' was being created from Dandakaranya (India) to the Himalayas (Nepal).[6]

For us, meeting the leaders of the CPI (ML) PW and the MCC was perilous as they were being hunted, and so were we. We would meet them at different locations across India to elude surveillance. However, our relations were primarily of an ideological and political nature; we were not involved in the subversive issues that jeopardized Nepal–India relations. My first impression of the CPI (ML) PW members was that they looked knowledgeable and technologically savvy, while comrades belonging to the MCC looked more traditional and naive. Often, we used to mediate between them and encourage them to come under one party.

In September 2004, they finally merged into the Communist Party of India (Maoist).[7]

We also helped facilitate the formation of a Maoist party in Bhutan. These parties were curious about the fast development of the PW in Nepal and were particularly interested in knowing how our base areas functioned. They wanted to know how we had fused the issues of class and other forms of oppression.

While in India, I met many senior leaders of the CPI (Maoist). I still remember Com. Kobad Ghandy who used to come and meet us frequently. We used to get along quite well, perhaps because we came from similar intellectual backgrounds. He was arrested in 2010 while propagating the activities of his party. I also met Com. Azad (Cherukuri Rajkumar), one of the senior-most leaders and spokesman of CPI (Maoist). Later, we learnt that he had been killed in an encounter in 2010. I even met Com. Ganapathi (Muppala Lakshmana Rao), the then general secretary of the CPI (Maoist). I thought he would be much older but was surprised to see such a young face. I remember having discussed how the Maoist movement in Nepal was geared towards socialist-oriented capitalism, while in India it was directed towards achieving socialism.

The RIM outpost in Europe also helped in mobilizing the Nepalis working in Belgium. They were instrumental in stopping the sale of 5500 automatic rifles to Nepal by the Belgian government. Belgian former health minister Magda Aelvoet, in fact, resigned in protest against a government decision to allow the sale of machine guns in August 2002.[8]

People representing the RIM took a keen interest in understanding the ideological trends, strategic issues and the inner struggles waged within Maoist parties in different countries. We were particularly curious to know about what was happening inside the Peruvian Communist Party (PCP) and the fate of its chairman, Guzman. We were careful enough not to repeat their mistakes of deification of the main leader. The debate with RIM helped us in naming/labelling our thought. There was a great debate on how to name the thought based on five years of PW experiences. There was ambivalence on whether to use the label 'Guiding Thought of the Party' or 'Prachanda Thought'. They were against using any form of 'thought' or 'ism' as it connoted universality. Ultimately, it was decided that the name 'Prachanda Path' would be adopted. Similarly, the debate with RIM helped us arrive at the correct position on the question of establishing leadership in the party. They had warned us about the consequences of deifying Guzman, particularly after his arrest from Lima in Peru. This helped us, too, to become cautious of deifying Prachanda.

I fondly remember an Iranian woman comrade from the Communist Party of Iran (Marxist–Leninist–Maoist) who used to often meet with the RIM team in India. She would give me books on women's issues, and we would discuss the activities of women guerrillas in different parts of the world.

However, despite their wide international experiences, the RIM had been adopting a rather dogmatic line. They seemed to believe that a revolution could be achieved through war and war alone.[9] They were against any kind of negotiations or dialogues. They were also not happy with our line: 'Development of Democracy in the 21st Century', which advocated that the revolutionary party should be subjected to investigation, monitoring and surveillance by the people. They were against the concept of accepting multiparty competition in a socialist state. For them, this was reformism. As a result, they were unhappy with BRB's line and more comfortable with Kiran's. It is important to note that the RIM had severed ties with the CPN (Unity Centre) in 1990 precisely because the latter had decided to participate in the national election after the first people's movement.[10] It was only when the CPN (Unity Centre) decided to boycott the election in 1994 that it was taken back into the RIM fold. The RIM was never in favour of a Constituent Assembly election. All they believed in was class war.

Notwithstanding our bittersweet relations with RIM, we were clear that revolutionary parties must learn from each other. We were equally clear that revolutionary movements must develop and pursue their own policies and programmes suited to their concrete conditions.

When the party HQ shifted to Nepal from India in 2004, the international department, too, moved there. I was excited to be able to finally work in Rolpa, the epicentre of the PW!

15

Tears in Phuntiwang

pain from one's own

When I reached Rolpa in August 2004, I found a marked change from the time I had visited in 1995, before the PW. The revolution had spread across Nepal. However, its epicentre was mid-western Nepal. As a prelude to the formation of the Maoist base area, a 'special region' had already been formed, bringing together nine districts—Rolpa, Rukum, Salyan, Pyuthan, Arghakhanchi, Myagdi, Gulmi, Baglung and Palpa. This was to take the shape of the Magarat Autonomous Region later. The creation of this special region was based on the high concentration of whole-time cadres, leaders, PLA members, the militia and strong mass support in the area. It was an area dominated by the ethnic Magar group. Of these districts, Rolpa, Rukum and Salyan became the core. In due course, the base area was created, earmarking fourteen villages in Rolpa and Rukum. Thawang in Rolpa district was made the capital of the base area of the mid-western region.

However, unlike our earlier trips, our visit to Rolpa in August 2004 was not so pleasant. Given the arrests of our leaders in India, there was a prevailing climate of suspicion within the party. This was reflected in the CC meeting held from 8–17

August 2004 in Phuntiwang, a village in Rolpa with a strong presence of Maoists.

Prachanda, BRB, Diwakar and I had left India for Nepal to organize the CC meeting. I could tell from the body language of both the top leaders that they were not at ease with each other. They would not even sit at the same table while eating. Even while walking, their pace was different. It was after reaching Phuntiwang in Rolpa that we came to know that Prachanda had started doubting BRB with regard to the arrest of our leaders in India. It was there that their differences began to spill out into the open. In the CC meeting held in Phuntiwang, BRB was subjected to heavy criticism. He was again accused of being a rightist, soft towards Indian expansionism and an anarchist. BRB's political line was aggressively attacked. The arrest of Com. Kiran, Com. Gaurav and others had made the inner party struggle unhealthy, and it was very clear in the Phuntiwang CC meeting. It was at this meeting that Devendra Paudel, a CC member and a close follower of BRB's line, was forced to resign without even a preliminary inquiry into his alleged crime. Prachanda's clique was suspicious of him because he was not arrested while most of the other comrades in Patna in India were arrested.

Prachanda again started moving away from BRB's line and slowly began falling into Kiran's. He started going against the spirit of the second national conference, in which autocratic monarchy was identified as the main internal contradiction of Nepal, against which the PW should be waged. Prachanda advocated Indian expansionism as the main contradiction of Nepal, which was Kiran's line. BRB's line of prioritizing the attack against the monarchy was abandoned. Instead, a 'trench war' was declared to prepare for an impending war with India. The cadres began to dig trenches in preparation for military offence, even as allegations and counter-allegations between the two leaders flew thick and fast. While those siding with Prachanda called BRB an Indian expansionist stooge, those siding with BRB called Prachanda the monarchy's stooge![1]

Prachanda also took the opportunity to revive the line he had proposed in the fourth extended meeting—the necessity of centralizing leadership. He wanted to implement this for all three instruments of the revolution: the party, the people's army and the united front. Not only that, he wanted to be the head of all the central departments of the party. His photos were put up everywhere alongside Marx, Engels, Lenin, Stalin and Mao. I repeatedly pointed out the fallacy of such a portrayal, as it indicated that the Prachanda Path had developed into an '-ism' or a distinct ideology, which was not true. With great hesitation, his photo was put aside. His quotations were put up in meeting rooms; almost all articles written had some reference to his quotations, and most of the speeches delivered mentioned his name.

I remember being particularly disappointed when Prachanda started backtracking from the political line approved during the second national conference. In despair, I once asked him at one of the CC meetings who coined the pseudonym 'Biswas'—meaning 'trust' or 'belief'—for him when his activities were sadly contrary to the meaning. Despite the political risk, I had asked this question boldly, but he did not respond.

The barrage of attacks on us was mounting. We were castigated for our 'bourgeois' degrees. I was picked on not only because I was the wife of BRB, but also because I was an educated, vocal and Kathmandu-origin woman. BRB would tell me to remain silent because whenever I voiced my opinion, they would say it was his voice, as if I did not have my own identity. Whenever the orthodox faction called me bourgeois, I would retort, 'Yes, I am. But it is one step better than being feudal.' This irritated them all the more. I found that most of them concealed a feudal mindset under the garb of dogmatic communism.

They accused us of being 'book philosophers'. Apparently, they wanted to create a false debate over which was correct: book philosophy or life philosophy. Life philosophy was looked upon as superior and revolutionary, with its followers believing themselves to be the upholders of the class war. Book philosophy was looked down upon as being bourgeois and anarchic. It was even said that we had a low opinion of PLA members, as they were the least educated. We were portrayed as snobbish scholars who hated the PLA and cadres from the lower classes. These were all baseless allegations, which we denied. Nevertheless, I was deeply hurt.

It was ironic that while BRB was often attacked for his degrees within the party, in public he was admired as a person who had joined the PW despite his excellent education. In fact, many bright students had left their schools and colleges to join the PW, drawing inspiration from him. His presence in the party during the PW added legitimacy to the movement. We often heard people saying that if a person like BRB had joined the PW, then the movement must be worth it. It was painful to see many promising cadres and PLA members being demoted, transferred and punished for supporting BRB's political stand.

BRB often complained that he had been treated like a Dalit inside the party during internal struggles. I admired his patience and often teased him by calling him a 'Marxist Gandhi', a Gandhian who suffered atrocities from his own class for their own sake.

During the PW, democratic centralization was difficult. Leaders and cadres were often discouraged from exercising democracy in the name of war. BRB was one of the few leaders who dared to question Prachanda on the methodology of his leadership. But this was not taken kindly.

Unable to compete with BRB's ideological and intellectual capacity, the followers of Prachanda's line used to say that BRB should be like Engels who followed Marx without self-interest. When CC member Janardan Sharma brought this up during a meeting, I replied, 'If Prachanda wants BRB to act like Engels, then Prachanda should first behave like Marx.' At one point,

I asked BRB to seriously consider taking over the reins of the party. But BRB said that it was not in his nature to aspire to leadership.

I respected his feelings and the stand he took, and never asked him about it again.

While Prachanda needed BRB's vision, intelligence and knowledge, he also made sure to keep BRB's position weak within the organizational structure. On the other hand, BRB also knew that he needed Prachanda and the party organization for the execution of his vision. BRB had his own style of fighting the internal ideological–organizational battles: he would pen critical articles exposing the wrong political stances and actions taken by the leadership, he would write notes of dissent and even resign from his formal position. But he took care to never indulge in activities that could split the party.

Prachanda's followers would get irritated when BRB was portrayed as an ideologue by the media. In 'political classes', which is the general Maoist term for closed-door lessons or lectures delivered by senior leaders to party cadres, if BRB's speech received a better response from the audience than Prachanda's, it was not taken kindly. Just after the palace massacre in 2001, BRB had written an influential and timely article analysing the event, titled 'Let's Give No Legitimacy to the Beneficiaries of the New Kot Massacre', which got published in *Kantipur* newspaper.[2] In the article, he had pleaded for institutionalizing the republic and exposed the massacre as a design of imperialism. Despite the newspaper being confiscated and the publishers arrested, the article was well circulated; we were told that it was photocopied and sold and resold in Nepal. I could see at the time that some of our comrades were visibly disturbed by the popularity of that article.

In the Phuntiwang meeting, almost all the CC members spoke one by one, condemning us for being bourgeois and stooges of Indian expansionism. I kept asking myself why we had been attacked when we had voluntarily come to serve the PW. The more I questioned myself, the more difficult I found it to control my tears. I started sobbing in the hall when I could no longer take the attacks on BRB and our line, and finally I left the meeting. For the first time, I felt that inner party struggle could be more hurtful than class struggle against the enemy.

Soon, BRB tendered his resignation from the URPC, the central schooling department and the publicity and publication department. In his resignation letter, he cited his opposition to the centralization of leadership and the monolithic tendency growing within the party. Subsequently, the question of centralization of the main leadership was suspended. The central women's department, of which I was the head, was also dissolved.

The Phuntiwang meeting left a bad taste in my mouth. That was the first time I had cried at a meeting.

16

Red Flag over Rolpa

the making of a new world

Amidst growing bitterness within the party, I found myself intrigued by life in the base areas. Before the PW started, it was envisaged that the base areas would be formed out of consolidated guerrilla zones. Building base areas was the central strategic issue in the PW. It was the very foundation of the PW, without which it could not be waged, sustained or developed. Base areas were needed in order to run a parallel government, under which people's courts, cooperatives, schools, model villages, communes, small-scale industries and developmental activities, including improved farming, could be set up, protected and developed. They had to be strong enough to resist any intrusion from the old state.

Although a decision to form a people's government in autonomous regions was taken in 2001, it was only in 2004 that nine people's governments in as many autonomous regions could be declared under the PLA's protection. These included the Magarat, Tharuwan, Tamuwan, Tamsaling, Newa, Kirat, Madhesh, Seti–Mahakali and Bheri–Karnali autonomous regions.

Before I went to Thawang, the capital of the Magarat autonomous region, I had a completely different picture in my mind of what it would be like. I had thought it would be atop a mountain, but instead it was located right at the base of one. It was protected by the mountains to the north and bordered by the Rhi *khola* (stream) to the south and a narrow tributary to the west.

Thawang had a long history of resistance against the Panchayat regime.[1] M.B. Singh, the veteran communist, had sowed the seeds of communism there in 1956. By 1959, all votes went to the communists in the national election. In the 1980 national referendum, an outcome of a students' revolt, Thawang village had voted against the monarchy. Again, in 1981, this village boycotted the elections for the Panchayat legislature. Once again in 1994, almost everyone in the village boycotted the mid-term election. The village also had a long history of militancy. The culture of fighting among the heads of different villages had been institutionalized before the PW started. Later, such fights took a political turn when the communists and those belonging to the Nepali Congress started becoming hostile to each other. Thawang village had had a long history of class struggle, with almost every household losing a family member to it.[2]

By the time I started working in Thawang, thirty-two Maoists had been killed by the state, while the Maoists had killed two people belonging working for the state during the PW.[3] This shows the intensity of the class struggle in the area. As a result, it was liberated from the old state before other areas during the PW. Women in Thawang had been particularly militant as the army often raided their village. This also helped in enlisting women in the political struggle.

Thawang met all the requirements to function as the epicentre of the base area. It had militant masses with a history of participation in radical politics; the masses had been steeled in the crucible of class war. Right from the beginning of the Panchayat period, people in Rolpa, particularly Thawang, had been practising defence, offense and underground life. Whenever a major police operation was launched by the state, the people knew how to retreat to the jungle, leaving the older generation to face the police when they swooped into villages. United, they knew how to sabotage local elections or punish renegades. It was constituted almost entirely of the oppressed ethnic indigenous community, the Kham Magars.[4] It had the most developed militia. Generally, the Maoist party worked under the concept of 'one village, one militia'. As time advanced and provinces were formed on the basis of ethnicity and region, the militia, too, was formed to reflect these ethnic-regional identities. For instance, in Rolpa, Rukum and Surkhet one could see the formation of the Magar militia under the banner of the Magar Liberation Front to support, protect and strengthen the Magarat autonomous region.[5] Normally, each household was expected to send/contribute one family member as militia personnel for protecting the region.[6]

We were taken to Lisne village in Rolpa to show us the remains of an intense fight the PLA had waged successfully against the RNA in the daytime, which was a first for them. There, we saw a tree which still had more than 100 bullets lodged in its trunk, a victim of the crossfire. The PLA captured two light machine guns, five self-loading rifles, one sub-machine gun, their bullets, as well as a cell of 81-mm mortar, maps and important official documents. Five RNA soldiers were killed. Six PLA members were killed.[7] In fact, they managed to chase away the rest of the RNA by the evening. We also learnt that many children were separated from their parents during the crossfire.[8]

It would be interesting to note how the party started outlining strategies for converting parts of the countryside into base areas. The process of forming the base areas had started with the withdrawal of the police, officials, teachers, businessmen and moneylenders who openly sided with the old regime. The void created by the absence of the old regime was quickly occupied by the new state run by the CPN (Maoist) by building parallel government structures. They set up a people's court, people's cooperatives, communes, a model hospital, model schools, roads, trekking trails and horse trails. While the *jana adalat* (people's court) was the institution of justice, it was the jana militia (people's militia) that actually executed the order.

One could see the red flag of the CPN (Maoist) atop mountains, on trekking routes, on huts and buildings. Checkposts were set up at regular intervals to prevent infiltration of the enemy, comprising the security forces of the old state, into the base areas. The checkposts also functioned as points of exchange of information through letters, notes and documents. They doubled up as resting places for party members, the PLA and the militia that travelled from one area to the other. Often, such posts were abandoned houses of families who had left the area or the homes of those sympathetic to the Maoists.

As the PW advanced, we required a more consolidated and specialized division of labour. The party and the URPC introduced labour, production and consumer cooperatives. Since the base area served as an important rear zone for the war, it needed to supply and manage logistics, food and other requirements. Before a battle, the base area would be buzzing with activity—people would be sewing PLA uniforms, preparing dry food, making *doko*s (conical baskets made from bamboo), assembling temporary stretchers, cleaning weapons, etc. Those injured in the PW needed treatment; hence, a hospital was constructed in the base area. Similarly, those who had been displaced by the war in the 'white areas', that is areas with strong state presence as opposed to the Maoist 'red areas', needed to be resettled. Even the families of the PLA members needed to be sheltered. This gave birth to several communes in Rolpa, Rukum, Jajarkot and other districts.

I had been to the Ajambari people's commune in Rolpa and the Balidaan people's commune in Rukum. There, families not only stayed together but they also worked together to farm and rear animals. I also visited the Jaljala commune where people lived in individual houses but shared the agricultural and animal husbandry work. It was in the Ajambari commune that I ate a mouse for the first time in my life. It tasted like any other meat, except that there wasn't much meat on it. It did not taste like the frog I had eaten in Kerala. That had tasted like chicken.

Magars are fond of eating meat, especially pork. We explained to them the benefit of eating salads. At first, they teased us and asked, 'Are you teaching us to eat *ghaans* (grass)?' But gradually, salad became a part of the diet in the base area.

I also saw pigs being reared in the cooperative near Thawang. I was told that earlier pigs used to be reared in each household. Pigs were fed human faeces through holes made in the terrace floor. This was an unhygienic process, which could cause diseases. After Rolpa became a Maoist base area, people were gradually taught to separate their living areas from the pigsties. Local units of the Maoist women's organization also taught people how to keep their homes clean. There were two whole-timer comrades who had degrees in agriculture studies. They not only trained people in farming and breeding of cattle, but were also actively involved in forming agro cooperatives. The dams made by the local community on the Rhi khola impressed me. Similarly, reforestation campaigns were conducted in the Jaljala forest to protect Thawang from soil erosion.

An ambitious construction project was undertaken to build Martyr Road (Shahid Marg), a 91-km-long road running from Dahavan, Rolpa, to Chunwang, Rukum. It was inspiring to see the valiance of the people constructing the road despite being attacked by RNA troops in helicopters. There would be between 500 and 800 people working on the road at any given time. One person from each household had to contribute physical labour for this task for at least a week. Building this road had an impact both within the country and outside. It was to illustrate that the party was not only capable of destroying the old state but also determined to construct a new one.

I remember the deafening silence in the remote areas of Rolpa. Looking at the rugged, naked mountain facing south, I used to think of how perfect the slope would be for mounting solar panels. And when I came across the deep gorges, I would think of how they could be a destination for adventure tourism. I thought of how the water streaming down the cliffs could provide mineral water.

I worked in the base area for six months. The CPI (ML) PW group in India couldn't help but be impressed by our advancement and determination in building the base area in such a short span of time.[9] They had started an armed struggle much before us, in the 1980s, but they still had a long way to go.

17

Liberation or Death?

gender issues

When the PW started, I was president of the women's front, ANWA (R). After completing this tenure, in 2001, I was appointed as the head of the women's department of the CPN (Maoist). This gave me the opportunity to work on matters at the policy level. I had the advantage of reading the draft documents of the CC through either BRB or Prachanda, before they were finalized. My input in making the documents gender-sensitive was usually ratified by the party. I used to write regularly on women's issues in various newspapers and magazines. I continued writing on class, Dalit, ethnic and gender issues in the *Worker*. I remember having written a book review on *Five Sisters: Women Against the Tsar*.[1] I also translated various materials on women and communism from English to Nepali. I was very passionate about gender issues. I even wrote a poem, which got published in Nepali and translated in Hindi in some newspaper around 2000, an excerpt of which is:

> **We don't need to . . .**
> We don't need to be scared of bloodshed in war
> We have been shedding menstrual blood.

121

We don't need to be told to leave homes for war
We have been leaving our maternal homes.

We don't need to be taught to fight against inequality
We have been struggling against it from womb to tomb.

As the Liberation Tigers of Tamil Eelam (LTTE) movement in
Sri Lanka was at its peak in the 1990s, I was particularly interested
in knowing the role of women in that organization.

It was widely reported that LTTE fighters carried cyanide
capsules with them in case they got caught.[2] The Maoists in
Nepal used the slogan 'mrityu wa mukti (death or liberation)'.
They were motivated to fight till the end, leaving survival
to matters of chance, but not at the cost of betraying the
revolutionary cause. They used martyred bodies as examples
of their defiance against the state! They sent across a very clear
message of political supremacy over the military and, hence, at
no time did any leader prescribe giving cyanide capsules as an
escape from arrest, torture, rape and death by the police or the
army. The party has acknowledged that when caught by security
forces, women generally did much better than men in keeping
party secrets and not surrendering.[3]

The recruitment of women for the PW, in fact, led to the
recruitment of women in the RNA, too. The degree of women's
participation in a movement of nationwide impact was in fact
unprecedented in Nepal's history. One of the first rare moments in
the country's political history, where a woman emerged as a leader
of a social movement, was the case of Yogmaya Neupane.[4] She was
a spiritual woman who led a movement against the Rana oligarchy,
demanding social reforms in 1918. In 1941, she, along with her
sixty-eight disciples, jumped into the Arun River in eastern Nepal
and died as an act of rebellion when the Rana rulers did not heed
their call for reform. Another commonly acknowledged instance
of women's participation in the national struggle was the Battle of

Nalapani in Dehradun (now in India), fought between the British East India Company and Nepal, where they fought hand in hand with the men to defend their country.[5] Similarly, women have been participating in various movements against the monarchy and the Panchayat regime.

However, the PW was different from the previous upheavals. For the first time, a policy was made to ensure compulsory participation of women in the PLA and the embryonic revolutionary government in the form of the URPC. During the course of the PW, more than 3000 women were martyred.[6] Such was the level of women's participation. This makes one wonder: what made them participate in the PW in such numbers?

Despite being burdened by all forms of oppression and juggling their jobs and homes, they found no recognition, neither at home nor at their workplace, or in society. The multifaceted role of women, taking into account all forms of oppression, came to the forefront when the PW brought them into the public sphere for the wider public good. The war gave their efforts a sense of purpose, a wider perspective, and participation in all spheres of life gave them the recognition they were seeking.

The PW also gave the women an alternative vision of their work, body, family, life and death. Entering a situation of total war helped them expand their outlook beyond a conventional women's movement into ideological, organizational and military struggle. One important contribution of the PW towards women's empowerment was that it not only exposed the intertwined nature of class and gender oppression within the old state, but it also familiarized the women with the functioning of the new state where women's liberation was to become an integral part of a revolution's success. At the micro level, many practical problems faced by women were duly addressed. For instance, liquor sale was banned in public (although home-made liquor was tolerated, especially amongst indigenous households). Men who molested,

raped were kept in labour camps. Similarly, men who married
without divorcing their previous wives were criticized before the
public and assigned labour. Husbands thrashing their wives were
sent to labour camps. It is to be noted that women members of the
Maoist sister organization have also actively participated as jury
members and judges in the people's courts, which have been set up
to resolve local disputes.[7]

On the political front, the women's question was considered
to be of strategic importance right from the beginning. Before
the PW started, there were only two women whole-timers, Purna
Subedi (who became deputy speaker of the Constituent Assembly
in 2008) and Pampha Bhusal (who became a minister), in the
party. Before the PW, even within communist parties, there
was a general trend of men becoming whole-timers while their
wives were normally encouraged to support the family. The PW
overturned this division by making wives whole-timers as well.
Women were found to be participating on virtually all fronts: from
the infantry to the international department. The creation of a
separate women's department inside the party gave a boost to their
voice at the policy-making level. Two women managed to reach
the politburo level, Pampha Bhusal and myself, though there were
none at the Standing Committee level. At one point, the CC had
nine women members.[8]

Women attained much higher ranks in the military wing
than the political fronts. To start with, it was mandatory to
have at least two women in all military formations. But soon,
the numbers swelled. At one point, there was even an entire
female platoon force. Many women became commanders
and commissars at various levels, from section to platoon to
company to battalion to brigade. The highest level the women
reached in the PLA was as commissars at the battalion level.
An example is Onsari Gharti Magar, who later on became the
first female speaker of the Parliament of Nepal and was elected
unopposed. However, none reached the level of commissar or

commander of the division level, the highest rank in the PLA. However, to make the same mandatory, to have at least two (or even one) women in various layers of the party structure was not encouraged. As a result, women lagged behind men in all the layers of party structure.

On the economic front, women constituted the main workforce in running community-based farms, cooperative-based production such as dry food, dry fruit, shawls, cotton bags, papermaking, etc. They mobilized people in villages using the slogan 'one village, one unit, one product'. They invested in small-scale cottage industries and small-hydro projects. In fact, the women's front was considered to be one of the richest fronts in the base area. I particularly remember Manu Humagain, who was vice-president of the cottage industry department in Rolpa. She was from Kathmandu and one of the few women who were brave enough to leave behind their families to join the PW. Before joining the PW, she was running a small-scale industry in Kathmandu, producing pashmina garments. After the PW ended, she became the acting president of the National Women's Commission in Nepal.

On the administrative and social front, I found that women were more eager to learn, more organized and more committed than most men. They ran crèches. They organized literacy programmes. The formation of autonomous regions based on identity and power exercise also gave women an identity, in addition to the one based on their oppressed ethnicity and region. Inter-caste, inter-regional and inter-religion marriages took place. There were some third gender people, too, who participated in the war. Women's participation in the base areas had been phenomenal. They organized women using slogans like 'one village, one organization, one house, one member'. The ANWA (R) worked in tandem with local parties to build gender-friendly model villages, where they facilitated giving of parental property to daughters.

I often went to different parts of Nepal to give 'political lectures' to ANWA (R) activists and the PLA. One of the most fulfilling moments was when the women's department, under my initiative, conducted a national survey during 2002–03 on the condition of women in the party, both the PLA and URPC.[9] Nine sets of questions were asked. They were related to personal background, organizational background, family background, personal interest and experiences, gender-related questions, mental and physical health-related problems, organizational problems, method of solving problems and miscellaneous questions. It was empowering to see the comprehensive response women gave from the battlefield through the in-charges of different regional commands of the party.

The survey revealed that most of the women participating in the war were nineteen to twenty-five years old, and they represented the first generation of Maoist women activists. In terms of educational qualification, a large percentage of women had stated that they had attended school up to Classes 6–10. Hence, they were not entirely illiterate, as most people assumed. It was found that the majority of women belonged to an oppressed ethnic, Dalit or regional group. Amongst them, Madhesi women were the least in numbers. The survey also revealed that a majority of women were unmarried. Among those who were married, more than half had children. With regard to their class background, it was found that more than 50 per cent of women in the Maoist movement identified themselves as belonging to the lower class, or the proletariat.

This survey also revealed that more than 80 per cent of women in the movement were whole-time party workers. Majority of them had joined the Maoist party after 1996. Regarding their past political background, most of them claimed to have had no political affiliation; only 19 per cent of women had previously been associated with the UML, while about 1 per cent had been affiliated with the NC before becoming Maoists.

The percentage of women in the party's CC was found to be only about 1 per cent.[10] Inside the military wing, the PLA, less than 1 per cent reached the level of battalion commander. As far as mass fronts were concerned, women's presence in their central committees was found to be about 5 per cent only.

When asked about their family's political background, more than 75 per cent stated that their family had left leanings; less than 10 per cent of women revealed that their families were NC supporters. More than half of the women who participated in this survey affirmed that their family members were also a part of the Maoist movement in some role or the other. More than 40 per cent of married women were found to be working in the same region as their husbands.

In response to what their main reason behind joining the PW was, more than 60 per cent stated 'rebellion against class oppression', while more than 15 per cent mentioned 'rebellion against gender oppression' and less than 10 per cent mentioned 'ideological commitment'. If they could choose which party wing they wanted to join, most of the women revealed that they would choose the military wing.

When asked about what they liked the most about the Maoist movement, more than 35 per cent mentioned 'devotion and sacrifice', about 30 per cent mentioned 'commitment towards goal and ideology' and around 20 per cent mentioned 'equality between men and women'. When asked to identify their favourite woman leader of the international communist movement, most of them chose Jenny Marx, some chose Rosa Luxemburg, while around 15 per cent said they had no idea about these leaders.

Regarding their experience of gender discrimination within the movement, more than 70 per cent said they had experienced it in minor ways, while less than 5 per cent stated that such discrimination existed immensely. About 20 per cent said it did not exist at all. More than 25 per cent revealed that discrimination was felt most inside the PLA. More than 20 per cent mentioned that it existed in the party. Interestingly, nobody mentioned mass fronts as an area where they faced discrimination.

Similarly, the survey asked women to assess which 'outlook' was dominant within the Maoist movement—'egalitarian', 'feudal' or 'capitalist consumerism'? Interestingly, about 45 per cent women felt the 'egalitarian' outlook was dominant in the party, around 30 per cent chose 'feudal' tendencies, while about 15 per cent saw 'capitalist consumerism' as the dominant tendency.

The survey also revealed that more than 60 per cent of women favoured 'love marriage', about 30 per cent preferred marriages arranged by the party, while around 5 per cent women preferred marriages arranged by the family.

Regarding the major obstacle that married women faced in the movement, more than 35 per cent mentioned 'looking after children', more than 20 per cent stated 'husband's intervention' and about 15 per cent mentioned 'health-related problem'.

When asked if they felt physically and mentally weaker/ inferior to men, more than 65 per cent mentioned that they did feel inferior sometimes, and more than 20 per cent said they never felt that way. When asked if they felt their reproductive health affected their performance, more than 60 per cent stated 'yes', around 15 per cent said 'no'. It could perhaps be deduced that a majority of women felt they were weaker than men because of reproductive health-related issues.

The survey also asked unmarried women to classify the grimmest health-related problem that they had to face. More than 60 per cent mentioned 'menstruation', more than 20 per cent stated 'unavailability of sanitary pads', and about 10 per cent revealed that 'lack of good diet' affected their performance in the party.

The survey also made some eye-opening revelations regarding the development of women's leadership within the Maoist movement. More than 60 per cent mentioned that not enough efforts were made for the upgradation of their ideological and political knowledge. About 10 per cent women felt that the men had a problem with accepting women as their leaders. Within the PLA, more than 25 per cent women felt that their male counterparts regarded women to be physically weak; around 20 per cent stated that women considered themselves to be weaker than men. As far as the *jana sarkar,* or people's government, was concerned, it was revealed that more than 40 per cent women were not satisfied with the low participation of women, and more than 15 per cent stated that men found it difficult to accept women leaders in state functioning.

These revelations expose the immense challenges that women face to establish themselves as leaders in all the three organs of the movement—the party, the PLA and the parallel government.

The survey also asked women to select what measures must be taken to increase their participation in the movement. More than 55 per cent felt that women should be identified as the leading agents of revolution, about 15 per cent stated that women should be given special rights within the organization, and around 10 per cent women felt that the participation of family members of the top (male) leaders in party activities could be the best way of attracting other women to the movement.

Regarding the efforts that the party should make to develop women's leadership, the majority of women saw regular discourse on ideological and political knowledge as the most significant step to enhance their leadership. About 10 per cent felt that a special campaign to promote women leadership in various wings of the party would be more effective. About the same percentage of women felt that men's hesitation to give responsibilities to women in military and non-military tasks must be put to an end.[11]

Survey results came in from all the regions except the far-western region, which was under the command of Pampha Bhusal. I had expected more cooperation from her but was quite disappointed when she did not take an eager interest in conducting the survey. Later on, I found out that she had deliberately not given out the survey forms to cadres in her region. She considered the survey to be bourgeois and belittled its significance because it looked like an NGO/INGO questionnaire.

I felt sad to hear such thoughts coming from the senior-most woman leader.

18

Love, Marriage and Children

the morality question

In a country that has been ruled by the autocratic monarchy for hundreds of years, feudal values were bound to come in our way. In a society where polygamous relationships existed despite legal penalizations, and men could easily get away with infidelity, it was natural that the Maoist movement in Nepal would be faced with concerns regarding marriage, love and sexual relationships.

I remember BRB telling me how he was sick of hearing repeated allegations of extramarital affairs against M.B. Singh in the fifth national convention of the CPN (Masal) held in 1984. It seemed as though Singh, the general secretary of the party, was being punished for the same issue twice.[1] He was allegedly involved in an illicit relationship with a female leader. Delegates from the RIM, too, were invited to attend the fifth national convention. BRB had been given the task of translating documents, speeches, etc., from Nepali into English for the foreign delegates. Even the members of the RIM had asked him, 'Why are you all only talking about a sex scandal at your convention?'

What I found so 'feudal' and disagreeable about the way these issues were dealt with in communist parties was the hypocrisy,

double standards and conservative attitudes displayed in formal
meetings and outside. With the launch of the PW, would the
Maoists be in a position to break away from these feudal cultural
tendencies besetting the communist movement in Nepal?

The answer, sadly, was not in the affirmative. Within the
first year of the PW, many top leaders started having extramarital
affairs. Of these, the one between Badal and Pampha Bhusal,
also known as Himali, created the biggest stir within the party,
not only because Badal was one of the senior-most leaders of the
party but also because he was very close to Prachanda. So was
Pampha Bhusal, who was then the only woman CC member
in the party. Badal was married while Pampha was not.[2] When
they fell in love, the right to get a divorce became an important
debate. I was in favour of granting this right while Sita Dahal,
Prachanda's wife, was against it. Finally, the party took action
against both Badal and Pampha by demoting them. In most
cases of extramarital affairs, often termed as 'cultural deviation',
it was a senior married man falling for a junior, single woman
comrade. Punishments meted out were relative to their rank
in the party. Badal had to earn his living by doing computer
work in Dehradun, India. Pampha got herself a job in a dot-pen
manufacturing factory in Calcutta.

I recall that soon after, Shittal Kumar (Haribol Gajurel),
another CC member, was found to be having an illicit relationship
with Shila, another married comrade working under him. While
the party was taking action against these two, another comrade,
Sudarshan (Hemant Prakash Oli), who was already married and
on the verge of being promoted to a CC member, was found to
be involved in an illicit relationship with an unmarried comrade.[3]
The party took action against him shortly after. I remembered
asking myself how Sudarshan's conscience allowed him to hide his
relationship when he knew he was being promoted, and after three
CC members (Badal, Pampha and Shittal) had been demoted on
similar charges. He could have just revealed the relationship. These

episodes made me think how hypocrisy was deep-seated in the communist movement: we say one thing but do something else!

Interestingly, these incidents led many wives to leave their jobs and go underground to be with their husbands. Nainkala left her teaching job to join her husband, Badal. Similarly, Savitri left her job as a lecturer to join Shittal Kumar. However, not all wives joined their husbands for these reasons alone. Many wives who had initially hesitated to join the PW were forced to team up with their husbands when the police and the army started torturing them at their homes to get them to reveal the whereabouts of their husbands.

When such extramarital affairs started getting exposed more and more at the leadership level, BRB wrote a political article, *Janayuddhalai Prem Garna Sikoun* (Learn to Love the People's War)'.[4] The gist of this article was: revolutionaries should devise their own ways to use sexual energy for more constructive social and political purposes.[5]

In an other article, *Naitiktako Prashna ra Janayuddha* (The Question of Morality and People's War)', I wrote that sexual energy must be converted into energy that can help accelerate the PW. When deeply engaged in the PW, if sexual energy cannot be controlled, I suggested masturbation as a means that could be used to satisfy such urges.[6] It created quite a debate within the party! Some of the leaders went on to say that I befitted the role of a health worker rather than a leader. I remember asking an Iranian comrade from the RIM for her opinion. She said that biology was not the answer; rather the issue should be tackled ideologically. When asked to elaborate, she said that relationships should be based on monogamy for both men and women. Thus, the right to get a divorce should be granted to both men and women in order to maintain monogamous relationships.

The ruling government and the state tried to take advantage of these issues within the party. The RNA made an exaggerated claim that they had found volumes of condoms in a PLA member's bag. This was done with the aim of defaming the PLA as a lustful and immoral organization. Similarly, they used to often ridicule the women in the PLA using terms like 'petticoat battalion'.

There have been romances that have ended in happy marriages, too. One such courageous love story worth mentioning involved Sunita Regmi and Prakash Rijal. Sunita, the platoon commander, aka 'Yojana', had fallen in love with the brigade vice-commander Prakash, aka 'Basanta', and married him when they were training together. He had rescued her after a gruelling attack on the RNA left her leg injured with a bullet wound. He could not save her leg, but he was just in time to save her life. However, she lost her husband at Kotgaon in Rolpa while fighting against the RNA. She later married her martyred husband's friend Dhrubaraj Adhikari, 'Rajan', a battalion commander from Kaski.

However, not everyone was as lucky. I met Poonam in Parbat, where she was working in the district party organization. She had lost her husband in the PW. She had left her daughter with her parents and was working in a vulnerable place. I, somehow, had an intuition that she might get killed, too. She was martyred less than one month after I met her. I felt very sad when I heard the news. There were many such brave couples that were martyred during the PW. Many children were orphaned.

There were occasional debates on marriage, divorce, remarriage and children inside the party. One such debate centred around whether women in the PLA should bear children or not, and if yes, then how many? How soon or how late? I had read books on the LTTE war in Sri Lanka. I was curious to know how they had handled this issue in their movement. I found that they had strict rules on matters of marital relationships. They did not encourage combatants to have children. Similarly, I found that Indian Maoist leaders were mostly unmarried. And those who were married seldom had children. However, our party did not stipulate this policy. Instead, it said that the revolutionary life should not be dull and rigid; rather, it should be allowed to blossom. I agreed with this stance but had some concerns, too. Giving birth to children did affect a woman's political, military and organizational career. A man would seldom be affected in the same manner. I soon started campaigning for women and men to postpone childbearing for as long as possible. A woman leader/cadre going through pregnancy and maternal care would have to give up her position or fall behind. It was also difficult to maintain a crèche in a war zone.

Many cadres lost their partners during the PW. A debate arose on whether spouses of martyrs should be allowed to remarry. There was both support and opposition for whether a martyr's spouse could retain the status of being a 'martyr family member' (*shahid pariwar*) after remarriage. Some liberal comrades supported remarriage and recognition of the martyr family status while conservative comrades were against it. My own position leaned towards the former. Eventually, the party took the decision to grant martyr family status even after a remarriage.

Men and women in the PLA were relatively free to communicate their feelings to each other through letters, which often became love letters. The party would also occasionally help in finding a match for unmarried members. The marriageable age was twenty years for both men and women. Sometimes, these age restrictions were flouted, especially by the PLA. Marriages were hastened so as to make sure that both combatants focused on war activities. While love marriages were treated liberally inside the PLA, those working in the party and its sister organizations at local levels were under more scrutiny when it came to romantic affairs. After being reprimanded for their affairs, the party used to marry them off to avoid unnecessary gossip and criticism from the local people. However, I did not feel comfortable with it. I would encourage underage girls to postpone their marriage as they would be more adversely affected by such early unions.

In the base areas, party cadres and PLA combatants found the atmosphere conducive to safely bear and raise children. The children of the PLA members and whole-timer party workers were put in schools and hostels run by the party in the base areas. Communes would also shelter lactating PLA and whole-timer mothers. However, for those working outside Maoist base areas, it was not easy to raise children. Newborn babies had to be left behind with their family members or sympathizers, which was more challenging.

I found that most of the children of party comrades showed maturity at a very young age. They were observant, disciplined and serious. I think it was because they were aware of the risk their parents took every day. I had been told stories of how children as young as one year old would not cry once while their mothers marched quietly at night along with the others. I had observed the psychology of children: those who had both their parents active in the movement were hospitable to the comrades who visited them. However, where one of the parents objected to the movement, children were found to be uncooperative with the comrades who visited them.

To defame or criticize the movement, the government and other agencies have often raised the question of children's presence in the PW. What is often ignored, forgotten or unknown is that many children became part of the movement, not as cadres or combatants but in search of security as many of the family members of Maoist leaders/cadres/supporters would be hunted down by the police and army.[7] The reasons for children being part of the PW were many and different. They mostly joined not because of any ideological conviction but out of compulsion. Also, there were many children who were born out of wedlock; some had lost both parents, some had to live with a stepmother or stepfather under difficult conditions, some had been abandoned. Some had left home because of poverty while some helpless parents had deliberately sent their children away. And some had joined the movement out of sheer curiosity and excitement. I had met some of them hovering around the PLA camp, doing all sorts of work.

What attracted some children to the PW was the respect and sense of responsibility they got from the party. They were called by their actual names, prefixed by the title 'comrade' instead of the common belittling names like *kale*, *bhunte* or *phuchche* (like 'blackie' or 'shorty'). They were attracted to the egalitarian community activities and the sense of purpose that the PW provided. Their help was well acknowledged, and they were given food, shelter and security. They were mostly involved in running errands, including some intelligence-gathering work. Those who were talented in music and dance joined the cultural front. They were also given training in basic self-defence.

Coming from Kathmandu, it was rather upsetting for me to see the sad state of children in the remote mountains of western Nepal. I saw young girls dressing up stones, imagining them to be dolls. I also saw young boys using matchboxes and sticks to make toy guns. They were scantily dressed, with undone hair, running noses and infected wounds. I once washed the face of a child around four years old with a simple saline solution when he had an infection on his face. I was surprised to see him recovering fast. Sometimes, even the application of toothpaste on festering wounds was found to be effective. Most of the children were undernourished, with a bulging stomach and thin arms. It was the very sense of identity, respect and basic necessities of life that these children missed or were denied in their own homes, which they found in the Maoist party.

I felt sorry for those who said that children had been used as combatants in the PW against their will.

19

Rape, Rebellion and Resistance

tempering the steel

One of the reasons why so many women joined the PW voluntarily was because of the rampant gender discrimination and violence in Nepal. And when they did join the PW, the security wing of the government would use rape as an instrument to punish them. Rape and murder of women increased manyfold when the state of emergency was declared with the mobilization of the RNA.

For women, violence is an everyday struggle, specifically for those who are poor, powerless and belonging to any minority group, Dalit or ethnic community. The more women try to fight against it alone, the more humiliated and helpless they become. It is only when they fight it politically, locally and globally that they feel safer and more empowered. From the womb to the tomb, they have been subjected to discrimination. In fact, discrimination and violence often go hand in hand. For women, violence takes many forms and only women know how it has affected them. The PW became one of the instruments to fight against this gender violence.

My own father, despite being politically conscious, was not satisfied with only one son. He wanted another one. I was told that he was rather disheartened when his seventh child turned out to be a daughter again. And that was me! He did not even look at my mother's face or mine, and instead left for Calcutta to get a vasectomy.

At a very young age, I had seen violence in my own house. I had seen my mother being confronted by my father. He would throw things at her. My sisters used to hide her when my father got drunk and angry. My sisters told me that my parents had shared both happiness and sorrow during the anti-Rana period. But after my father became a minister, my mother became a victim of his violence.

My sisters had warned me about molestation at a young age. When I was seven or eight, I was told to be careful with a distant grandfather who had come to visit us from Darjeeling. He used to give me toffees and caress my hands and legs. I only got to know that he was molesting me when my sisters warned me not to go too close to him. Later on, he became a monk and seldom visited our house. I became even more sensitive towards gender issues when I saw incidents of sexual harassment in India.

My involvement in rescuing women who were sold to brothels in India, together with my research on gender issues, made me firmly believe that women's oppression was not only related to their lack of access to the economy but also to a lack of political power. Women in South Asia generally have low esteem, they are significantly invisible in national accounts, they face early marriages.[1] The Maoist PW gave women the opportunity to struggle against this. The PW was successful in disseminating the idea that the feudal state was the instrument of violence, whereby the oppressed lot was subjected to various forms of violence in the name of caste, gender, religion, region and ethnicity. This became clearer when women were being rampantly raped, tortured and killed during the PW.

The poorer the country, the less the reach of the state into women's lives. In Nepal, their domestic domain could hardly comes under the radar of state responsibility and support. Even if it did, the poorly equipped and overstretched police and judicial system could not cater to the rampant violence against women. On top of that, generally the police force, too, was mostly misogynist and an upholder of patriarchy. Their intervention often made matters worse for the women. In fact, gender violence was hardly ever reported, and even when it was reported, it was often suppressed.[2] This was the situation in Nepal before the PW started.

In war, women were trophies for the winning soldiers. Officers often allowed their soldiers to rape captured women as a reward for their service. Often, cultural norms made circumstances harsher for women. In Iran, for instance, it was believed that virgins went to heaven, hence radical female political activists were raped before being put to death.[3] In Nepal, particularly among the Khas Aryas,[4] where virginity is worshipped, the act of rape represented ostracization of the whole family or community. Thus, the act of rape represented social isolation for a woman.[5] The police used rape as an instrument of coercion to curb the rebellious masses. However, the more they used these tactics of suppression, the more number of women joined the PW. The Maoist party tried to impart class and gender consciousness in the PLA by making them answerable to the masses. It was often found that when men were unable to exercise control over other men, they indulged in violence against women. This was found to be true with regard to members of the state's armed forces, who not only raped Maoist women but also indulged in violence against the women at home.

The PW had been successful in unleashing the fury of women. It had been able to transform the individual sacrifice made by a woman in the name of protecting the family and private property of her husband into a larger sacrifice for social justice. Take the example of Com. Lali Rokka, the vice-president of ANWA (R),[6] who was allegedly taken away by the police from a health post where she was administering polio drops to children. She claimed that she was taken to a nearby police station. She also mentioned that she was tortured and raped repeatedly. Yet, she did not reveal the information they were trying to get from her. She was subsequently killed.

Com. Sunsara Budha, the wife of a key PLA leader, was allegedly subjected to extreme torture in front of her two-year-old daughter and then killed in the most gruesome manner. According to some reports, she was burnt alive in front of her child in Rolpa on 4 December 1996.[7]

Com. Dila Thapa from Jajarkot was allegedly killed in Surkhet on 11 May 1998. We were informed that after being raped, her breasts were lacerated and her body was left on display for days. She was a member of the guerrilla unit. She, too, did not divulge the information that the police force was looking for.[8]

Com. Sita Chaudhary, from the oppressed Tharu community in Terai, Dang district, was killed on 22 June 2002. She was nine months pregnant when she was allegedly tortured and shot dead. She was working as a party member in a local unit.[9]

Similarly, many people from urban areas had left their well-paying, secure jobs to join the PW. One such woman was Indira Tiwari, born in Kaski district.[10] She even left her husband and three children behind to join the PW. She was killed after being captured in Syangja district on 20 July 2002. She was a central committee member of ANWA (R). There were several cases where women were made to dig their own graves after being raped and then buried alive.[11]

Of course, there were some disappointments along the way. There was a woman called Com. Mukti. She was sent to India for treatment of heart disease, which was quite expensive for the party to bear. She did not return after she recovered. In fact, her Maoist husband, too, never returned. Eventually, they both left the Maoist movement.

There are other stories that never fail to inspire. On 30 March 2001, a historic jailbreak by six brave Maoist women from a strongly fortified jail in Gorkha made big news.[12] They were all whole-time party workers who were imprisoned on different dates and under different circumstances. Uma Bhujel was the main planner of the jailbreak. She was a platoon commander—she had been arrested from her shelter while the rest of her team escaped. The second member of the team, who worked hard to implement Bhujel's plan, was Kamala Naharki. She had been arrested while transporting some publication materials of the party. She dug the tunnel all by herself while the others stood guard. The other helpers were Mina Marhatta, Rita Biswokarma, Sanju Aryal and Anjela Biswokarma. As the date neared for their planned jailbreak, they were able to contact comrades from outside to coordinate with them. They had started constructing the tunnel on 26 December 2000 and their plan was to escape on 12 February 2001, the fifth anniversary of the PW. However, they finally made it out on 30 March.[13] On the whole, in my opinion, women were more resilient and rebellious than men when they faced the enemy.

The masses, particularly women, did not fear the Maoists as much as they feared the state's security forces. Maoists, too, abducted 'class enemies' sometimes, but they never used rape as an instrument of torture. They were more political in their approach and they punished the culprits in front of the public, explaining his/her wrongdoings.

20

'Are You a Newar or a Nepali?'

the nationality question

In the base area, I was surprised to learn that at one time the Magars in Rolpa were sceptical to form the Magar National Liberation Front (MNLF). After the launch of the PW, Prachanda had a difficult time convincing Maoist Magar leaders like Barshaman Pun (Ananta), Santosh Budha Magar and others to make the MNLF a strategic partner of the new people's state in the base area in Rolpa.

The basis for such a reluctant attitude towards the nationality question can be traced back to the early political teachings given by veteran communist leaders. M.B. Singh had visited Thawang, Rolpa, as early as the 1950s and delivered political schooling.[1] Thereafter, Mohan Vaidya (Kiran), too, had been imparting political classes in Rolpa. The Magars here had been indoctrinated in a strictly class-based communist line. Hence, they had been trained to look at class issues as the panacea to all ills of society. Ethnicity- and nationality-based oppression, on the other hand, had been looked upon as divisive tactics undermining the class issue. The outlook of M.B. Singh, till today, is anti-federal, anti-nationality. So, it was after a lot of persuasion during the PW that the Magars in Rolpa became sensitive to their oppression based on nationality/ethnicity, in addition to class oppression.

Magars are the largest indigenous group (*janjati*) in Nepal. They made substantial contributions to the PW. Out of the four deputy commanders of the PLA, two were Magars—Nanda Kishor Pun 'Pasang', a Kham Magar hailing from Rolpa (who is now the vice-president of the country), and Barshaman Pun 'Ananta', also from Rolpa (now a minister). Out of the seven division commanders of the PLA, three were Magars—Kali Bahadur Kham, Sukh Bahadur Rokka and Rajesh. Magars were legendary fighters who were exploited by kings to expand their bases but were never given due recognition.[2] In many parts, the Magar language was coercively suppressed. Magars belonging to Baglung, Parbat, Myagdi, Arghakhanchi and Gulmi districts were prevented from speaking their language by Khas rulers. They applied tough measures whereby those who sang songs in the Magar language had their tongues cut off.[3]

However, in Kathmandu, Maoists belonging to the Newar indigenous nationality were more sensitive and conscious about nationality–ethnicity issues than class issues. They had already formed an ethnicity-based Newar united front named 'Newa Khala' around 1997, when other ethnic groups within the party had not even imagined doing so.[4] Through Newa Khala, they broadened the base for incorporating other Newars belonging to different schools of thought. In fact, as early as 15 September 1999,[5] a *swaniga bandh* (Kathmandu Valley strike) was called by the Nepalbhasha Sangharsha Samiti, including Newa Khala, to assert the rights of the Newar community. This was the first strike called by the Maoists through this frontal organization. It was only when the party formally took a decision to form various regional and ethnic fronts that Newa Khala was dissolved and the Newa Rashtriya Mukti Morcha (Newar National Liberation Front) was established as a frontal organization for the Maoist party in 2003.[6]

The CPN (Maoist) had already produced a political document on nationality issues, asserting the right to self-governance in the year 1997, a year after the PW started.[7] In fact, the hallmark of the PW was that it was able to identify the specificity of Nepali society, where class oppression was manifested through oppressions based on gender, caste, nationality/ethnicity, language and region.

My visit to many districts in Nepal during the PW made me realize how rich the Newar culture was in terms of language, art, music, architecture, urbanization, culinary art, jewellery, clothing, industry, commerce and other aspects of life. Newari nationality, with its rich art, architecture and literature, is in a way synonymous with Nepal's identity. No wonder that in the United Nations it is the Ranjana script, a Newar script, which has been registered as the formal script of Nepal for recognition as a free nation. Newars have their own calendar called Nepal Sambat, which is based on the lunar calendar. The division of labour within the Newar community is so elaborate and institutionalized that they possess all the elements needed for making a separate nation. They have an elaborate *guthi* (community organization) system to take care of their economic, social, cultural and religious tasks.[8] Newars have been linguistically and culturally oppressed by the state since the occupation of Kathmandu Valley by King Prithvi Narayan Shah in 1769.[9] The Shah kings are credited with the unification of Nepal, but it was at the cost of brutal suppression of different indigenous nationalities/ethnic groups and their cultures, often through selective exclusion and inclusion in state affairs.

Once the nationality issue was fused with the class issue, the PW spread rapidly throughout the country. The party gave legitimacy to struggles against nationality and regional oppression by treating these extra-class issues not only as an instrument for revolution but also as a vital part of revolutionary state functioning. The party had endorsed the formation of nine autonomous provinces based on regional and nationality identity. The provinces based on regional identity were Seti-Mahakali and Bheri-Karnali in the far-western region.[10] The other seven based on nationality identity were Madhes, Tharuwan, Magarat, Tamuwan, Tamsaling, Newa, Kirat, and later Limbuwan. Depending upon the level and strength of Maoist presence in these provinces, they had been classified as having reached either the consolidated stage, the transitional stage or the propaganda phase. Magarat province reached the consolidated stage within a short span of time.

The sense of ownership imparted by these provinces to the nationally and regionally oppressed people gave further impetus to the PW. Added to this were the special rights given to women, Dalits and Muslims, which boosted their enthusiasm to fight for an inclusive new state.[11] No wonder the majority of imprisoned, martyred, 'disappeared' and injured people during the PW were Adivasis, Janjatis, Dalits and women. They fought not only for the new democratic revolution but also for their autonomous states.

Unlike the consolidated autonomous Magarat region, the Newa autonomous region was only at the initial 'propaganda' stage of the revolution. Kathmandu, the capital of the old state machinery, was regarded as a 'white area' with heavy concentration of security forces, bureaucracy and international forces. Hence, working in the Kathmandu Valley was very risky. Newar cadres, being local inhabitants, were more closely watched. However, the sympathy of the Newar community towards the communist movement once again helped in sustaining it within the valley. Historically, though a segment of the Newar community has been co-opted, the larger community has mostly been anti-establishment.[12]

During the PW, I was in India most of the time because of the nature of the work delegated to me. However, I remember asking my comrades from Kathmandu about the numerical strength of the Newar leaders or cadres in the party; how many of them had been arrested, 'disappeared', martyred and how many had deserted. In the central committee, initially there were only two

Newars from the valley: myself from Kathmandu and Rabindra Shrestha from Bhaktapur district. Later on, I came to know that five local Newars had been martyred and twelve of them had been 'disappeared' by the old state within the Kathmandu Valley.[13]

I was aware of the strategic importance of the Kathmandu Valley for future urban insurrection. I had reason to be inquisitive because, at one point in history, Kathmandu was the base of the communist movement. The founding general secretary of the Communist Party of Nepal was Pushpa Lal Shrestha, a Newar. Not only that, the remaining four founder members also came from the Newar community. In order to invoke their history, the oppression of the Newar community needed to be addressed. I, in fact, encouraged BRB to write one article, *'Janayuddha ra Newar Jatiko Muktiko Prashna* (People's War and the Question of Newar Ethnic Liberation)'. I then translated it in Newari language, which got published in *Sandhya Times*, a daily published in Kathmandu, in February 1997. I was told the issue sold like hot cakes in Kathmandu.

One of the reasons why I was passionate about Newar nationality was because at an early age, my father, Dharma Ratna Yami, had made us aware of the oppression based on our language, ethnicity and religion. His sensitivity regarding national oppression issues is well documented in the books written by him.[14] My uncle Chittadhar Hridaya[15], my father's cousin brother, who was a Newari literary figure and a crusader of the Nepal Bhasa Movement, or Newari language movement, accentuated our quest for Newari language rights. Both were leaders of the Newar movement of their times. But my father was known more as a rebel (against the oligarchic Rana rule) and later on as a politician, while my uncle was known more as a leader of the Newari language movement. My father was jailed several times and his property was confiscated for engaging in the anti-Rana political movement. My uncle was jailed for five years for writing poems in Nepal Bhasa (Newari), because literature in Newari language was banned by the Rana regime.[16]

Most of the names of my sisters—Timila, Nhuchhey Shova, Chirika Shova, Kayo—and my own name, Hisila, are Newari or Tibetan names.[17] In fact, the names Timila and Hisila are derived from an epic poem/opera *San Dey Ya Lisa* (Reply from Tibet) written by my father in 1930. It has now been translated into Nepali, Chinese and English. It was written after he came back from Lhasa, Tibet, and while he was under Rana detention. As a kid, I had seen my sisters participating in Newari literary competitions and cultural programmes. In addition to all these influences, our surname 'Yami' added a sense of belonging to not only the Newari language but also to Kathmandu city. In Newari language, 'Yen' means Kathmandu and 'Mi' means person. The person who comes from Kathmandu is called 'Yami'. My father used the title 'Yami' as a surname, instead of Tuladhar, in his twenty-five books. We were by profession a trading community; our actual surname 'Tuladhar' literally translates as scale-bearer.[18] We belonged to the Buddhist Newar clan within the Newar community. We were aware of the imposition of Nepali and Sanskrit languages, and Hinduism, since an early age. We had to hire home-tutors for these two languages in order to pass secondary school.

I had often heard my father denouncing hill Brahmins for their conspiratorial, cunning and manipulative methods and their monopoly in state affairs. We had a hill Brahmin family living just across the road from our house. They used to pester us to trim the branches of our tree to let the sunlight come into their house. They used to let their cows out, leaving the whole street in chaos. Despite the general aversion to them, they used to be respectfully also called *Baje* and *Bajyai* (grandpa and grandma). They were called chokho mukh, meaning 'pure mouth'; words coming from their mouth were considered final because they were considered pristine!

I had also seen those involved in the Newar movement being disappointed when my father married a hill Brahmin woman after my mother died. In fact, his prestige in the Newar movement was severely dented because of this. I had also overheard him saying that the Newars were too narrow-minded to be political. Chittadhar Hridaya had been exclusively active in the Newar movement, and I have overheard him blaming politicians for not fighting enough for the Newar identity.

We were hurt that Newari language, our mother tongue, was not made compulsory while Sanskrit, the ancient language not in daily use, was imposed on us in school. I remember, during the 1990 movement, we had burnt Sanskrit books as a symbol of protest against the imposition of a language of the hill Hindu *Khas Arya*. The movement was also against the idea and practice of a homogenous nation, which advocated one language, one religion, one dress and one culture.

When I was studying in Delhi around the 1970s, my normal question to the Nepali students I met in the city would be, 'Are you a Newar or a Nepali?' All of them, including BRB, would find this amusing and ask me back, 'What do you mean by Nepali or Newari? Are not all Newars Nepali?' I genuinely thought being a Nepali and a Newar were not the same. I had difficulty communicating in Nepali language. Even to this day, my fluency in Nepali language is not smooth. I have had altercations within my party on the language issue. When I spoke in Nepali language, the Nepali-speaking comrades would often make fun of my grammatical and pronunciation mistakes. I would then challenge them to speak in Newari language, if not English, in the hope of making them realize the pains of conducting politics in a language that was not one's mother tongue.

I was sensitive about not only being a Newar but also a Buddhist when I was a child. At seven to ten years of age, I was already rebelling against most of the Shrestha, Rajbhandari and Joshi students who not only followed Hinduism, which was the state religion, but also belonged to the highest caste within the Newar community. Those belonging to the Tuladhar, Shakya and Sthapit, etc., clans were Buddhists, and were generally defensive.

I used to be the most vocal while defending Buddhism on behalf of the students from our clan. Later on, I came to know that my father had written many books on Buddhism. However, he never imposed it on us. I remember as a child when I offered money in a temple, imitating my relatives, my father had vehemently restrained me. His argument was that the money would go to those who did not deserve it. My parents never allowed us to be swayed by any religion, nor did they allow us to practise unscientific cultural traditions. For instance, we were never introduced to the 'Gupha' ritual, which is still rife among the Newar community, whereby a girl, before her first menstrual period, would be kept inside a dark room for a week. No contact with the sunlight and boys would be allowed. Similarly, we were not made to follow Bel Biwaha, a Newar ritual wherein a girl is symbolically married to a bel fruit (wood apple or the Bengal quince). Thus, without our knowing, my parents had already injected in our minds the tenets of secularism.

During those days, girls were generally discouraged from attending schools for fear that they might elope and bring disgrace to the family and entire community. However, my mother would always encourage us to study hard, saying that it was the best jewellery she could give us: jewellery which could never be lost, snatched or destroyed. She would narrate how her personal life suffered because she did not get an education. Thus, she made sure that all the seven children in our family were given a good education. Not only that, my father used to boast to my relatives that he would get his children married to people from different ethnicities, classes, castes and religious backgrounds. His wish got realized to some extent.

My eldest sister, Dr Dharma Devi, became an oncologist; she had a love marriage with a Rajbhandari, a Hindu higher-caste Newar. My brother, Bidhan Ratna, became a civil engineer and married within the same caste. My second eldest sister, Timila Yami, became an electrical engineer and was an assistant professor and dean of IoE, Pulchowk; she had a love marriage with a Thapa-Magar who belonged to a different indigenous ethnic group. My third eldest sister, Nhuchhey Shova, became an assistant professor of mathematics and also was a campus chief of IoE, Thapathali; my fourth eldest sister, Chirika Shova, became a professor of chemistry and later the dean of the science faculty at Tribhuvan University. Both of them married within the same caste and ethnic community. My fifth eldest sister, Dr Kayo Devi, a microbiologist who also became the chairperson of the Civil Services Commission, had a love marriage with a hill Khas Arya Brahmin. And I, an architect, too got married to a hill Khas Arya Brahmin. Considering the feudal set-up under which we were born, we, especially the six daughters, were lucky to have such liberal parents who encouraged and enabled us to get higher education.

With this background, I joined the Maoist PW. My knowledge of oppressed nationalities was further widened thanks to my interactions with Indian students from the North-east Indian states, and professors and intellectuals of DU and JNU, who were sympathetic to the North-east nationality movement in India. My participation in an international seminar organized by the All India People's Resistance Forum (AIPRF) in New Delhi in 1996 further sharpened my outlook on the issue.[19]

21

The Oppressed of the Oppressed

the Dalit question

Manchhe manchhe yeute ho ni, farak kina ho?
Shram chalchha, seep chalchha, pani nachalne bho . . .[1]

(All humans are the same, why the differences?
The labour is needed, the expertise matters, but the water
remains untouchable)

—a popular song

My interest in Dalit issues started right at home, where we had
a Newar 'chyame' (scavenger), a Dalit whom we all called Haku
(dark-skinned). Her name was Ram Maya Nepali. My father and
mother were not only rebels but also great social reformers. They
were secular and totally against untouchability. After my father
became a minister in 1951, my parents, particularly my father,
dared to bring a Dalit woman helper into our house. One incident
particularly shocked the Newar community. After my father became
the second person from the Newar community to be appointed
a minister[2]—Ganesh Singh was the first—he called members of
the Newar community for dinner to celebrate his tenure in the

government. When our Dalit maid, Haku, served them food, half of the invited Newars walked out. Those who stayed on and ate left soon to bathe and purify themselves after having eaten food served by an untouchable. I also remember Haku getting angry with my relatives when they rewashed the utensils washed by her before plating the food. My father was a great admirer of Dr Bhimrao Ramji Ambedkar, the Indian leader who raised the issues of the Dalits at the national level. In fact, Ambedkar had stayed in our house in 1956 when he visited Nepal to participate in an international Buddhist conference.[3] My father was often invited by Ambedkar-related societies in different parts of India to speak about and to support the Dalit cause. Once he almost made a *khor* (pigsty) for the pigs inside the compound of our house but later refrained when there was a lot of opposition from our relatives. In fact, they used to call my father *wein,* meaning 'madman', because of his radical, non-conformist views. And we were called *weinya masta,* meaning 'children of madman'!

BRB, too, had serious concerns about the Dalit issue in Nepal. He had seen how Dalits were treated at the hands of the Brahmins and Chhetris in his village. He had also witnessed how the oppressed Adivasi Janjatis treated Dalits as second-class beings on the instigation of Brahmins and Chhetris. I also remember that at BRB's house in Gorkha, I often saw Dalits squatting on the floor of our *aangan* (front yard), not even daring to touch the threshold. My mother-in-law always showed generosity towards them by giving them some food when they came. But she would not touch the people. They were not allowed to come and sit in the veranda of our house. Once I invited one of them to sit on a bed in our veranda, but I was told not to do so by my father-in-law. This was before the PW started.

The agenda of radical social transformation championed by the PW attracted the Dalit community towards the Maoist movement. It would not be an exaggeration if one were to say that Dalits stood as a strong foundation for the PW. They not only participated in it with enthusiasm but were also most helpful during the period of heavy state suppression against the Maoists. The party organized them through the Dalit Mukti Morcha (Dalit Liberation Front) at the local and national levels. The party also encouraged inter-caste marriages between Dalits and non-Dalits.

During police or military operations launched against the PW, Dalits gave shelter to PLA and Maoist leaders, cadres and sympathizers, while most of the upper-caste people refrained from giving either logistic help or shelter. Being the poorest of the poor and relegated to untouchability, they readily gave shelter and helped guide us to safety, even undertaking great risk. They were happy that Maoists entered their house, which had been shunned by society till then. Indeed, many Dalits had been martyred during the PW. The first PW victim was a Dalit child called Dil Bahadur Ramtel, who was killed by the police when he tried to save his non-Dalit teacher from getting arrested in his school in Gorkha in 1996.[4] Similarly, an incident that occurred at Malkot village in Kalikot got attention from the national media. Unarmed Dalit women had seized rifles from patrolling police men. Three policemen died after falling off a cliff when the local Dalit women fought against them in 1998.[5]

Being Dalit implies belonging to the lowest strata of a hierarchical caste system, as inscribed in the *Manu Smriti* and institutionalized in Nepal by the 1854 Muluki Ain, or the country code, promulgated by the first Rana ruler, Jung Bahadur. The Dalit issue is not only to do with inequality, but inequality with landlessness and social ostracization. So intense was the discrimination within their own religion (Hinduism) that many Dalits turned to Buddhism, Christianity and Islam. They represent the oppressed of the oppressed lot, especially Dalit women who face class oppression, gender oppression and social exclusion. What makes the Dalit issue more complicated and painful is the divisions created between them within their own community. In Nepal, they are divided regionally between Madhesi Dalit (belonging to the Terai region) and Pahadi Dalit (belonging to the hilly region). Within regional differences, there are lingual differences as the Pahadi Dalits speak Nepali language, the language of the ruling class and the state, while Madhesi Dalits speak languages used within the Madhesi community and the Newar Dalits speak Newari language. Of all the Dalits, the Pahadi Dalits had been taking advantage of the limited facilities that the state had been giving in the name of Dalit upliftment, because of the advantage of language and the region they come from. Biswakarma, also known by Kami, is the largest caste within Dalits spread across all ecological zones—they are found to have better access to education, jobs and property, and thus are found to have greater access to state perks and other opportunities.[6] Dalits such as Baadi and Dom are lesser in number; they have poorer access to education, health and property, and hence they are generally left out of state perks.[7]

Communists in Nepal were aware of the Dalits' class position and their social exclusion right from the time when the communist party was formed in 1949. They often revolted against their own Brahmin Chhetri culture by entering into a Dalit's house, drinking liquor and eating pork in the house. This was considered a revolutionary step. However, their revolutionary steps did not go far enough to marry Dalit women or men. In fact, in many cases, so-called communists went out of their way to stop marriages between their siblings and Dalits, even the siblings of Dalit communists. But this trend was broken during the PW.

During the PW, when I was taking a trip to one of the remote villages in Rukum, I came across one young woman. She was walking ahead of me with a rucksack. She looked young and had an energetic gait and upbeat body language. I thought she must be a university student who had left her studies to join the PW. I walked faster to catch up with her. I asked her name, her level of education and the place she hailed from. She was uneducated, came from a remote village in Rolpa district and was a Dalit named Shiwani B.K., about seventeen years old. She looked so confident and beautiful. Later on, when I inquired about her, I felt extremely sad to learn that she was killed in an ambush.

Had I not joined the PW, I would have known very little about Nepal. The war took me to almost all of the remote districts. I remember going to Kalikot, where Dalits reside in large numbers. The dry, rugged mountains and the hard and dry nature of the soil helped me understand why extreme conditions beget extreme steps. The small huts scattered here and there in those steep mountains defied what we had been taught in architecture—that houses should not be built over very steep slopes. I saw women planting corn with ropes tied around their waists so that they would not fall into the deep gorge. My comrades had told me how they had lost their wives, who had fallen into ravines while tending cattle. I have heard a woman describing how cattle died when they lost balance. Once I myself fell off a cliff when I was chased by a cow. Luckily, the cliff was not too steep and so I escaped a deadly fall with just a few bruises. My comrades informed me how security forces had killed captives during the PW by throwing them into such ravines and how our comrades jumped to death to avoid capture. A woman comrade told me how she saved herself after falling on to the branch of a tree.

Dalit settlements were often located in higher, remote and steep places in the village. I remember we were amidst one such Dalit settlement in Rukum. The deafening silence there stunned me. The only sound I heard was the tinkling of the bells put around the cows' necks when they left for grazing around 9 a.m. and when they came back around 6 p.m. Beyond that, I would hear nothing. I was, in a way, both scared and excited. Scared, because I, as an extrovert used to crowds and urban civilization, was suddenly amidst isolation; excited, because it was a new and different experience. At night, hailstorms made raging sounds. I nearly thought our roof would be blown off. So strong were the winds that we would hear it wailing. I couldn't help but think what a spot *National Geographic* was missing!

A young Hisila with her family in Kathmandu in 1962

At the School of Planning and Architecture, New Delhi, with her friend Rekha Trivedi in 1976

A letter from BRB (Baburam Bhattarai) to me, part 1

BRB's letter to me, part 2

<u>Marriage declaration</u> of Baburam Bhattarai
& Hisila Yami

On this occasion of our publicly declaring our mental, physical and emotional attachment to each other (which has been traditionally termed as 'marriage'); we pledge by our free conscience to exercise the human capabilities inherent in us with utmost rationality and to fulfil our roles as agents of progressive transformation of human society to higher social formations with utmost sincerity. We unequivocally renounce all forms of exploitative mechanisms of religion, communalism, casteism, superstition etc. introduced in human relations by persons in positions of power in different periods of human history, and on the contrary are committed to live a conjugal life free of any sexual discrimination and marked by absolute freedom of thought and action of both the partners. We have entered into this special human relationship by our own free volition at a state of our full consciousness and pledge to maintain it so long as it fulfils our mutual aspirations and contributes to the realization of our higher selfs. With effect from this day we declare ourselves as man and wife.

(Hisila Yami)   (Babnram Bhattarai)

Date 29-3-1981

A rather faded photo of our marriage declaration

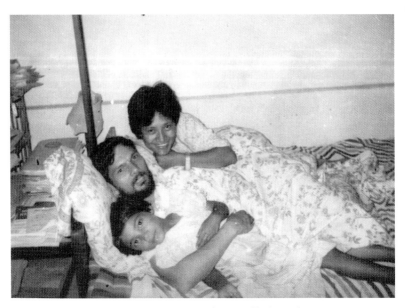

BRB, Manushi and I at our residence in Kathmandu in 1991

The three of us at our residence in Allahabad, India, in 2002,
when we were living underground

On 11 May 2002, the Royal Nepal Army released photographs of
Maoist leaders Pushpa Kamal Dahal 'Prachanda', Dr Baburam Bhattarai,
Ram Bahadur Thapa 'Badal' and me in western Nepal, declaring
us war criminals and offering Rs 50,00,000 (Nepalese rupees)
to whoever captured us alive

The notice given by the home
ministry declaring us terrorists and
mentioning the price on our heads

Me in combat dress in Thawang,
Rolpa, Nepal, in 2004

4th March 1999.

Dearest Asmita,

We felt very nice meeting you. I am particularly satisfied that your Rai sir & madam are noticing you by your good behavior & that they seem to care for you. That is exactly what we want. We want people to respect you & treat you like adult, responsible person. Ofcourse for earning that responsibility you yourself have to behave responsibly.

Talking of your cool & serene character your father said you are like his father, our hujurba. It seems he too is saintly like you, never asking anything for one - self, cool, calm & composed. How unlike me!!

My dear ovulating lady I would like to give you some tip regarding your ladyhood:

→ When you are menstruating you may get some cramp like pain in your abdomen. This is normal, unless the pain is intolerable. You must understand why such mild pain comes. Once you know the source, you can easily tackle the pain. The mild pain is the result of convulsions the uterus goes through to shed off the blood with your unfertilised egg so that at the end of the day your uterus remains clean after your menstruation period is over. So how do you combat that mild pain?? This is where our famous DR. Einstien comes into the picture. Remember his theory of relativity? Well inorder to make the pain less painful you have to engage in some activities which will make your mild pain relatively less. This means you have to be doing some physical exercise, may be walking, jogging so that your outside movement makes you forget your internal movement. Also remember pain is often psycological; the more you think of it the more it dominates. The more you divert your attention from it the more you forget about it. Ofcourse severe pain one cannot write off so if such pain occurs & means there is some problem inside the uterus, in such case you must consult the physician.

My letter to Asmita, the pseudonym our daughter, Manushi, used in India

→ During menstruating period make sure you have enough sanitary towel, if you happen to not possess it when you menstruate donot hesitate to ask for menstruating towel from other female member if you happen to be outside your hotel. Also remember, for emergency you can use any clean "Jalo" which should be observant. If you happen to stain your cloth, don't panick, just be aware that you avoid such situation as far as possible. Heavens will not fall if the stain happen to appear. Instead try to change the cloth as soon as possible or try to wipe the stain with your pullover or bagpa or some sort of hide up act.

DO NOT BE ASHAMED OF YOUR WOMANHOOD !!

I WANT YOU TO BE A PROUD WOMAN !!

I donot ask anything from you except that you should not feel hesitant to ask for anything or say anything. I truely look to you as my trustworthy friend rather than mother. Really Asmi your matured behavior sometimes make me feel like a child (but I don't mind as long as I don't behave that way to others). Ofcourse you father then tells me that I am special in my own way & that I should not compare. He is right, isn't he?!

Of late, he has been very thoughtful about you. We were reading a book in which there was a description of father by a daughter. We thought it may be interesting to send you. Discover for yourself who the father is & who the child is.

your
Ama.

P.N.
Asmi when you ring up for therapy make sure you dont tell where you are speaking from, just say you are speaking from Darjeeling.

A continuation of the letter

Woman soldiers of the People's Liberation Army (PLA) of Nepal posing for a photo in a remote village

Me with the women members of the Central Committee of the CPN (Maoist) in Phuntiwang, Rolpa, in 2004

Post Bahadur Bogati, Prachanda and BRB in Phuntiwang, Rolpa, in 2004

Children in a base camp

BRB during the second round of peace talks with the government on
29 January 2003 in Kathmandu

Shahid Marg (Martyr's Road), 91 km from Rolpa to Rukum, being built by
the locals in Rolpa in 2004

A wooden bridge made by the people's militia in Rolpa in 2001

(Left) Thawang village, the epicentre of the PW capital of the base area in Rolpa; (right) some of the residences burnt by the security forces of Nepal. These photos were taken in 2004

Anekot Smriti Sanskritik Company performing during a programme organized in a village by the CPN (Maoist)

A typical checkpost on the way to the Kharibot base area in Rolpa. The signboard says: 'This is a people's war checkpost. You are requested to present proof of identity before entering.' This photograph was taken around 2002

BRB and I relaxing after reaching a base area in Rolpa in 2001

The first open mass programme organized by the CPN (Maoist) in Tundikhel, Kathmandu, in June 2006

Giving a speech in Kathmandu for the CA
elections in 2008

एकीकृत नेकपा माओवादीको दोस्रो चरणको आन्दोलनको अन्तिम दिन शुक्रबार राजधानी
घेराउ कार्यक्रममा नाच्दै माओवादी नेता दम्पती बाबुराम भट्टराई र हिसिला यमी।

A rare photo of BRB dancing for the first time (or the
last time?) in Kathmandu in 2009, outside the Singha
Durbar compound

The litigation I won against the editor of *Crime Today* magazine, against whom I filed a defamation case in the Kathmandu district court

This was taken in 2014 when I visited Sarlahi district in Terai, where I found ex-PLA women living as housewives. The woman with short hair was a staff member who had accompanied me there

My husband, when he was the prime minister of Nepal, and I with former US President Barack Obama and his wife, Michelle Obama, on a US visit in 2011 to attend the UN General Assembly meeting

Generally, Dalit settlements lacked proper sanitation because of rampant poverty. The number of flies in and around the households amazed me. They would compete with the breeze inside the house; many of them buzzing and swarming around. We would often use poison to kill them.

The health facility was so bad that I would say people were surviving based on mere luck. Surprisingly, not even a single doctor had joined the PW, although there were many engineers in the party. However, the health assistants who joined the movement did an excellent job. In due course of time, they became as good as doctors due to the intense practice of operating on and tending to the sick, both within the PLA and among the masses.

As the PW intensified and spread, Dalit settlements started becoming more hygienic. Also alcoholism, which used to afflict Dalits more than other communities, reduced.[8] I also came across many Dalit Maoist women marrying Brahmin/Chhetri men, and Dalit men marrying Brahmin/Chhetri women. I was particularly surprised to find some Brahmin women marrying Baadimen. This was simply unthinkable earlier because the Baadis belonged to one of the lowest rungs, even amongst the Dalits. Brahmin women marrying Baadi men would have been considered blasphemous. Thus, the number of inter-caste marriages between Dalits and non-Dalits was increasing during the PW. This was because the PW gave the Dalits confidence and dignity. It also removed internal discrimination within the Dalit community.

The PW gave more space to the Dalits, which was generally lacking in preceding political movements. It gave them special rights to participate in running state affairs at different levels. Their traditional skill of blacksmith work found room in the making and maintaining of local guns, traditional weapons and ammunition. Their traditional work of sewing and making dresses found space in making uniforms for the PLA, and bags and cover for weapons, etc. Similarly, their skill of construction work found use in making of bridges, roads, buildings, etc. Their tannery skills found use in making shoes and leather bags. And their customary talent of singing, dancing and playing musical instruments found space in revolutionary cultural activities during the PW.

The PW particularly inspired the Dalits to fight against discrimination, from a class as well as a caste perspective. Untouchability was not tolerated and was punishable. The very act of carrying weapons and using them made them feel empowered. The state army never allowed this; in fact, Dalits were given low-level jobs. They were made to shine the shoes of military officers, clean utensils in the mess and dispose of waste.

The Dalit Mukti Morcha, a front to organize Dalits, was very active in the base areas. They made trekking trails, *chowtaras* (raised platforms used as a resting place), houses and halls for meetings. To boost their confidence and enhance their fighting spirit, they often resorted to march pasts, playing their traditional musical instruments and carrying weapons through village after village as a way of displaying their strength and talent.

People readily accepted Dalits into their houses in the base areas. Outside base areas, people allowed Dalit PLA members to enter their houses, perhaps out of fear. Often, the same could not be said in the case of local Dalits who were still discriminated against. However, the PW made a qualitative leap in the transformation of Dalits and raised the level of their political consciousness.

22

A Twenty-First-Century Political Sati

emergence of a stronger me

While I was enjoying my job as the secretary of the people's power consolidation department in Rolpa, I slowly started feeling alienated. I had designed houses that would stand in place of those burnt down by the state's security forces in Thawang. I had also designed an extension wing of the Ajambari commune, as requested by its members. I had always enjoyed teaching and practising architecture, so I was very happy when I was told to design the building for Janabadi Namuna School (People's Democratic Model School), which I did with great fervour. However, I soon realized that the party was not executing any of my designs.

Slowly, women started commenting on my daughter, Manushi. They said that while I was bringing up a child, I was discouraging others from having children. They criticized me for sending Manushi to school while other children were participating in war. Some alleged that I was not a Maoist, but a feminist who was always raising women's issues in the party. Others considered me to be merely the wife of BRB. I remember Pampha Bhusal once telling me that I was like Jenny, Karl Marx's wife; meaning I was just the wife of a political leader. I had retorted, 'Why can't you develop yourself as

159

Rosa Luxemburg?' She did not reply. My question could have been demeaning for her because Rosa, according to her, was anarchist and rightist. In inner party struggles, Pampha had consistently sided with Kiran's dogmatic line. She also took ultranationalist positions. I, on the other hand, was castigated as bourgeois and rightist.

My political career had been different from most of the women of my own ranking in the base area. Except a few, most of the women had studied up to secondary level or below that. I had not only come from an educated urban background but had also studied abroad. I had little organizational experience. Hence, for most of the people, I was like an outsider. I had a language problem, too. I spoke Newari and English fluently, but my Nepali was poor. Often, they made fun of my speech in Nepali. I had to assert that I was a Newar and that Khas Nepali was not my native language. People continued to call me capitalist and rightist. My reply would be: 'I may be capitalist, but you are feudalist, which is a step behind.' This made matters worse. I did not know that my frankness would be harmful to both BRB and me. BRB kept insisting that I speak more tactfully.

Later on, I came to know that my work in the base area was in fact a stopgap for the major event that was waiting to happen. And that event was the Lawang meeting in January 2005, where the Prachanda faction took action against us in an unfair manner. While BRB was charged on political grounds, I was accused of instigating him.

Thawang, being predominantly inhabited by the Magars, had strong community-based solidarity. This sentiment eased the practice of strong centralization within the party. However, when it came to handling inner party struggle, they appeared to be quite intolerant and inflexible towards differing ideas. Criticism of Prachanda was not stomached well. Consequently, we were looked upon with suspicion.

Nevertheless, it is important to know the string of events that led to political action against us. After being attacked aggressively in the Phuntiwang CC meeting, I started reading more classical communist texts. I also began understanding the past inner party struggles vis-à-vis ideological trends and tendencies. I became convinced that these struggles existed because of tensions between two ideological paths: one was based on the concrete analysis of situations and the other was based on a dogmatic understanding of Marxism. Moreover, it became clear to me that these were not because of personality clashes between Prachanda and BRB. From then on, I began to steel myself by becoming more political and less personal/emotional when it came to inner party struggles.

After the Phuntiwang meeting, BRB also started becoming serious about the fate of his ideological position. He was more worried about this than the threat to his own life. Henceforth, he decided to jot down his ideological stances and formally register them in the party. To start with, BRB wrote four points of disagreement on 11 November 2004 and submitted the paper to Prachanda.[1] His main argument was against over-centralization of leadership at the cost of suffocating democratic practice. The same year, on 30 November, it was further augmented with another thirteen points under the subheadings 'ideology and philosophical question', 'political and military question', 'organizational question' and 'cultural question'.[2]

We sensed we were being closely monitored by the PLA. BRB contacted Partha (Surendra Karki) who was in Delhi. BRB translated the points into English so that the PLA members overseeing us would not be able to understand the content. When the points of disagreement got published in a newspaper, the party's vigilance over us increased. The news drew national and international attention. Then on, events started unfolding one after the other: satellite phone was confiscated from BRB; the revolver given to him for his protection was confiscated.

BRB wrote another article, 'Princely Tendency and Democracy', in the national daily *Kantipur* on 19 January 2005,[3] in which he categorically stated: '. . . there is no other alternative for the genuine democratic forces in both the parliamentary and revolutionary camp than to abandon all the prejudices of the past, to reach common understanding on the minimum program of the *democratic republic* (emphasis added) and to fulfil the historical duty of defeating the autocratic monarchy and foreign interference.'[4] This created a huge political debate in the country. He also criticized princely tendencies that were growing within the top leadership in all political parties, thereby subtly exposing the same tendency within his own party. Prachanda took this as a personal attack on him, making the inner party struggle all the more intense and bitter. This created a big ripple within the party. Sensing that political punitive action may be taken against him, BRB further wrote a document titled 'The Two-Line Struggle inside CPN (Maoist): Background and Present Situation',[5] in which he summarized the inner party struggles from 1991 to 2004. He presented it in the extended politburo meeting at Lawang in Rukum on 29 January 2005, in the presence of available CC members, politburo members and central advisers.

All these culminated into disciplinary actions against BRB, Dinanath Sharma and myself. We were demoted to being general party members.

Essentially, action was taken against BRB for his organizational stand on a more democratic way of functioning within the party and his political stand against the monarchy and the appeal for a 'democratic republic'. To conceal this, the chargesheet stated that BRB was running a 'parallel headquarter' to fulfil his personal ambitions, making external contacts to add strength to his ideological stance, and that he was against Prachanda as an individual. We were shocked to hear these accusations. Action was taken against me because I was said to have instigated BRB to defy the party leadership. I was appalled that I could be charged on such flimsy grounds. I took it as political violence against me since the charges had nothing to do with the political or ideological stance that I had sided with.

Unlike the previous inner party struggles, this time, I couldn't help but laugh. I laughed loudly when such ridiculous charges were levelled against me. I told everyone: 'Long live twenty-first-century political sati!'[6] I was being reprimanded for inciting BRB to act against the party leadership! If BRB could be affected by my instigation, then I congratulated the party leaders for finding me capable enough to be his leader! Com. Dinanath was blamed for facilitating the leaking of BRB's document to the press just because his son-in-law happened to be an editor of a weekly newspaper. It was such a flimsy charge! We all left the CC meeting hall with out taking on any tension. Rather, we laughed. In our review meeting later, we came to the conclusion that we could have working relations with Prachanda and his team only till we achieved our immediate goal of turning Nepal into a democratic republic. After that, we needed to part with him.

Unlike the Phuntiwang CC meeting where I had cried, this time I felt more empowered when action was taken against me. Why had I cried in Phuntiwang, and why was I laughing in Lawang? I realized that in Phuntiwang, I was taking the inner party struggle as a personal struggle, which made me feel sentimental. However, during the Lawang meeting, I had taken the inner party struggle as an undertaking for correcting the trends, strategy and leadership within the party. This made me look at things more holistically and purely from a political and ideological point of view. It was a great discovery for me to know how taking inner party struggles personally led to sentimental feelings while viewing them ideologically led to a liberating feeling.

On 1 February 2005, we heard on BBC Radio while in Lawang that King Gyanendra had staged a coup and assumed executive powers. This sent shock waves both within the party and outside. Meanwhile, it was reported that Prachanda's allies were hobnobbing with the royalist forces in Kathmandu to arrive at some form of understanding.[7] The purpose was to agree to share power with him and abandon the PW. But what he got instead was a coup! Prachanda's game plan came to naught. It was crystal clear why he wanted to remove BRB and his associates from the top leadership.

When action was taken against us, the Prachanda faction started avoiding us. The PLA section, which had been accompanying us, was replaced. The new PLA unit guarded us strictly; they would not leave us even when we had to use the toilet. Rumour had it that we may flee to India.

After we were reinstated, I was particularly interested to know the after-effects of our detention on the people who supported our line. In conversation with some of the middle-ranking party cadres, I was told that many leaders and cadres who dared to question our virtual detention by the party were either transferred to remote areas or faced disciplinary action. Apparently, some of them even left the PW out of dismay. I had asked some PLA members in Rolpa about the whereabouts of Com. Samersen. He was one of the PLA members assigned to our security post before the action against us. Samersen was a good student; he said he had left school to join the PW with BRB as inspiration. I remember finding his handwriting to be really neat and clear. He was fond of reading books. I was disappointed to hear from them that he had left the Maoist movement after he was transferred to another security post. Till today, I have been inquiring about him but to no avail.

We heard similar stories from elsewhere, too. Many comrades had to go without their monthly allowances because they happened to be supporters of BRB. Some departed from the movement because they could not bear to see the way BRB was being mistreated. Take the case of Com. Thakur Devkota 'Asim'. He was asked to pen a piece of self-criticism for indulging in regionalism just because he happened to come from Gorkha, the same district that BRB came from. All because he asked why BRB was removed from the top party leadership. According to him, his monthly allowance amounting to Rs 500 was stopped and there was constant surveillance on his activities till we were reinstated. Asim was a rare case of a 'red and expert' party member, a combination of revolutionary fervour and thematic expertise. He was a graduate in agricultural studies and had left his job to come and work in a base area in an agricultural cooperative. In base areas, those who were educated and had a degree were generally looked at with apprehension.

After the Prachanda faction took action against us, we were later told, everyone had to denounce us in party meetings. This was particularly expected from those who had sided with us. Inside the PLA, leaders imparted political coaching where we were denounced as careerists, rightists and stooges of expansionism. Some of the commanders reportedly said we should be buried alive.

While we were going through these experiences, in eastern Nepal another couple, Devendra Parajuli (a regional bureau member and ex-president of the students' front) and Kalpana Dhamala (sub-regional bureau member working with the women's front) had already fallen victim to such action by the Prachanda faction. Both husband and wife were whole-timers. Their fault was that they escaped detention while others were caught in Patna, India. They were punished separately. Dhamala went through mental torture in Udayapur, while Devendra Parajuli got physical punishment, no less than what the RNA would give to the captive Maoists, in Bhojpur. According to Parajuli, he was subjected to all kinds of physical torture except electrocution.[8] Parajuli's additional crime was that he was both political and ideological. He had said that nobody should be punished within the party for conducting debates on ideology and political strategy. That was taken as support for BRB. Both Parajuli and Dhamala went through a longer period of confinement, and more physical and mental torture than us. This punishment was meted out to them despite the fact that they belonged to the Masal group led by Prachanda. At one point, Dhamala had insisted they leave the movement and the party. But Parajuli did not agree.[9]

I must also mention Biswadeep Pandey's grit. He had been sent to work for BRB by his father, Bhakti Pandey (a CC member and later a CA member, who succumbed to cancer), at the early age of seventeen. He was a very hard-working, sharp young boy. He stayed with us during our trying days, throughout our confinement period. He, too, had been attacked at some point or the other because of his commitment to BRB and his line.[10] Similarly, Om Sharma, a regional bureau member of the party, needs to be mentioned. He was the editor of *Jana Ahwan* newspaper. He became a victim of the actions of the Prachanda faction in August–September 2001, when he republished BRB's article that had already been printed in *Kantipur*: 'Let's Give No Legitimacy to the Beneficiaries of the New Kot Massacre'.[11] The valley's bureau in-charge, Badal, and the secretary, Rabindra Shrestha, often targeted him because his paper printed BRB's articles regularly. Rabindra even threatened Om saying that he was the party authority, and that if he did not stop the publication, he would not hesitate to exercise his authority to deal with him! When Om continued publishing it, Rabindra took action against him and suspended him for six months. Om was forced to stop publication of *Jana Ahwan* in August 2001. Similarly, another senior party journalist, Manarishi, was threatened verbally several times for working with *Jana Ahwan*.[12]

We were formally attached with the HQ based in Rolpa, but we kept a distance. Wherever we shifted, we had cordial relationships with the villagers. Being an extrovert, I used to meet people. I met several ex-army men who had served in the Indian military. We shared each other's experiences in India. I also met many families who had some member or the other working in different parts of India. However, I felt bad that despite working in the Indian Army, or in India, for so many years, there was hardly any improvement in their lifestyle and economic status.

Meanwhile, I used the confinement time (January–July 2005) to read and discuss politics and ideology with BRB. I was also able to stay with him throughout the six months of detention, a luxury I did not get often. We played badminton regularly. Most of the time, he used to read and write. We would also talk about architecture. We never regretted being architects despite taking this rough political path. In architecture, you need to have a proper balance between theory (art) and practice (engineering), between space and time. War, too, comprised a dialectical relationship between theory and practice; science and art; party and the people; leaders and led; concrete analysis of concrete situations; playing with contradictions (in architecture, it means dealing with opposite forms); dealing with unity in diversity; dealing with illusion and reality (like art); inner party struggle (dealing with contradictory forms), etc. We also talked about philosophy.

Soon, we saw troops of the PLA entering Rolpa from other districts. Later on, we came to know this was in preparation of the attack on the military camp in Khara in Rukum.[13] It was a centralized plan, directly monitored and supervised by the HQ.[14] Prachanda, as the military chief commander, was supervising and monitoring the plan for the first time. We were told that for this attack, the best cadres and commanders from the western division, under the division commander Prabhakar, and the middle division, under the division commander Pasang, had been mobilized. It was one of the biggest concentrations of PLA troops. Prachanda gave them regular political and military lectures.

In the beginning, Prachanda had promised to take us along to a site from where we could watch the battle. But later on, he went by himself. However, we could hear the bombardment and gunshots from where we were stationed. The battle of Khara was important for taking an offensive measure against King Gyanendra, who was now at the helm of all affairs in Nepal. It was important for Prachanda to win this battle, both for the class war as well as the inner struggle within the party. He needed to score a point against

King Gyanendra who had ditched him. Similarly, he needed to score a point against BRB. However, the Khara battle turned out to be a debacle. It was a mighty blow for the party, particularly for Prachanda. We were told that one of the reasons the battle was lost was the lack of coordination between Pasang and Prabhakar on the battlefield.[15] Later on, we were also to learn that there was a big contradiction between the leaders and cadres belonging to Rukum and Rolpa on the matter of supremacy of each district.

It was during the retreat from Khara to Kotgaon village in Rolpa (where we were kept in a hut) that we watched another battle at close range. I saw PLA troops from the Gandak region eating in a mess close to our hut. They were preparing to defend their troops from the RNA's offensive attack. I was keen to call Basanta (Prakash Rijal), who was commanding the Gandak PLA, and give him my best wishes. BRB prevented me from doing so as he felt it would be better not to appear close to him. Anybody close to us was treated with suspicion. I felt very sad to hear that he was killed in the same battle. He was one of the bravest battalion commanders we had. He was politically close to BRB.

I also saw many trenches being dug in the middle of school premises, in open spaces, and even in front of houses in preparation for a probable war with India. At that time, Prachanda had taken the stand of viewing Indian expansionism as the main enemy of the revolution.

After the defeat in the Khara attack, the relationship between Prachanda and BRB started getting better again. BRB's political stance of joining hands with parliamentary political parties to fight the monarchy had been validated. Hence, most of the time both Prachanda and BRB were seen busy contacting leaders of other parties within the country.

By April 2005, we had to go to India, along with Krishna Bahadur Mahara, to contact leaders of parliamentary parties of Nepal and to lobby with the political leaders of India. All this while the political action against us, which took place three months ago, had still not been revoked. At first, we were hesitant to go to India as it could provide fodder to the royalists and Prachanda's henchmen to smear us with their habitual accusation of us being 'pro-India'. However, since it was our own political line that was going to be implemented, we shouldered the responsibility.

We started reaching out to various civil liberties activists, intellectuals and media persons in both Nepal and India once we reached Delhi. While we were taking our work seriously in India, we were once again very disappointed when we heard about a videotape aired by the RNA on the Internet. The tape was about the coaching given by Prachanda to the PLA troops before the Khara attack. In that tape, as I recall, BRB was as usual castigated and smeared as working against the revolution and collaborating with India.[16]

I was shocked to hear that. I remember telling BRB to leave the party and Prachanda. I just could not take their venomous allegations any more.

23

When I Saw the Siberian Birds

triumph of republican agenda

Our efforts in India to bring the together different political forces of Nepal were gradually yielding results. Slowly, but steadily, leaders of various political parties came in contact with us.

Around the middle of June, we had a very important meeting with senior leaders of the NC and the UML in Delhi. Prachanda was called from Rolpa to join the high-level meeting. In the summit meeting, joined by G.P. Koirala and Prachanda, it was agreed upon that the NC and the UML would accept the republican agenda and the Maoists would enter peaceful politics. Subsequently, both sides would formalize this understanding in their respective party forums in the following months.

It was around the same time that we met Tamrat Samuel, who was representing the UN in Nepal. He had come to discuss the modality of a peaceful solution to the conflict in the country. We were also in contact with civil society members and Indian sympathizers of our cause through the People's Solidarity Forum.

All these events took place against the backdrop of King Gyanendra's increasing fascist tendencies. The World Trade Center attack (11 September 2001) in the USA emboldened him to take up the offensive 'anti-terrorism' agenda against the Maoists.

From October 2002 to mid-April 2006, the country was virtually seized by King Gyanendra. Backed by the army, he sacked the elected government on 1 February 2005. He imprisoned leaders of the major political parties, curbed the media and Internet, and suspended the rights of the people to organize and assemble.[1] These activities had not only antagonized political parties inside Nepal but had also alienated the international community, particularly India. The interaction of our leaders with strategically placed Indian intellectuals and bureaucrats had also influenced the Indian authorities to abandon the 'two-pillar theory' (the idea that the two institutions of monarchy and parliamentary, 'democratic' forces were the main pillars of a stable Nepal) in favour of a 'one-pillar theory' (of abandoning monarchy for complete democracy).

While we had failed to convince the main parliamentary parties, in Siliguri in 2001, to accept the agenda of forming a republic, we were successful in bringing them on board the republican agenda in 2005 in Delhi. King Gyanendra actually needs to be thanked for providing us a favourable opportunity to convince the parliamentary parties after his coup d'état!

Meanwhile, Prachanda also tried to pacify us about the leaked videotape where he had spoken ill of BRB. We did not react to his explanation. By now, we were used to his double-talk.

After getting a positive response from all sectors in India, we left for Chunwang village in Rukum for the CC meeting in October 2005. Unlike our previous trip to Rolpa in August 2004, this time the body language of both leaders showed that things were amicable between them. Whenever they got tired, they rested together and wherever they were hungry, they ate together.

The atmosphere at the Chunwang CC meeting evoked positive responses from all; it was totally different from the Lawang meeting. What had also made the Chunwang meeting different was the battle won at Pili in Kalikot by a division of the PLA under the western command headed by Com. Prabhakar. In this battle, '129 RNA personnel and twenty-six PLA [soldiers], including a battalion commissar, were killed. PLA captured many ammunition and arms.'[2] After the lost battle of Khara, it was important to boost the morale of the PLA. The victory at Pili was at that time important both politically and militarily. It also increased our credibility in the eyes of the parliamentary parties.

This time, the document proposed in the CC meeting charted BRB's political line in place of the earlier Prachanda–Kiran line.[3] The strategy endorsed by the second national conference (2001), regarding the republican agenda, was evoked and developed further. This time, the party focused on achieving the immediate: making Nepal a democratic republic.[4] This democratic republic was to be neither a bourgeois parliamentary republic nor a traditional communist-style people's democratic republic. In short, it was to play the role of a transitional state, which addressed class, gender, national/ethnic and regional oppression through total restructuring. It envisaged an interim government, an interim Constitution and a new Constitution through an elected Constituent Assembly. This scheme had already been approved in the second national conference where feudalism/monarchy was recognized as the principal barrier in Nepali society. This had paved the way for creating a united front, with the parliamentary political parties against monarchy.

When the document was presented in the Chunwang meeting, BRB was visibly happy because Prachanda had made a bold shift towards his political stance. Later on, we came to know that Mani Thapa, who had earlier stood by BRB's ideas, did not like this Prachanda–BRB bonhomie. Similarly, Rabindra Shrestha, who had always backed Prachanda's proposals, did not like the adoption of BRB's proposition. It was strange that two opposing trends (of Mani and Rabindra) converged to criticize the new alliance. Similarly, Badal reasserted his allegiance to Prachanda saying that he had acknowledged defeat. Earlier, he had supported Kiran's stance of identifying nationalism as the main contradiction as opposed to BRB's stance of ascertaining monarchy as the main contradiction in Nepali society. I could see that Kiran's arrest in India at the time of the Chunwang meeting had left those following his beliefs suppressed, and they eventually tailed Prachanda in following BRB's political line.

When my turn came to speak at the meeting, I gave a political speech buttressed by the books that I had read during our confinement. I spoke mainly on the international situation: about how our party's unilateral ceasefire in 2005, for about four months, had isolated King Gyanendra, and about the support we gained from the UN and other countries. On the question of leadership, I quoted Georgi Plekhanov, 'A great man is great not because his personal qualities give individual features to great historical events, but because he possesses qualities which make him most capable of serving the great social needs of his time, needs which arose as a result of serving general and particular causes.'[5] I also said that any person's weakness must not be determined by his/her personal setting but by his/her class position. And the dominant class in Nepal is the petty bourgeois class, which characteristically swings from one extreme position to the other. I also spoke about my own class background and my struggle to overcome any class traits that hindered my obligation towards the revolution.

BRB withdrew his notes of dissent. Prachanda also withdrew his charges against BRB. It was a liberating experience not only for us but also for the other leaders and cadres in the rest of the country, who had silently suffered all kinds of discrimination and humiliation for siding with us. The unity in the meeting hall was so strong that when Prachanda asked all CC members to voluntarily undergo one-step demotion, everybody agreed. From ninety-five members, the CC was brought down to thirty-five members. This kind of voluntarism is rare in the communist movement in Nepal.

It is worth recalling that during the fourth extended meeting of the party in September 1999, Prachanda's supporters had tried their best to prop him up as the centralized leader, but they could not succeed. However, this time, in the Chunwang meeting, without the issue of leadership being explicitly mentioned, Prachanda was elevated to a higher level rather agreeably.

After the CC meeting, when all of us came out of the meeting hall, I saw a beautiful flock of Siberian birds flying just above us. I had heard about such flights elsewhere but not in Nepal. I expected it the least in Chunwang. The V-shaped flight pattern of the Siberian birds was mesmerizing. I said, 'Comrades! Look at the flight of *karyangkurung* (Siberian migratory birds)! Look at the pattern of flight and the leader heading it! Isn't it trying to send some political message?' Indeed, the pattern indicated the strength of collectivity. The strength of leadership, which changed periodically in the flock, mirrored the periodic change of leadership in the party under the line adopted by our document 'Development of Democracy in the 21st Century'.

Right after the meeting was concluded, Samana Pariwar, the central cultural troupe, presented a cultural programme along with other pariwars in the open air. It was set against a perfect scenic surrounding. The weather was clear. This was to be the famous cultural programme in which almost all top leaders of the party, the PLA and the united front were found sobbing uncontrollably.[6] It was an opera based on the brutality of the state and the determination to avenge the comrades we had lost in the war. The main actress who performed extraordinarily was Com. Deepa Pun (at the time of writing, in late 2020, she was a provincial assembly member of province five), who had recently lost her husband, a PLA commander, in the Khara attack. She had danced and acted with her child (barely one year old) tied to her back. Every time she raised her fist to express determination to fight back, the child too would imitate her, raising her little fist! This made everyone sentimental. Prachanda, BRB, Post Bahadur. Bogati, Pasang and Barshaman Pun—all were shedding tears. I had never seen BRB crying. After the programme ended, I went behind the curtain to congratulate Deepa Pun. Hugging me, she burst into tears, remembering her martyred husband. The child, too, cried watching her mother cry. I couldn't stop my tears either as I held both mother and child. I will never forget that scene![7]

During the cultural programme, I saw an interesting couple. The husband was a singer in the Samana Pariwar while his wife was a company commander in the PLA. It was a role reversal of the traditional division of labour where the wife was usually the cultural activist and the husband a PLA combatant.

After the Chunwang meeting, Prachanda, BRB, Krishna B. Mahara, Rabindra Shrestha and I went back to India. Comrade Sunil, a CC member, had come to provide security cover to us all the way from Rolpa to the border between Nepal and India. Somehow, just when he was going back, I had an uneasy feeling that the RNA or the armed police might target this fine, tall fighter whose wife and daughter were brutally assaulted by the police.[8] I had told him and his team to travel safely. Later, when we reached India, we heard that he was killed on the spot when an RNA military plane ambushed them in Rolpa. He was hit in the head by a bullet. I felt very sad. I thought it was better to die in war, fighting for a just world, than to die having done nothing.

When I was in the base area, I had felt that I was bleeding abnormally during my period. Once, I even felt dizzy when we had to flee to the nearby jungle when a RNA airplane started targeting our shelter. So, when I went to India, I went for a check-up at a government hospital in Chandigarh. There, I was diagnosed with a benign uterus tumor and asked to get it operated immediately. The day I had to undergo surgery, BRB's mother passed away in Nepal in March 2006. BRB broke the news to me after I regained consciousness from the surgery. I remembered her strong uterus, which bore seven children; three of whom had passed away. I remembered what a strong figure she was in her family and village. She had once taken the risk to clandestinely meet me with a glass of milk in my shelter in Gorkha. I could not control my tears, knowing that I would not be able to see her any more. BRB, as usual, did not show much sign of distress, but I knew how he felt deep inside. His mother adored him; she wouldn't take her eyes off him whenever she met him and would proudly brag about her son to others.

In the meantime, Rabindra Shrestha was made in-charge of the overseas bureau (OB) in India. I was to be the assistant in-charge. We used to send contingents of Nepali workers, cultural activists and whole-timer party cadres from India to Nepal to join the armed struggle. Shrestha, who was not happy with the outcome of the Chunwang meeting, was also unhappy with his new posting. He was not happy to see Prachanda aligning with BRB and wanted to work in Kathmandu. Gradually, he started opposing the party's line, leadership and defying his responsibilities. Mani Thapa joined him. He, too, was not happy to see BRB aligning with Prachanda. They had clandestinely started forming their own clique, which they later named as 'cultural revolutionary group', within four months of the Chunwang meeting.[9] Through this group, they started criticizing both Prachanda and BRB's character and the work culture. When repeated warnings didn't work, the party took political action against them.

Meanwhile, the increasing repression of political parties in Nepal and King Gyanendra's short-sighted moves on foreign affairs further created space for bringing major political parties together. The political strategy adopted in the Chunwang meeting additionally created an environment for this. Most of the leaders had either been placed under arrest by the king or had fled to India. The Maoist leadership invited UML leaders such as Bamdev Gautam and Yubaraj Gyawali to the base area. A joint statement was issued by the Maoist party and the UML to fight against the tyranny of the king. The Maoist party also invited the leader of the Nepali Congress (NC), G.P. Koirala, to come to the base area to agree upon the same agenda. However, Koirala declined, citing health issues and the risk of travelling to the war zone. In fact, this agreement created the basis for the twelve-point understanding between the Maoist and seven other political parties. The historic understanding between the Maoists and the Seven-Party Alliance (SPA) was signed in November 2005 in Delhi. The agreement clearly spelt out the new agenda: abolition of autocratic monarchy and restructuring of the state by eliminating all oppression based on class, gender, national/ethnic and regional identities. This triggered the historic second people's movement in April 2006, which lasted for nineteen days and paved the way for the election of the CA and declaration of the country as a democratic republic.

Finally, I entered Nepal in July 2006 through Tanakpur, travelling all the way from Delhi by bus. I straightaway went to a place called B.P. Nagar in Doti, a far-western district, where others had also gathered. There, we waited for our leaders, Prachanda and BRB, to come from Kathmandu in a helicopter accompanied by the then home minister, Krishna Prasad Sitaula. The historic peace process had finally begun. In Doti, I met Bhojraj Bhat who represented *Nepal* magazine. He was the first Nepali journalist to interview me in the country after ten years of the PW.

24

Dhai-Futte Sena

PLA narratives

When I came to Rolpa for the first time after the PW had been launched in 2001, a PLA woman was appointed to look after my security. Her name was Kushal Rakchhya and she was around eighteen years old; she was a section commander then. She came from Rolpa and belonged to the local Magar community. She was short and sturdy, about four feet tall. I remember asking her, 'How can you fight the NA with such a short height?' She promptly replied, 'Yes, they tease us by calling us *dhai-futte sena*! But we retaliate by saying that we have *saye futte bichar*'. ('Dhai-futte' means two and a half feet and 'saye futte bichar' means a hundred feet in thought.) That was an apt reply. I was quite impressed after hearing it. She said that while the enemy may carry sophisticated arms, they carried the weapon of ideology. Indeed, they had been given lessons in Maoism, such as 'it is right to rebel' and 'without the People's Army, the people have nothing'. Besides, the PLA gave women teeth to fight against male chauvinism, male authority and feudal patriarchy.

While away from the war zone, I had read *The Art of War* by Sun Tzu to understand the phenomena of the PW. I had never directly participated in a war. I had not fired a single bullet, not even out of curiosity. A staff member of mine used to carry a gun with her. One such staff member, Neema Chowdhari, had accidently shot herself in the thigh with an automatic machine gun when she was trying to sling it from one shoulder to the other. That was the closest I came to seeing a gun being fired, that too a mishap, and saw an injured PLA member right in front of me. Luckily, she survived with a thigh injury. My job within the PLA was to give political coaching, to inspire them to fight and to arm them with ideological bullets. The only time I felt like a combatant was when I had to wear the combat dress while travelling and coaching the cadres.

I was a curious cat regarding the PLA and its structure. Sometimes, they used to tease me, 'Didi, you look like a war journalist asking all sorts of questions!' My interest in women in the PLA dated back to the 1980s, when I read Evelyn Reed's book *Is Biology Woman's Destiny?* (1971). She had written in depth about how women are biologically stronger than men. Taking inspiration from her book and others, I had written an article, '*Ke Mahilaharu Sharirik Roople Nai Kamjor Hun Ta?* (Are Women Really Physically Weak?)', in 1994.[1] I was told that this article became quite popular among women PLA members. Whenever I gave them political lectures, I used to share with them the latest findings on the capabilities of women. For instance, I used to tell them that pregnancy could be postponed and how sperm could be stored in a sperm bank and retrieved. Whenever I had time, I liked to give them a head massage. I also showed them some self-defence moves. All these were skills I had learnt in the UK.

I found women PLA combatants to be very vibrant, curious and dedicated. I remember some of the male division commanders narrating how brave and enthusiastic women commanders were. They tried to save some of the promising women commanders by pacing their direct involvement in war. But the women commanders refused to stand in the margins. Instead, they positioned themselves on the front line. Consequently, many promising commanders lost their lives.

It would be interesting to know how the concept of waging a war evolved within the communist movement in Nepal. It was the Jhapa revolt in the early '70s that can be considered as the first organized armed struggle by the communists in Nepal, but it did not last long. People were then attracted to the CPN (Masal) led by M.B. Singh because he used to talk about waging an armed struggle. Gradually, people saw through it as M.B. Singh never put his words into practice. This eventually made way for the formation of a new party, CPN (Mashal), led by Kiran. This Mashal group tried to initiate armed struggle by attacking some police posts in Kathmandu in 1987. But it was a failure leading to many leaders and cadres being arrested. After this, the CPN (Mashal) and other communist groups joined hands to form CPN (Unity Centre) in 1990.

It was in the sixth national congress held between 22 November and 6 December 1991 that a rural-based protracted PW was mooted. It was in the third extended meeting (1995) that the military line was finally passed to execute the PW. It was clearly spelt out that the main form of organization would be the army and the main form of struggle would be the PW in order to complete the 'new democratic revolution'. In the CC meeting held immediately after the third extended meeting, an elaborate first plan to initiate the PW was drafted in 1995. In it, Mao was quoted: 'Political power grows out of the barrel of a gun.'[2] This statement was repeated several times during the PW to make sure that it did not degenerate into roving guerrilla warfare.

A lot of preparations had taken place before the formal launch of the PW. The Young Communist League (YCL) had been formed. This was the youth wing of the party, which existed before the PW and played the main role in forming combatant forces,[3] defence forces and voluntary forces. In fact, volunteer groups were already active in fighting against local goons backed by the NC and the UML before the formal declaration of the PW. The old state had no clue about its linkage with the PW that was to be declared soon.

In the party's CC meeting, it was decided that fighting squads would be formed and supervised under the district committees, village defence forces would be supervised under area committees and volunteer forces would be supervised under cell committees. The concept of primary area, secondary area and propaganda area was formulated. Accordingly, the primary area protected by a squad unit would concentrate on guerrilla warfare, the secondary area covered by a defence force would concentrate on sabotage activities and the propaganda area covered by a volunteer force would concentrate on propaganda-related activities.[4] All these exercises ultimately helped in launching the PW on 13 February 1996, with hundreds of simultaneous actions taking place within a day of initiation.

When the PW was launched, the intensity of war was so great that strikes, attacks and ambush used to take place almost every day in some part of Nepal or the other. This was the first phase of the PW's defence strategy. The party struck a fine balance between political and military attacks by using offensive military strike and dialogue (in the form of peace talks). It also maintained a balance between military offence and defence to sustain the PW.

Within two months of initiation of the PW, the fighting squad was converted into a guerrilla squad. Using the guerrilla warfare ploy of 'hit and run', the guerrilla units launched surprise attacks on vulnerable police posts in remote villages, particularly in western Nepal. This strategy was adopted to strike at the enemy's weakest spot while avoiding decisive war with the state. 'Hit' signified harassing the enemy while 'run' stood for consolidating one's strength. Guerrilla squads laid ambushes on police patrols. This forced the government to centralize its forces by bringing together police posts of different villages under one umbrella in an area. This carried on till August 2001 and resulted in clearing villages of reactionary, repressive, intelligence operators, police, loan sharks and other opponents of the PW. The local units of the people's state (Maoist parallel government) then filled the deserted village state organ.

In the second national conference held in February 2001, it was decided to prepare for mobile warfare while relying on guerrilla tactics in order to achieve strategic equilibrium. After a significant increase in clearing posts and accumulating weapons seized from police posts, the PW reached the strategic equilibrium stage. People's states now started replacing district headquarters. In big cities, urban squads, too, started operating daringly, striking strategic installations and army personnel.

The capture of Dunai, the headquarters of Dolpa district, on 25 September 2000, with the help of a guerrilla force indicated a qualitative leap and a high level of skills achieved by our guerrilla force within the strategic defence phase. This was the first successful strike on a district HQ.[5] This forced the government to form the Armed Police Force (APF), a paramilitary force to combat the Maoists, in October 2001. However, the assassination of the first chief of APF, Krishna Mohan Shrestha (then serving as the additional inspector general of police), in 2003 by the Maoists's special task force (STF) demoralized the government further.[6] Additionally, the impressive presence of women combatants in the Maoist PW forced the government to recruit women in the police, APF and RNA, too.[7] It also forced the government intelligence agency to recruit women in their surveillance activities.

On 24 September 2001, the creation of the PLA was formally announced. The PLA, thus formed, had a double command system: the military command and the political command. The formation of the PLA gradually expanded from squad to division over the years: the lowest rung was the squad, consisting of seven to thirteen men. Three squads made up a platoon, three platoons made up a company, three companies made up one battalion, three battalions formed one brigade and three brigades made a division, the highest formation in PLA. The party provided them with food, dress and shoes. They were also given a monthly allowance (Rs 150) for logistical support.

On the day of the formation of the PLA, the formation of the 'people's militia' was also declared. The militia was like the community police. They were trained to provide security to the villagers by giving intelligence information about the enemy to the PLA. They worked as sentries, in tandem with the PLA, as a supporting force when needed during the war. They did all sorts of logistical work like helping to prepare food, carrying the injured away from a war zone, etc. They helped in production work, assisting the needy in sowing seeds or harvesting the yield. They also worked in health camps. They didn't wear uniforms. Children as young as fifteen to men and women as old as sixty to sixty-five were given militia training. They generally, however, did not carry weapons but were given sockets for self-defence. They underwent physical training (PT) and took self-defence courses. They also acted as enforcers of law and order, whereby they helped in punishing the culprits as ordered by the people's court. The competent ones were promoted to the PLA. Many times they also participated in an ambush and made grenades. There were part-time and full-time militia. The masses, too, were involved in making crude bombs by mixing chilli powder, pieces of iron, used batteries and broken earthen pots.

Immediately after the formation of the PLA, it attacked the RNA for the first time in Dang on 23 November 2001.[8] This resulted in the capture of huge quantities of arms and armaments. This boosted the morale of the Maoists both within the country and outside. But around the same time, the 9/11 attack took place. This alerted both national and international forces. A series of important events, such as the Royal Palace massacre in June 2001, the formation of the PLA in September 2001, the first successful attack on an army barrack in November 2001 created an environment for the mobilization of the RNA. Externally, the 9/11 attack helped King Gyanendra declare a state of emergency.

The RNA was mobilized for the first time against the Maoists, along with the declaration of a state of emergency, on 26 November 2001.[9] The RNA had boasted that the PLA would be defeated within three months of emergency rule. However, it turned out to be a hard row to hoe.

By the end of 2001, the government forces were limited to district centres and highways.[10] They could not enter villages. Finding it difficult to face the Maoists on land, the RNA started relying more on air strikes (perhaps influenced by the US army).

As the war intensified, I remember leaders telling commanders not to attack the police, APF and army personnel who had come to their villages to meet their families. In fact, cadres were encouraged to meet family members of state security personnel to try and win them over to our side, so that they could encourage their husbands to join the PLA. Many ex-Gurkha soldiers from India and Britain came forward to teach the PLA the art and technology of war.

Periodic calls were made by the party members to the homes of security personnel, to encourage them to leave their jobs and join the PW. As a result, many security personnel from the RNA, police and APF came to join the PW. One such man was a sub-inspector, belonging to the Nepal Police, working in the communication sector in the western part of Nepal. He left the force in 2001 to join the party. According to him, at that time, there were ten to fifteen of them who had left the state force to join the Maoist party. Eventually, a few thousand personnel belonging to the RNA, police and APF joined the movement. Some of them even brought weapons with them. After the sub-inspector left his job, the party made him an area secretary in Kailali district.

Bhakti Pandey was one of the main people who dealt with ammunition and other logistical supplies. According to him, in the beginning, arms were taken from villagers, particularly from feudal lords who hunted in jungles. As the PW intensified, ammunition started coming from India, Burma and China. The main source of supply was North-east India. Pandey and his team often bribed men in the lower rungs of the Indian Army, railway staff and the police to get their supply through different points.[11] According to him, the Indian government started intervening when US-made ammunition started getting into Nepal through Burma. Pandey and his team had to be on high alert when thirteen suitcases of ammunition were caught at Guwahati station in Assam, India, in 2002.[12] According to him, they got a consignment of small arms from Khasa, a bordering town of China. But this led to capital punishment being meted out to the Nepali supplier.[13]

Pandey told me one interesting incident where he had saved himself from the jaws of death. He had been approached by an acquaintance in Gorakhpur, who had told him that he could be supplied with ammunition at a cheap rate. He had been taken to a place about 7 kilometres away from Gaya railway station, to a hotel adjoining a huge temple in the middle of a lake. It was some Hindu religious organization that was to supply him ammunition. But they put a condition that the guns should be used against Muslims and Christians. When he didn't agree to their condition, he felt that they were hatching a plot to kill him and throw him into the lake. Pandey threatened them saying that his comrades had been following the person who had brought him to the hotel, and that the person, including his family, would not be left alive. That was how he had been let off!

The police had a strength of 63,000, while the armed police had 18,000 members. Previously, there were seven fighting brigades in the RNA. At the time, there were fifteen operational brigades, including one in Kathmandu and excluding the increase from 53,000 in 2001 to 83,000 in early 2005. Each year, 5000 soldiers were added till 2010, thus bringing the RNA's strength to 1,00,000. The budget for security and home affairs was substantially hiked and took up a big proportion of the national budget.[14]

In June 2004, the Maoist party's CC meeting decided that it was time to enter the strategic offence phase. On 15 January 2005, a daring and successful PLA attack took place in both Thankot and Dadhikot within the Kathmandu Valley, the 'white area' for the Maoists. This prepared the ground for fusing guerrilla warfare with urban insurrection. For this, not only was it necessary to increase PLA recruitments but high-range mortars were also required to offset enemy planes and helicopters. Several cadres from mass frontal organizations, including those from autonomous nationality/ethnicity and regional states started joining the PLA force. At this stage of the strategic offence, a round of attacks in the form of a ring was planned, from the east and the west, to finally concentrate on the Kathmandu Valley. This plan was called *dhadma tekera tauko ma hanne* (climb on the back and strike the head).[15] The mission was to launch an attack on the 'head'—the district headquarters, city centres, while the 'back' referred to regions surrounding the district headquarters and urban peripheries.

The ultimate target was the Kathmandu Valley, the 'head'. The surrounding districts outside the valley, including highways leading to Kathmandu, were considered to be the 'back'. Highways were targeted to starve the security forces. Headquarters of districts surrounding Kathmandu were targeted to weaken the central state.

On 5 April 2006, the PLA attacked Malangwa, the district headquarters of Sarlahi district in Terai, a place considered to be strategically important.[16] In fact, an RNA helicopter was downed there. On 23 April, the PLA attacked the district headquarters of Sindhupalchowk. Key police posts in Kavre district were also targeted.

All these events helped in initiating the second people's movement in April 2006, which lasted nineteen days in the Kathmandu Valley. PLA combatants and the militia in civil dress were sent to intermingle with the masses, along with cadres of parliamentary parties, for a decisive insurrection in Kathmandu.

Meanwhile, the movement started burgeoning in other urban centres. Throughout the country, nineteen protesters were killed, over 400 were arrested and dozens of civilians were injured.[17] But before the insurrection could reach its peak, the parliamentary parties called off the movement. Unlike my direct involvement in the first people's movement, I was not present in Kathmandu during the second one. I was in Doti district in the far-western region.

With the partial success of the second people's movement in April 2006, a ceasefire was declared and the peace negotiation with the SPA coalition government was initiated.[18]

25

Drums, Pen and Rifle

the cultural front

The Maoist cultural troupe played an important role when the party entered the peace process after the Comprehensive Peace Agreement (CPA) was signed in November 2006. In the heart of Kathmandu, they introduced the culture of revolutionary zeal and action. Gradually, they started transforming the psychology of the cadres and the masses from war to peace by focusing on consolidation of the gains made by the PW. Likewise, there was also gradual transformation in the nature of the cultural performances. Slowly, the dancers started applying make-up, wearing shiny jewellery and colourful, bright dresses to attract the attention of the masses. The content of their performance also started revolving around patriotic songs, love songs with social themes, laced with class war and hatred for the class enemy, etc. As time passed, there were instances where the artists started drifting towards commercial performances. While some did it out of choice, others were forced by circumstances.

Cultural troupes were also in demand when the CA election took place. Once again, they were called to attract the masses, not for war but for state restructuring and for inculcating inclusive democracy in people's mindsets. Cultural programmes depicting various ethnicities not only brought colourful variety to the programme but also educated the masses about the multicultural composition of the country. In short, the Maoist cultural troupe helped in filling the transitional gap between war and peace as much as it had helped in launching the PW.

During the PW, the Maoist cultural wing also helped in fusing guns and bombs with drums, pen and paintings. The following poem was composed and sung by martyred Com. Chunnu Gurung,[1] one of the most admired cultural activists:

'Tyo rato chhitijko pahilo kiranma
ma ladirahanchhu mukti yuddhama.
ladda laddai yo jiwan gaye gaijala
timi sangha gahiro maya basyo jaljala!'

(In the first rays of that red horizon
I will remain fighting in the war for liberation.
Even if I die while fighting, let it be!
I have fallen in deep love with you, dear Jaljala!)

Indeed, Chunnu Gurung died a martyr's death! Jaljala is a mountain in the Maoist heartland, Rolpa, which has a symbolic connotation for the revolutionaries. Chunnu truly dedicated her life in the spirit of the song she sang. She, who came from the marginalized Gurung (Tamu) indigenous ethnic group, hailed from a very poor family in Palpa district. She had very little formal education, but she was a multitalented woman. She sang, danced, wrote poems and articles and was a very good orator as well. She was truly a member of the proletariat, materially as well as spiritually. No wonder the RNA targeted her: she was killed in Syangja in May 2002.[2] At that time, she was the president of the Jana Sanskritik Sangh, Kaski district. Her death was a great loss for the PW. She had barely recovered from the loss of her husband who had been martyred less than a month before she herself was

killed. After their marriage, they had barely stayed together for
one month when she heard about his death. I remember having
read her article, in which she wrote about her late husband;[3] it
was so emotional and moving that everybody was talking about it.
I had known her long before she joined the PW.

I took a great interest in cultural activities during the PW,
even though I was not directly in charge of them. My interest
in the cultural field was inborn. I got my first exposure at IIT
Kanpur, where students and children of professors were introduced
to music, songs and dance at an early age. Top vocalists, musicians
and dancers used to come there to perform. I had a good voice,
and I participated in a singing competition that was held by the
Central School at various levels. My singing talent was one of the
reasons why I was chosen as the cultural secretary of the AINSA
in Delhi.

After coming to Nepal, I had been a backstage singer and
occasionally a dancer in the programmes organized by the party.
I had never taken dance classes. It came naturally to me. At times,
I had also choreographed and taught singing for local cultural
groups. I had been observing how cultural activities had a direct
link with various movements in Nepal.

Cultural programmes had been one of the strong instruments
of propaganda, successfully used by underground political parties
against the Rana regime, monarchy and the Panchayat system.
Mao had said that for any movement or revolution to set out, an
appropriate atmosphere should first be created; he was pointing at
the tasks of the cultural front during a revolution's foundational
period. Just as 'Ralfa', the first people's cultural troupe led by
artists Ramesh, Manjul and Rayan, had prepared the ground
for launching the Jhapa in the 1970s, the Samana Pariwar,
established in 1990 under the leadership of Khushiram Pakhrin,
Chunnu Gurung and Mani Thapa, had prepared the ground for
launching the PW in Nepal.[4] Songs like *Krantikari! Nepal Mukta
Banaideu* . . . (Revolutionaries! Liberate Nepal . . .)' and, *'Huri*

Chaldai Chha, Aandhi Aaundai Chha . . . (A Storm is Breaking, A Hurricane is Approaching . . .)' sung before the launch of the PW indicated the impending political commotion.

Around the period of the PW's initiation, propaganda campaigns spanning three months were launched throughout the country. They involved mass gatherings, political awakening and cultural programmes in a three-in-one package. For instance, the *Bhalka Abhiyan* (Bhaktapur–Lalitpur–Kathmandu campaign) was launched just before the PW started in order to psychologically prepare the people for the war. *Sija Abhiyan* ('si' for Sisne and 'ja' for Jaljala mountain in Rukum and Rolpa, respectively) was launched before the PW started. Likewise, other such movements were launched throughout the country.

After the PW was launched, I was amazed to see the rapid expanse and variety of cultural activities, which lasted throughout the PW. Cultural activities provided a platform for many talented singers, dancers and actors/actresses (especially to those coming from remote areas and poor families) to show their talents and dedication. Their consciousness was raised to the point where they did not want to be considered as mere entertainers or cultural activists but wanted to assert themselves as revolutionary cultural cadres who were there to advance, enhance and strengthen the PW for a constructive breakthrough. Before the PW was kicked-off, cultural performances were often interludes between long speeches. However, as the PW picked up, the programmes worked as a psychological and physical force to build up, advance and strengthen it. They were not merely of instrumental use but of substantive worth. Hierarchically, it expanded from the local level to the district-, regional- and central-level cultural teams. Cultural activities also inculcated in the masses awareness about their rights and duties. At the same time, they attacked feudal structures and bolstered communist values. They glorified sacrifices made during the PW by the people, the PLA, the women and the martyrs.

Dalits were very enthusiastic when it came to cultural programmes, as they were traditionally singers and experts in playing various indigenous musical instruments. *Panchey baja* (a band consisting of five traditional musical instruments), as popular in contemporary times as it used to be in the past, was profusely used during the PW.

In many places, cultural performances became the first instance where the masses came into direct contact with the party. In many ways, it became a recruiting centre. The increasing influence of cultural activities on the masses became apparent when Maoist cultural troupes started incorporating different ethnicities and regional cultural performances to truly embrace the spirit of federal restructuring and inclusive democracy. This, in fact, not only increased the volume and quality of cultural activities but also presented a scope for building new national unity by celebrating diversity. This was particularly visible when the first United Revolutionary People's Council (URPC) was formed in Kureli in Rolpa. There, different cultural groups representing Tamsaling, Magarat, Madhesi and Seti–Mahakali regions performed their presentations and showcased their distinct, vibrant forms of art. From then on, cultural activities became multi-ethnic and multiregional.

With the demarcation of nine provinces by the CPN (Maoist), cultural teams dedicated to each ethnic and regional province started developing. For instance, in the Newa province, Baikuntha Chet Narayan Sanskritik Abhiyan was formed in memory of martyrs Baikuntha Shrestha and Chet Narayan Shrestha. Similarly, in Tamsaling, Chyang Sanskritik Abhiyan was set up in memory of martyrs Krishna Sen and Chyangba Lama. In due course of time, cultural troupes were formed within the PLA. Cultural platoons, companies and brigades were formed to fight directly alongside the PLA. The PLA and the cultural troupes perfectly complemented each other. The cultural activists added emotional and zealous spirit to the PLA, and the PLA in turn imparted further emotional, dynamic and creative ideas and techniques to sharpen their ideological and cultural instincts. During the war, people often quoted Prachanda's saying, '*Hansda hansdai rune, runda rundai hasne* (While laughing one has to cry, and while crying one has to laugh)'.

This reflected the dialectical relationship between ecstasy and grief during the war.

The reason why cultural activities were particularly important, and why they flourished, during the PW was that they received institutional support at the highest level. Com. Kiran, also known as Chaitanya, took great interest on the cultural front.[5] He was an established revolutionary literary critic even before the PW started. During the PW, publication of all mass organizations like those of women, Dalits, students and various autonomous ethnic and regional fronts were published and circulated on a regular basis. There was a spurt of talent in writing poems, memoirs and stories. I, too, wrote a couple of poems. One of them was on women's biological and social strength. Diaries of PLA combatants used to be full of unpublished poems, memoirs and stories. Many a time, diaries left by the slain army, police or APF personnel, too, were found to be filled with such writings. Thus, the war had unleashed talents in literary expression on both sides. Occasionally, journalists, guests, and even foreign tourists, would get access to watch cultural programmes by the Maoists. Seeing this, even the security personnel of the old state started organizing their own cultural programmes.

There were instances when state security forces targeted cultural troupes because of their vital role in the PW.[6] Thus, for their safety, they were given self-defence courses and armed with sockets for self-defence. They participated in attacks by helping to be messengers, motivators and entertainers. They were also called upon to boost the morale of the workers involved in construction sites, such as trekking trails, Martyrs' Road[7] and chowtaras. They also helped Maoist cadres assimilate in new places by adopting the cultural activities of that locality. I remember being pleasantly surprised to see *mayur* dance (peacock dance) in Rolpa, when one couldn't even find a peacock in that region. I saw dancers sticking peacock feathers on their backs and also wearing colourful Rajasthani costumes!

As many as 160 cadres and leaders of Maoist cultural groups were killed, either in groups or individually, during the PW.[8] The numbers escalated when a state of emergency was imposed. In Anekot in Kavre, a cultural troupe consisting of seven artists was ambushed and killed on the spot in 1999. Similarly, eleven artists constituting a cultural troupe were killed on the spot at Bhawang in Rolpa in the same year. Artists had been killed at Gumchal in Rolpa, at Binayak in Achham, at Chheda in Doti and at Basikhora in Bhojpur.[9] Amongst those martyred, Krishna Sen 'Ichhuk' represented the senior-most cultural activist. He was the editor of the Maoist mouthpiece *Janadesh*. He was also a progressive writer and poet. He was the coordinator of Akhil Nepal Jan Sanskriti Sangathan, the central cultural front of the Maoists. He was arrested in Kathmandu, tortured and eventually murdered in police custody. Similarly, D.B. Thapa, Sharada Shrestha and many others were also arrested and killed by the police.

Seeing the effective use of cultural programmes as a morale booster for the PLA, the old feudal state also started using mainstream artists like Komal Oli, who hailed from Dang, in state-sponsored programmes. In such programmes, love songs were often sung and dance programmes were staged. Sometimes, patriotic songs evoking the heroic deeds of the government forces were played. The aim was probably to entertain and divert the attention of the security forces, bureaucrats and the general masses. However, in my opinion, such programmes could not fulfil their aim nor were they as effective as the performances of the revolutionaries. After all, the Maoists had an appealing mission to build a new society, new government structures—a new Nepal with new and progressive cultural values.

Part III

A NEW BEGINNING

26

Maoists in Kathmandu

wooing the middle class

After ten years of underground politics, I finally entered my hometown, Kathmandu, in July 2006. I had briefly visited the city during the PW, but I had not been able to walk around freely then. This time, it was different. The first thing that I noticed was the appalling traffic congestions. This was in great contrast to what I had been seeing in western and far-western parts of rural Nepal, where I had been travelling before arriving in Kathmandu. Used to seeing scant traffic flow and deafening silence in the rural hinterlands, I was rather nervous travelling around the Kathmandu Valley.

Prachanda and BRB had already arrived a month before I reached. I found Kathmandu to be a concrete jungle—overcrowded, unplanned and noisy. Ten years ago, I could easily carry my daughter on my bicycle around Kathmandu. Now, I hardly found bicycles on the road. I found the core city area, viz. Ason, Chhetrapati, Wongal, etc., turning into urban slums with the indigenous Newar inhabitants moving out to the peripheries and poor urban migrants settling in. The cozy and comfortable *galli*s (lanes) running through the core area had become narrower with too many people and high-rise buildings. The beautiful, traditional Newari dwellings had been replaced by the concrete jungle. Many traditional *baha*s (courtyards with temples, stupas, water wells, etc.) had been pulled down and turned into shopping complexes. Not to mention pollution of all sorts—water, air and sound. The ring road that used to be uncongested had become the busiest lifeline for the growing city. The sacred Bagmati and Bishnumati rivers had shrunk and were polluted, reduced to mere rivulets owing to garbage heaps and filth. High-rise buildings and settlements coming up on the hills surrounding the valley had dwarfed the towering Dharahara and Swayambhu landmarks. Consumerism was on the rise. I felt I was not coming to the old Kathmandu that I had left ten years ago but a different 'Concrete-mandu'.

Later on, I came to know that one of the reasons for this rapid increase in population, along with urbanization, was migration of people from the PW-affected areas. I saw the Newars being pushed into becoming a minority in their own homeland because of the influx of outsiders from the rural districts. Not only that, I also observed that most of the Newars were not teaching their children the native Newari language. I also saw the mushrooming of private-run schools and colleges. I was particularly surprised to see girls studying in private schools wearing pants, shirts, ties and coats as uniforms. That had not been the scene earlier. I realized that Kathmandu had remained very much the mushrooming capital of a rather centralized state, of course with some modernity. Everything was centralized here, all kinds of facilities and opportunities. It was a bustling city amidst a rural sprawl.

I was curious about Kathmandu Valley from a political perspective, too. Kathmandu was an important centre for the frontal organizations of our party, particularly for the students' and women's wings. While the students' wing fought to stop rampant mushrooming of private schools and regulate rapid increase in fees, the women's front was active in checking unbridled use of alcohol and gender violence.

During the PW, I had heard that this valley was a stronghold of Kiran's supporters. Rabindra Shrestha was seen taking the dogmatic line and condemning BRB's political line while witch-hunting those who supported BRB. He went out of his way to promote Badal, as he was in-charge of the valley bureau during the PW. Rabindra was found to be hobnobbing with the royalists while he was in jail.[1] He was given special facilities in jail because of this connection, which was not appreciated by other inmates. In fact, a special meeting was called to solve the inner party struggle in the valley.[2] Later on, Rabindra Shrestha left the party to join the UML, after the party took political action against him.

After coming to Kathmandu Valley, the first thing I was keen to know was the level of participation and the contribution of the valley inhabitants during the PW. Through the Informal Sector Service Centre (INSEC), a human rights organization, I came to know that thirty-seven Maoists had been killed, ninety had disappeared and two had been disabled within the Kathmandu Valley.[3] I was also keen to know how many actions had taken place within the valley. On the very first day of the initiation of the PW in February 1996, the Pepsi factory, a multinational company stationed in Kathmandu, was struck as a symbol of attack on imperialism. After the formation of the STF by the Maoists in Kathmandu Valley, the chief of the APF, Krishna Mohan Shrestha, along with his wife and bodyguard, were shot dead in Lalitpur, an adjoining district inside the valley on 16 January 2003. The same year, on 12 September, the Maoist STF ambushed a RNA patrol troop in Tokha, in Kathmandu district, killing five RNA personnel and seizing their weapons.[4] Similarly, the STF gunned down a DSP right in the heart of Kathmandu district in Gongbu on 6 July 2004. In Sankhu, east of Kathmandu district, the STF attacked a police post, seizing weapons and gunning down five policemen, including an inspector. A DSP and three other policemen were shot down in Kathmandu on 27 February 2005. On 14 January 2006, two police posts in Thankot and Dadhikot were attacked by the STF, gunning down twelve policemen, including a police inspector, and capturing thirty firearms.

It is worth questioning why the Maoist party had decided not to mount a decisive attack on the Kathmandu Valley. In fact, many actions in the valley were taken to divert the attention of the security forces from the rural areas, where an intense class war was taking place. The valley, besides being the national capital, was the centre of international activities. It was felt that even if the party successfully seized the valley, retaining/sustaining its hold over the capital would be quite difficult and challenging. Also, militarily, it was increasingly felt that neither could the PLA have a decisive victory over the RNA nor could the RNA completely defeat the PLA. Thus, the party kept itself open to dialogues with the parliamentary parties, which later culminated in a mutual agreement to launch a people's movement in Kathmandu Valley.

I also came to know from my stepmother, Savitri Dahal, that she had been taken into custody and her house had been raided repeatedly by the police and army. Before the launch of the PW, my mother's house had sheltered our party's students, workers and women's organizations' offices, and they remained there during the PW, too. My sisters, too, had been supportive of the PW. They helped in finding shelters for our comrades. I actually have to give credit to BRB. It was he who instilled political awakening in my maternal family by bringing out the book *Dharma Ratna Yami Smriti Granth* in 1989. He had encouraged my sisters, particularly Timila, to bring out the book on my parents' life and their contributions to the country. That exercise had paid off; as a result, none of my family members went against the PW. Similarly, my sister-in-law, Durga Neupane, helped in relaying messages to us in some way or the other by contacting us in India or in the base areas.

When I entered Kathmandu Valley in 2006, I realized that I was the only local Newar from Kathmandu proper who was a CC member of the Maoist party. I was assigned the task of being assistant in-charge of the Kathmandu Valley Bureau. Then, our party divided Nepal into five commands: eastern command, special command, middle command, western command and far-western command. The in-charge of special command, comprising both Tamsaling and Newar regions, was Barshaman Pun 'Ananta'.

We had produced an elaborate three-month plan under the banner of *Ganatanrik Janasambandha Sudridhikaran Abhiyan* (campaign to consolidate our relationship with the people) to spread our influence among Kathmandu's middle class. It included a comprehensive plan to improve the city's physical infrastructure, to strengthen security in the city, to make the city more green, to mitigate traffic congestion, etc. Besides these, economic activities, such as rearing pigs, ducklings, poultry and vegetation were undertaken by the YCL on the peripheral riverside land.

We had made a month-long security plan for the valley and set up a crime control campaign. The leader of YCL in Kathmandu, Com. Sagar (Chandra Bahadur Thapa), took the lead and cracked down on around fifty dons (leaders of criminal gangs) as well as other goons, kidnappers, petty thieves and extortionists operating in the valley. The YCL confiscated guns, kukris, various weapons, golden chains, cash, mobiles, etc., which were displayed to the media and handed over to the police. We gave political coaching to all the detained goons, told them to be good citizens and let them off eventually. During the PW, some local goons and thugs had joined the PW and become good commanders in war. Some of them even sacrificed their lives. Hence, for us, it was not difficult to understand their psychology and find ways to mold them into revolutionaries. Naya Bazar in Kathmandu, which was known to be a crime-infested area, experienced some relief when our HQ was stationed there. The presence of the PLA provided a sense of security to the residents of Naya Bazar as well. Similarly, the YCL had opened a drug rehabilitation centre at Balaju to control, manage and rehabilitate addicts for up to six months.

As a part of the cleanliness campaign, we used Tundikhel, an open-air theatre right in the centre of the city, to kick off our initiative to make Kathmandu clean and green. Core areas of the city and the Bagmati and Bishnumati were chosen for this campaign. Volunteers were mobilized from the YCL to facilitate smooth flow of traffic in coordination with the local traffic police. Also, actions were taken against ignominious massage parlours, dance bars, and so on with the help of the party's women's front. Often, the police helped us; but when faced with political pressure from the NC and the UML, the police looked helpless and hopeless. Soon they started making big noise about Maoists continuing to run a parallel state even after the war had ended.

Special plans to mobilize local Newars in the Kathmandu Valley became indispensable. During the PW, the Newa region was the only one where we had not practised any form of parallel governance. It had been used only as an area to carry out propaganda-related tasks. Hence, we found ourselves with very few local Newar cadres and leaders. Even among the limited Newar cadres we had during the PW, many had been killed or had disappeared. The founding member of the Newa Rastriya Mukti Morcha had died within the four walls of a prison during the PW; CC members such as Chet Narayan Shrestha, Shiva Shrestha, Tika Shrestha, Asha Kaji Shrestha, Sabin Shrestha had been martyred.[5] Similarly, CC members Arjun Lal Shrestha, Rajendra Mali, B.K. Shrestha, Arjun Maharjan, Bhim Maharjan had been 'disappeared' by the RNA during the PW.

The party gave us permission to set up a separate committee constituting only members of the Newar community. This was a bold step; very few communist parties in the world would allow this (as this ran counter to the concept of the party as the vanguard of the proletariat class). This step indeed helped in grooming Newar cadres and leaders, although this special committee was allowed to function only for nine months. A daily Newari language newspaper, *Swoniga*, was brought into circulation. And 1 June was designated as 'Black Day' in the history of language movements in Nepal, as it was on this day in 1999 that the Supreme Court had barred Nepal, bhasha (Newari language) from being used in local bodies. This became a special day for Newari language activists to stage protests. We, too, became active participants in the Newari linguistic movement.

Spreading our support base in Kathmandu was important, as the valley had been playing a crucial and determining role in most political uprisings or movements in Nepal. It had been proven that it was the Newars, the local ethnic community, whose participation in any movement finally determined its victory.[6] And the Newars, who were not only advanced culturally and economically but also politically, had lost their autonomy after the rise of Prithvi Narayan Shah as the king of Nepal in 1769. They, thus, had the potential to become an important ally in the ongoing urban insurrection. Hence, it was not only important to increase the number of Newar cadres in Kathmandu, but it was also equally important to develop their leadership inside the party. Newa Rashtriya Mukti Morcha, a Newar front that had otherwise been lying dormant during the PW, was activated to work as an instrument of state functioning. To consolidate itself in the valley, it launched a month-long movement called *Ganatantrik Swoniga Abhiyan* (Republican Valley Campaign) in the core areas of the Kathmandu Valley, where we educated the people about the importance of a 'federal democratic republic' and why we needed a Newa province. An exclusively Newar cultural troupe called Baikuntha Chet Narayan Sanskritik Abhiyan was mobilized throughout the one-month campaign. For some time, the Newa Rashtriya Mukti Morcha also functioned as a people's court, sorting out many cases involving Newar people's litigations (with the dissolution of the people's state, as stipulated in CPA, it later stopped taking up litigation tasks).

All these activities paid off as we won a thumping majority in the first CA election held in 2008. I won from constituency 7 in

Kathmandu district. Earlier, in April 2007, when the party had participated in an interim legislative body, I was one of the eighty-three nominated legislative members. I later became the minister of physical planning and works under the then prime minister, Girija Prasad Koirala.

27

How Monarchy Was Abolished Inch-by-Inch

birth of a republic

In the first CA election held on 10 April 2008, we won 229 out of 601 seats and became the single-largest party to hold so many seats. The agenda of making Nepal a republic started becoming a reality.[1] It was the last phase of our journey to end monarchy. This republic, however, did not come to us easily.

As mentioned earlier, I developed a resentment against the monarchy not just due to political consciousness but more due to my gender sensitivity and social awakening. BRB, on the other hand, evolved as a radical republican democrat because he found the monarchical system to be unscientific and was determined to remove it. He and I had not become communists when we first met in Delhi.

The concept of the CA was incorporated in the tripartite agreement arrived at between the king, the NC and the Ranas in the 1950s, after the anti-Rana movement.[2] However, King Mahendra usurped this agenda by cleverly substituting it with a constitutional–monarchical arrangement in 1959. Unfortunately, the so-called democratic NC, led by B.P. Koirala, could not stop the king's move to abort the CA. Instead, it participated in the parliamentary elections. In 1960, King Mahendra toppled the elected B.P. Koirala government using emergency rule. He took upon executive power and banned all political parties.

Throughout the Panchayat period (1960–90), both BRB and I consistently opposed the monarchy system and were arrested many times. We found that M.B. Singh was avoiding placing the focus on eliminating the monarchy by taking up an eclectic position of identifying the principal contradiction in Nepali society with both feudalism and Indian expansionism, simultaneously. This resulted in the formation of a united front under the leadership of BRB in February 1990.[3] It was named Samyukta Rashtriya Janandolan, or United National People's Movement (UNPM). He became its coordinator as well as the spokesperson. It was a united front of radical left parties, which clearly stood for the republican agenda. For the first time, the demand for a Constitution through a CA was made, a clause in the ten-point demands put up by the UNPM. Similarly, Samyukta Bam Morcha, a united front of left parliamentary parties was formed, which joined hands with the NC to fight for a constitutional–monarchical parliamentary state.

The people's movement in 1990 settled for a constitutional–monarchical parliamentary system.[4] It was the product of a political agreement between the king, the NC and the parliamentary left. Under the monarchical parliamentary system, the king still wielded power, as he and his family matters were considered to be above the law. The king was also the executive head of the military force. He had his nominated members within the parliament. Dissatisfied with the constitutional–monarchical parliamentary system, we joined the Maoist PW in 1996 to establish a people's democratic, republic state.

As mentioned earlier, there was a long and bitter inner struggle within the Maoist party to arrive at the republican agenda through the CA election. It did not come easily. This was because many communists considered making a new Constitution through the CA to be a rightist agenda. This concept was deeply entrenched and overtly stated in Kiran's line and covertly in Prachanda's line even before the PW started. This had an impact even while the SJMN, led by BRB, was drafting the forty demands to be presented to the Deuba-led government as a prelude to the PW. Eventually, these demands did not make an explicit mention of the CA. BRB had to insert it indirectly by dropping a line that said, 'Constitution would be made through elected representatives.'

Within the party, BRB stood for a democratic republic by firmly adhering to the drafting of a new Constitution by an elected CA. Kiran, on the other hand, stood firmly for a people's democratic republic through a protracted PW. Prachanda vacillated between the two lines.

It was finally in the second national conference (February 2001) that the political line of holding a CA election was adopted by the party. The massacre of King Birendra and his family in June 2001 and the ascendance of King Gyanendra had weakened the monarchy's support base even further. Conversely, it strengthened BRB's line.

Thereafter, the Maoist party called a meeting in Siliguri, West Bengal (India) on 15 August 2001, in which all parliamentary parties from Nepal were invited for a dialogue. There, the republican agenda was floated. However, none of the party representatives endorsed it. So far, all the peace talks within the PW had failed precisely because of hesitations regarding the rationale of the CA to institutionalize the republican agenda. BRB's line was further boosted when King Gyanendra launched a coup in February 2005, eventually isolating all parliamentary parties and by default making them realize the need for abolishing the monarchy.

Prior to King Gyanendra's usurping executive power, a string of arrests of Maoist leaders, including Kiran's in India, had jolted Prachanda. We observed that he had started reverting to Kiran's line by addressing Indian expansionism as the main threat and had started hobnobbing with the 'nationalist' King Gyanendra.[5] We were deprived of leadership positions in the party and virtually

confined to the makeshift shelter by the Prachanda faction, all
because of the stand we took on the republican agenda in January
2005. The promulgation of an emergency in February 2005 by
King Gyanendra had disrupted Prachanda's plan of sharing
power with him.[6] The strategic loss in the Khara attack (April
2005) in Rukum further weakened Prachanda. Additionally, the
unfortunate Bandarmudhe mishap in Madi, Chitwan district
(where thirty-four common people were killed when a passenger
bus was bombed), damaged Prachanda's image all the more within
and outside the party.[7] All these factors facilitated the adoption of
BRB's line of 'democratic republic' in the Chunwang CC meeting
in September 2005.

Eventually, a twelve-point understanding between the SPA
and the CPN (Maoist) was reached on 22 November 2005 in
New Delhi.[8] However, the NC was not yet ready to yield to the
republican agenda in one stroke. The twelve-point understanding
had carefully avoided mentioning the establishment of a republic;
instead it mentioned the inevitability of 'bringing the autocratic
monarchy to an end'. In fact, the NC and the UML wanted to
promulgate a reformed Constitution by making some amendments
in the 1990 Constitution to slice down the king's power but not
completely abolish monarchy.

Meanwhile, King Gyanendra used the announcement of
local elections (February 2006) as a last stunt to hoodwink the
international community and to legitimize his own democratic
claims.[9] The political parties panicked and sought Maoist help to
sabotage the elections. They asked Maoists to attack local police
posts and make the elections unsuccessful. Finally, the concerns
regarding the local elections abated, as they did not yield the
expected result. With a dismal voter turnout, it was a total fiasco.

The local elections further alienated parliamentary parties and
paved the way for the second people's movement in April 2006.
Unlike the first people's movement of February 1990, which was
limited mainly to the Kathmandu Valley, and where the king was

strongly defended by the RNA, the second people's movement was launched on the strength of the rural-based PW.[10] In Kathmandu people from all walks of life joined the movement, particularly indigenous communities, garment industry workers, cadres and sympathizers of different political parties who opposed monarchy. For the first time, the RNA stayed neutral in this movement.

On 24 April 2006, King Gyanendra was forced to make a proclamation to the nation stating that 'the source of state authority and sovereignty of the kingdom of Nepal is inherent in the people of Nepal'.[11] He was forced to reinstate the House of Representatives, which he had dissolved four years back (May 2002). G.P. Koirala was declared the prime minister (his fourth tenure) the same month.

This was immediately followed by the reinstatement of the House of Representatives on 18 May 2006, which proclaimed its sovereignty 'as mandated by the people' for exercising all rights until other constitutional arrangements were introduced.[12] It went on to state that all the executive powers of the state of Nepal would henceforth be vested in the council of ministers and not the king. The newly reinstated Parliament stripped the king of his title of the supreme commander of the army, which would now be known as the Nepali Army (NA) instead of the Royal Nepalese Army. All other 'royal' prefixes were removed: the Royal Nepal Airlines became Nepal Airlines, and the kingdom of Nepal became the government of Nepal. The Parliament's resolution stripped the king of all his authority and privileges; the royal privy council was disbanded; about 2500 palace personnel were brought under the Public Service Commission Act; and all royal properties were brought under the tax net of the government. Also, Nepal was declared a secular state; it no longer remained a Hindu kingdom.[13]

We were very excited by this proclamation. We went around making sure no government office hung portraits of the king and queen. However, we were ill at ease to discover that the NA was still carrying the symbols of royalty and displaying photos of the monarch in the office walls.

On 16 June 2006, an eight-point agreement was signed between the Maoist party and the SPA.[14] This was another vital step as it stipulated the formation of an interim Constitution, created a conducive environment for the Comprehensive Peace Agreement (CPA), the formation of an interim government and holding the CA elections.

Eventually, the CPA was signed between the government of Nepal (GoN) and the CPN (Maoist) on 21 November 2006. It became one of the most important accords for making Nepal a republic, as this agreement, unlike the twelve-point understanding, clearly stipulated that no powers should remain with the king. It specified that the fate of the monarchy would be decided by a simple majority of the CA. It also paved the way for drafting the interim Constitution, which was promulgated on 15 January 2007. On the same day, the interim Legislature–Parliament was formed consisting of eighty-five NC members, eighty-three UML members and eighty-three CPN (Maoist) members. I, too, was nominated as a member.

At the political level, three members played a leading role in formulating the interim Constitution: Baburam Bhattarai from CPN (Maoist), Krishna Sitaula from the NC and Pradeep Gyawali from the UML. They were the main team who worked day and night to arrive at a consensus. The interim Constitution was a landmark achievement in Nepali history as it made departures from the 1990 Constitution in many fundamental ways. According to the preamble, the sovereign and state authority was vested in the people and not in the king. From a Hindu nation, Nepal became a secular country. It advocated restructuring of the state in order to end oppressions based on class, caste, nationality/ethnicity, gender, religion and region. I remember I arrived in the nick of time during a meeting that was finalizing the interim Constitution, when leaders were debating on the percentage of women's candidacy in CA elections. Some of the members of the left parties, even ex-PM Sher B. Deuba from the NC, were pleading for 33 per cent reservation of seats for women but were being overpowered by those against it. There was not a single woman present in that meeting. It was at that time that my support for, and insistence on, reservation for women finally led to a provision for the same in the interim Constitution. It was then that I realized the importance of the presence of women leaders at strategic times and places.

By April 2007, the Maoists joined the interim government led by G.P. Koirala.[15] Soon, conflict started developing between the Maoists and parliamentary parties on the question of declaring Nepal a republic and the modality of elections to the CA. We wanted to declare Nepal a republic before going to the CA elections. We also wanted a fully proportional system for the CA as opposed to a first-past-the-post electoral system. When this was not heeded, the Maoist party withdrew its support to the government for four months as a form of protest. Finally, a solution was reached whereby a mixed form of electoral system was agreed upon. Similarly, it was decided that Nepal would be declared a republic by abolishing monarchy in the first meeting of the elected CA through a simple majority.

However, stipulated dates for elections to the CA had to be postponed twice. Finally, the date of the election was declared: 10 April 2008. The Maoist party won the highest number of seats. In the history of Nepal, this day in 2008 would be marked as a historic day (or night) for all the republican forces in Nepal.[16] The first meeting of Nepal's first-ever elected CA was held. The government of Nepal tabled a resolution for the establishment of a federal republic at 11.22 p.m. on this historic night. Out of the 564 assembled CA members, 560 voted in favour of the resolution.[17] Only four delegates from a royalist political party voted against the move. Thus, Nepal was formally declared a federal democratic republic by legally abolishing the monarchy. All the privileges of the king and his family members were declared null and void.

All the property inherited by the king as officiating monarch was to be nationalized by bringing it under the Nepal Trust. The CA declared '15 Jestha' (28 May) as Republic Day, to be celebrated throughout the country. It also declared the conversion of Narayanhiti Royal Palace into a national museum.

Monarchy was finally abolished after nearly 250 years.

That night, I was reminded of Nehru's famous 'tryst with destiny' speech, which he gave at midnight when India got freedom from British rule.[18] What a coincidence it was. We, too, became a federal democratic republic at the stroke of midnight. Our country was reborn and was carving out its own destiny.

BRB was the happiest person that night. His dream of thirty years had come true; his political line of Nepal becoming a democratic republic had finally materialized. I was equally excited. The whole country celebrated with jubilation.

In July 2008, the CA was to elect the first President of the country. The Maoists had fielded the candidacy of Ram Raja Prasad Singh, an old, firebrand Madhesi republican figure who had won the seat of the graduate constituency reserved in the dummy parliament during the Panchayat regime in 1971. Despite being elected, he had been barred from attending the Parliament and also had been arrested for his republican belief. However, this time he lost to Dr Ram Baran Yadav, the NC general secretary who was elected to become the first President of the federal democratic republic of new Nepal.[19]

Thus came about the end of the Shah dynasty, which had been reigning since 1769 in Nepal. It did not end in the French style where the king was beheaded, nor did it end as in Iran, where the Shah had to be airlifted to Egypt. In Nepal's case, the monarchy was abolished for good through a series of events triggered by the strength of the PW, the joint people's movement and finally the elected CA. Thus, inch-by-inch, the Nepali monarchy was pushed out. So much so that when the king was finally and formally deposed, it hardly drew any response from the national audience or from international forces. King Gyanendra left the palace to go and live as an ordinary citizen in the Nagarjuna palace, one of the nationalized summer palaces on the fringe of Kathmandu Valley, on 11 June 2008, with police security.

Despite our victory in the first CA election, it was only after four months that we were allowed to form a government under Maoist leadership. Prachanda became the first prime minister of the Republic of Nepal in August 2008.

I was the happiest person when Narayanhiti palace was turned into a national museum in May 2008. I remembered all those martyrs who had sacrificed their lives to end monarchy. I remembered all those who had been 'disappeared' and those who had suffered injuries, brutality and disability due to tortuous imprisonment.

Today, when I travel in the streets surrounding the Narayanhiti museum, I remember those days (before the PW) when I used to cycle around the palace with Manushi behind me, wishing that someday this palace would turn into a museum. After almost two decades, my dream had finally come true!

28

Bungee-Jumping My Way to a Republican State

being a minister

In April 2007, I was one of the eighty-three members of the Maoist party in the interim Legislature–Parliament. There were a total of 330 members from all parties. When I entered Singha Durbar compound (which houses the prime minister's office [PMO] and other important government offices) and stood in the legislature hall, my mind sailed back to the memory of my mother.

In 1949, she had just delivered her second child, Bidhan Ratna Yami, my brother. My father had gone underground and the Rana regime was all out in hot pursuit of him. When they did not find him, they caught my mother instead. However, because of her frail condition, they could not imprison her; instead, she was obligated to show up for daily attendance at Singha Durbar. In the chilly winter, she had to walk for an hour all the way from Khyokeba to reach Singha Durbar. She later developed asthma because of this ordeal and died at the age of forty-nine. Now, I was entering the same compound after fifty-five years as a member of the interim legislative body!

During the Rana regime, Singha Durbar was a symbol of oligarchic rule. From 1950, it was mainly a symbol of authoritarian monarchy. During the PW, we saw the Durbar as the emblem of authority of the 'white area' (as opposed to the Maoist 'red area'). Post-PW, we entered this building viewing it as a symbol of a new state that would be republic, democratic, secular and inclusive. My first impression of the legislative hall was that it was a dingy space crowded with seats arranged in three aisles. The big pillars with foliage-like relief work actually reminded me of trees; the dark hall also reminded me of the underground meeting halls that we used during the PW. Inside the hall, we appeared to be outsiders—not knowing how to speak, what to speak, what not to speak and how long to speak. During that period, I particularly remembered my father who had wanted me to study law. All my sisters and my brother had studied science in college. Because I was the youngest, he wanted me to follow his wish. During those days, science was considered to be superior in terms of both worth and prospects. So, I decided to follow my elders. Today, at times, I regret not studying law.

Inside the interim Legislature–Parliament, we used to be jeered at by members of other political parties, particularly the UML, for being inexperienced. They used to laugh at us because we were not familiar with the rules and regulations, which were supposed to guide our speeches in the hall. We were, in many ways, at odds with the new situation. I was particularly irritated that all the important clauses in the interim Constitution were tagged with the condition—'according to existing law'—so as to dilute the constitutional provision. Somehow, I kept thinking that the major leaders of the SPA, particularly the NC and the UML, were either not able to or did not want to catch up to the new spirit of change.

On 1 April 2007, the Maoist party joined the interim government under PM G.P. Koirala. I was assigned by my party to take over the ministry of physical planning and works (MOPPW) (April 2007–September 2007). Being a woman, I had to face many hurdles. Even after I was assigned the MOPPW,

I was requested by Prachanda to swap my ministry with the ministry of women, children and social welfare (MOWCSW), which was not my priority then, in order to make space for Khadak Bahadur Bishwokarma, another Maoist leader who was eyeing the MOPPW. Bishwokarma insisted that since I was a woman, it was more appropriate for me to handle the MOWCSW. To that I replied, 'Well, you are a Dalit, so this ministry is also a ministry of social welfare, which should suit you by the same logic. Additionally, as an architect, I have a more legitimate claim to the ministry of physical planning and works.' Ultimately, he had to accept the ministry assigned to him.

When I was sworn in as a minister, I had an assistant (commonly referred to as 'staff' by Maoists) who was an ex-PLA combatant and still carried a weapon on her. Her name was Bina Sherpa. She was from Bhojpur, a district in east Nepal. It felt strange to have personnel on one side and ex-PLA 'staff' on the other side, and then ride together in the government car. One day, some ex-PLA comrades from Rolpa hopped into my car. I wondered how they felt to see me seated with NA personnel. After all, till 2006, we were at intense war with the RNA (now the NA)! Later, when we went on to participate in the CA, some of us even carried guns with us. Lokendra Bista Magar, one such CA member who had a gun with him, was stopped from entering the CA premises. This news created quite a flutter. During those days, many Maoist leaders carried guns for security purposes. This double security arrangement came to an end later.

The fluttering of the small national flag on the government car reminded me of my father. My sister used to tell me that our father, when he had become a minister, would say that as a minister his two eyes were only hooked to the sun and moon printed on the flag. I suppose this suggested that one became single-minded in governmental work. It could also mean being cut off from the masses. Reminiscing on that, I decided I should be hooked to the people I was supposed to serve. One of the obstacles I came across was interference from the minister of finance, Ram Saran Mahat, a leader from the NC. I often had to struggle with him in cabinet meetings on one issue or the other. The Melamchi Water Supply Project was one such case where I had to take a firm stand against the finance minister's insistence on the appointment of a foreign company, Severn Trent, as a service provider. In this project, I helped in streamlining the fund flow amounting to Rs 40 crore, approximately US $3.5 million, meant to reach the people inhabiting affected villages in Sindhupalchowk district. Unfortunately, that money never reached them. It was being siphoned off at the district level by political representatives. Consequently, the agitating local community halted construction work. In fact, the locals beat up the public relations officer and the site office was shut down. I directly approached the villagers and was able to end the deadlock through dialogue.

Another instance of my struggle with the finance minister was when he was about to inaugurate the Rapti Highway in the mid-western region, which clearly fell under my ministry. When my assertion to inaugurate the road was not heeded, I had to threaten to halt the project. My threat worked. I even had to fight against the finance minister to get money transferred from the department of roads to the department of water within my own ministry.

Taking a cue from earlier campaigns organized by the Maoist party, I started getting members of the YCL to participate in developmental activities. For instance, YCL provided assistance in road-widening programmes, including that of Kalanki Junction in Kathmandu. The YCL also facilitated the distribution of drinking water during the acute dry season in Kathmandu. I also drafted a vision paper for the ministry, which is being followed till date in one way or another.[1] I am, by nature, a woman of action. The ministry of physical planning and works was one of the biggest ministries in terms of its scope, concerns and budgetary allocation. I kept myself busy to such an extent that the secretary of my ministry would ask me if I was missing out on the political–organizational meetings of my party. I would reach the ministry office every day at 9 a.m. and leave around 6 p.m., as if I was an obedient student attending school regularly.

What made my job more challenging was the spate of Terai-wide bandhs (strike) called by the Madhesi People's Rights Forum (MPRF).[2] There was pressure on us to find alternative routes as the agitation in the plains was bringing hardship to the people in the hills and mountains. One incident in March 2007 particularly touched me: twenty-seven Maoist cadres out of the thirty-one dead had been killed in a clash with MPRF supporters in Rautahat district.[3] Those killed were young men and women from different communities—Dalit, Adivasi Janajati, Madhesi, upper-caste Brahman and Chhetri. Most of them belonged to the poorest and most marginalized communities. I went to attend the mourning ceremony at Tundikhel in Kathmandu where their bodies had been lined up. The white linen that was wrapped around the bodies could not conceal the brutality. I had my hands smeared with blood when I touched their heads as a mark of respect. I will never forget that scene.

Providing physical infrastructure in all twenty-one camps (under seven cantonments) of the Maoist army, too, fell under my ministry. It was being coordinated by the ministry of peace and reconciliation under Ram Chandra Paudel, a senior NC leader. I remember that the finance minister was uncooperative and would use all kinds of excuses to avoid dispensing a budget to the PLA camps. He would behave as if the money had to be taken out of his own pocket. Krishna Bahadur Mahara, the then minister of information and communication, and I had to fight hard for every penny allocated. We, thus, could not be as efficient as we wanted to in providing basic amenities inside the camps. We had to face the wrath of the PLA cadres whenever we visited them. To add to this, Kiran's faction inside the Maoist party was feeding them all kinds of political jargon to make them disapprove of the peace process.

I tried my best to coordinate the tasks of the ministry at the local level through party channels. Often, I felt pained to see wrangling for road construction between our own cadres and leaders. This was particularly evident between the members of the Legislature–Parliament from Rukum and Jajarkot districts. I also felt uncomfortable when vested interests crept in to pressurize my ministry to first construct roads that would lead to the villages of leaders. I realized how the parliamentary system could indeed make politicians selfish and greedy. I also realized how important it was to adopt a rotational system in politics whereby the leader/minister's responsibility should be changed periodically; from governance to running the party organization intermittently and making space for the next generation of leaders to replace the old leaders. This evoked the importance of our party document, 'Development of Democracy in the 21st Century'.

On 18 September 2007, the party directed us to leave the coalition government. The Maoist party had made a demand for the formal declaration of Nepal being a republic through the interim Legislature–Parliament and a system of fully proportional representation before declaring the CA election. We again joined the government with the same portfolios on 30 December 2007, after our demands were met partially. Accordingly, 60 per cent proportional representation (PR) and 40 per cent first-past-the-post system was adopted for the CA election. Similarly, monarchy was suspended before the election. And it was agreed that Nepal would be formally declared a republic in the first meeting of the CA.

I must also mention my experience of working with PM Koirala, under whom I worked as a cabinet minister. Before I knew him personally, I did not have a very pleasant impression of him. Left political leaders disliked him for his anti-communist outlook. He was known as a *hawaldar* (a member of one of the lower ranks in the police force). Compared to his enlightened older brother, B.P. Koirala, who was known as a talented, sharp and visionary leader within the NC, G.P. Koirala was perceived as someone who only knew how to take orders from his brother. To my surprise, when I met him in person, I found him to be a man of few words but a doer. When he spoke, he spoke with determination and conviction, irrespective of how conservative he sounded. At the age of eighty-two, he was mentally alert. He was well-versed with the latest news. He took a bold stance to sign the CPA as the PM of Nepal despite opposition from within his own party. Another display of his boldness was when he gave a green signal for conducting the CA election. With the PLA still intact, there were many doubts being cast around within the NC and the UML when the CA elections were announced. Many NC and UML members wanted the Maoist party to disarm before the election. But the SPA, particularly G.P. Koirala, agreed to go ahead without the party being disarmed. The SPA needed the PLA as much as the Maoists because Nepal had not yet been declared a republic, and the SPA was still nervous about the Nepali Army's loyalty to the monarchy. Koirala and the Maoist party would often arrive at a gentlemen's agreement on various issues. One such agreement was to keep about 400 modern weapons with the Maoists even as the PLA had been sent to cantonments. Koirala was also aware of the inflated number of combatants put in cantonments.

Due to Koirala's poor health, most of the cabinet meetings used to take place at Baluwatar (at the PM's official residence) instead of Singha Durbar. Once, when I went to meet the PM in a private meeting room at Baluwatar to discuss my ministerial work, a journalist teased me that someday I may end up in the same residential building. Little did I know then that I would indeed be living in the same building four years later, when BRB became the thirty-fifth prime minister of Nepal.

Finally, the date of the first CA election was announced. The Maoist party's main electoral slogan was: *Arulai heryoun patak patak, maobaadi lai heroun yes patak* (You have tested others all this time. Vote for Maoists this time).

I won from constituency no. 7 in Kathmandu district. BRB won from constituency no. 2 in Gorkha district with the highest margin. Prachanda won from two constituencies, Rolpa-2 and Kathmandu-10. The Maoist party emerged as the largest party in the CA. Prachanda became the first prime minister of the federal democratic republic and secular state of Nepal (August 2008–May 2009). We were very excited.

This time, I was given the portfolio of the ministry of tourism and civil aviation. BRB joined the government as the minister of finance. It was a strange coincidence that, during the PW, both of us had been demoted due to political differences with the Prachanda faction. And now, in the post-PW period, we were both being rewarded with an opportunity to serve the people as ministers. We stayed in the ministers' quarters allotted to us separately. I had already started living in the minister's quarters when I was the minister of physical planning and works. I had my own staff, my own schedule, and I needed my own space. Before we knew it, rumours were being fed that BRB and I were not getting along because we were living in separate quarters. This shows the patriarchal mindset prevalent in the country.

As the minister of tourism and civil aviation, I became even more active. I was excited by the immense possibilities this sector offered in Nepal. I had already seen the potential of tourism during the PW. During the armed revolution, we were careful about not targeting tourists; not even a single case of abduction, killing, injury or extortion of tourists by the Maoists was recorded. In fact, we were well aware that many tourists wrote in their travel diaries about their experience of meeting Maoists or visiting Maoist red-areas. I even thought that some of the trails that we used in and around Rolpa and Rukum could be declared as guerrilla trails to attract people. I was happy when the Guerrilla Trek (aka The Shangrila Trek) actually came into existence after the PW, covering some of the important villages of Rolpa and Rukum, such as Thawang and Chunwang.

Since my early childhood, I had a taste for adventure and sports, which was accentuated during my tenure as tourism minister. Without any fear, I took the challenge of bungee-jumping into the 160-metre gorge of Bhote Kosi River. I also did paragliding, took an ultra-light flight in Pokhara and went on a six-hour trek to Panchase from Pokhara. I personally went for these adventure sports/trips to promote tourism.

During my tenure, the ministry granted permission for the commercialization of skydiving and the purchase of single-engine planes, which had multiple effects on the tourism sector. These decisions had been pending for a while. This resulted in the first skydive, which took place with the majestic Mount Everest in the background in the Khumbu region of Nepal in October 2008. It was during my tenure that *National Geographic* declared Nepal as the second most adventurous destination in the world after Brazil.[4] I also released the budget to develop Jaljala in Rolpa as a tourism hub. In the aviation field, for the first time, I initiated the purchase of two narrow-bodied and two wide-bodied airplanes through an open tendering process.[5] Until then, airplanes had been bought from companies without going through a competitive public procurement process; this had always been controversial because of the lack of transparency, and bribery and corruption allegations.

In 2011, I was made the minister of land reform when I entered the government for the third time. However, this tenure lasted less than one month. By then, PM Jhala Nath Khanal had resigned and BRB had become the PM, changing the political scenario, whereby more political forces needed to be incorporated. Anyway, in all the three ministries I headed, I made sure I produced policy papers and interacted with the media on a monthly basis to keep them aware of the activities of the ministry and its future plans. Being a member of Parliament twice and holding three ministries within a span of five years, I learnt about many aspects and crafts of state functioning. When I look back, I realize that my six months' experience in Thawang, as the secretary of the People's

Power Consolidation Department during the PW, helped me in carrying out my parliamentary responsibilities.

Indeed, I did feel that the government under a parliamentary system was the best instrument of managing the interests of the bourgeoisie. We tried to use our presence in the Legislature–Parliament and the CA to institutionalize the gains made by the PW. However, our honeymoon with the state machinery was quite short.

29

Fall of Prachanda

taste of power

We were sad when Prachanda had to resign on 4 May 2009 after only eight months as the PM. However, we also felt righteous and revolutionary because it was a principled resignation. The resignation followed PM Prachanda's decision to dismiss Rookmangud Katawal, the chief of army staff (CoAS) of the NA.[1] President Ram Baran Yadav asked him to stay on. This ignited a dangerous constitutional crisis since the ceremonial President was seen as directly intervening and bypassing the decision made by the council of ministers.

Although the Maoist party had been observing that national and international forces were trying hard to topple its government, it was Katawal who became one of the principal actors responsible for our fall from the seats of power. From day one, Prachanda was portrayed as a controversial PM. His first visit to China to attend the Olympic Games in August 2008 attracted a lot of criticism from the other parties who felt that he had broken the political culture of making the first visit to India as the PM. Apparently, he had revealed his proclivity towards China rather than India.[2]

The NA, especially Chief Katawal, was seen defying the PM's order. Katawal had a history of showing his displeasure towards the Maoists. When G.P. Koirala was leading the coalition government, Katawal had tried to ensure that the Maoists did not get an upper hand in state affairs.[3] Katawal was in essence against army integration in the manner it had taken place. He was also against republicanism, federalism and secularism in the way it had arrived. He insisted that all these issues must be decided through a referendum. He openly expressed his displeasure with civilian supremacy over the military by speaking against democratization of the army. I felt he was acting more as a politician than an army chief. He was, in fact, a royalist whose education had been sponsored and shaped by the palace from a young age. Perhaps this was the reason why NA offices still displayed royal portraits with reverence when all other government offices had removed photos of the royal family from their walls after the declaration of Nepal as a republic.

Relations between Prachanda and Katawal deteriorated further when Badal was made the minister of defence. The NA had lobbied hard to not give the defence portfolio to the Maoists. As a result, he used all tactics to defy the decisions made by Badal. Katawal kept harping before the national and international communities that the Maoists aimed to capture state power and destroy the NA.

Similarly, another incident triggered controversy. When the fifth national football tournament was to be held, the NA cancelled its participation at the last hour.[4] Previously, the police, APF and NA used to participate in the annual meet. However, when the Maoist combatants under the name 'PLA Club' decided to join the tournament, the NA backed out.

Katawal also insisted on recruiting more personnel into the NA when it had been clearly written in the CPA that no new recruitment in the security forces was to be allowed. Defence Minister Badal ordered the NA not to carry out this recruiting process. Katawal, however, defied his orders. It was widely perceived that even the courts did not restrain him.

After this defiance, PM Prachanda dismissed Katawal and appointed a new army chief. A lot of pressure was exerted by the other political parties to retain Katawal. The coalition partners, the UML and the MPRF, initially supported PM Prachanda's move but later backed out. President Yadav, too, was not in favour of Katawal's removal. At first, Prachanda asked for a formal explanation from Katawal regarding his defiance. Katawal wrote back a lengthy response in his defence, which read more like an open confrontation rather than a reply.[5] Thereafter, PM Prachanda immediately decided to relieve Katawal of his duties and appointed the second-in-command, Lieutenant General Kul B. Khadka, as the army chief on 3 May 2009.[6] However, President Yadav overrode the government decision and ordered Katawal to continue. As a ceremonial President, Yadav had no constitutional right to do so, but our partners in the government, the UML and the MPRF, too, backed the President's move. There was a lot of speculation about the President receiving the tacit support of India when he reinstated Katawal. I remember discussing how to deal with the situation if a coup was to take place. Prachanda had at one point thought of resisting the coup attempt by deploying PLA bodyguards inside the PM's residence. What also made things complicated was Kiran's consistent opposition to the whole peace process.

Katawal's reinstatement as the army chief impelled Prachanda to tender his resignation as PM in May 2009. BRB fully supported Prachanda's decision.[7] Subsequently, Madhav Kumar Nepal, a senior leader of the UML, headed a new government with support from the NC and MPRF. Previously, Madhav K. Nepal had lost in the first CA election from two constituencies. Ironically, it was Prachanda who had insisted earlier to bring Madhav K. Nepal to the Legislature–Parliament under the nominated quota. Had this not happened, Madhav K. Nepal would not even have been able to stake claim to lead the new government.

After resigning from the government, the Maoist party took to the streets, raising issues of civilian supremacy, national sovereignty and asking for the resignation of PM Madhav K. Nepal. It started attacking India overtly as the cause of the downfall of the Maoist government. In a grand mass gathering in front of the CA hall at Baneshwor, Prachanda asserted that the ascension of Madhav K. Nepal as the PM was a clear consequence of India's scheme and will. He further stated that if one was to go for a dialogue, then one would prefer to sit with the 'main master' (India) instead of the 'puppet' (Madhav K. Nepal).

The Maoist party's relation with the Indian establishment started deteriorating further. At one point, Indian ambassador Rakesh Sood was shown black flags, and the Maoist crowd also threw shoes at his motorcade at an airport in Solukhumbu.[8] Soon, the anti-India uproar started gaining ground. I remember seeing the Indian national flag being stamped on or thrown away in cultural programmes organized in Kathmandu by Maoist cultural groups. As anti-India sentiments started intensifying, India secretly called Prachanda to different parts of the world to mend the broken relationship. However, it did not materialize.[9]

In February 2010, the Maoist party held its CC meeting and decided to adopt an organized pressure tactic to speed up the removal of Madhav K. Nepal. It was decided that the party would call for an indefinite strike in Kathmandu. For this, the Maoist party mobilized its forces from all over the country. The date of 1 May, the International Workers' Day, in 2010 was chosen as the day to begin the strike. However, Kiran also took this opportunity to prepare for urban insurrection. Accordingly, he gave a notification to all the cadres coming to Kathmandu to also prepare for the ultimate insurrection to capture state power. Thousands of people from all over the country converged into the Kathmandu Valley to take part in the agitation. They formed a human chain around Singha Durbar, the seat of governance, as well as along the twenty-seven-kilometre-long Ring Road circling Kathmandu.

However, on the sixth day of the strike, Kathmandu's elite community under the banner of FNCCI (Federation of Nepalese Chamber of Commerce and Industries), civil society and various other organizations took to the streets protesting against the Maoist agitation.[10] Meanwhile, the party HQ received information that a meeting of the National Security Council was being called to mobilize the army to crush the agitation. Prachanda, in consultation with the Standing Committee of the party, decided to back off. He told the cadres that the aim of the strike was not insurrection but to bring down the Madhav K Nepal-led government. By then, about nine Maoist cadres had died either due to injury sustained while confronting the police or in road accidents while coming to Kathmandu. Upon hearing the Maoist party's retreat from its supposed insurrection, many cadres felt disappointed and disillusioned. They had been given the impression that this was the final stage for urban insurrection. The confusion regarding the actual purpose of the strike was natural because of Prachanda's eclectic stance. In many ways, this was a reflection of the party's extended meeting in Kharipati (2008), where Prachanda had succumbed to Kiran's line of insurrection while BRB had insisted that the leadership remain firm on the 'democratic republic' agenda and stand resolutely by the CPA.

Prime Minister Madhav K. Nepal ultimately resigned on 30 June 2010. This paved the way for elections in the CA for a new PM. The Maoist party decided to field Prachanda. Three candidates: Ram Chandra Paudel from the NC, Jhala Nath Khanal from the UML and Prachanda from the CPN (Maoist) were fielded for PM candidacy on 21 July 2010. Despite several rounds of elections, none of the three candidates could muster the minimum number of votes required to be elected as the PM. It was humiliating to see Prachanda, the winner in two constituencies and the chairman of the largest party in the CA, losing in these elections. Ultimately, when he failed to get elected even in the seventh round, he withdrew his candidacy. However, Paudel continued to contest even until the seventeenth time! Despite this, he could not garner the required votes as the UML had decided to stay neutral. Subsequently, the rules of the election were changed, and it was stipulated that no party could stay neutral and refrain from voting. Candidacy for a new PM was sought again.

The earlier pattern of voting had shown that the NC and the UML would not allow Prachanda to win the impending election. Apprehending this, BRB's supporters sought to make him the leader of the Legislature–Parliament. They wanted to field BRB's as the PM candidate. This time, there was a possibility of BRB winning the majority vote. As finance minister in Prachanda's cabinet, he had performed well. He had been credited for the incredible increase (33.3%) in revenue during 2009–10. It was a record-breaking revenue collection.[11] He had increased the social security benefit fund without increasing the tax rate. He had doubled the old-age pension, social benefits to Dalits and single women, and raised salaries for civil servants. He had waived all loans up to Rs 30,000 and interest on loans taken from government banks up to Rs 1 lakh by small farmers and entrepreneurs affected by conflict. He had increased the grant given to the local government from Rs 10 lakh to Rs 30 lakh. He had initiated a youth self-employment programme (Rs 2 lakh-loan granted without collateral). He had established consumers' cooperatives in all 4000 village development committees (VDCs), providing each with Rs 1 lakh as seed money. He had also came up with the voluntary declaration of income scheme (VDIS) under which Rs 15 billion (Rs 1500 crore) was declared and Rs. 1.5 billion revenue was collected.[12]

Accordingly, BRB's supporters lobbied for his candidacy as the next PM, but the Prachanda faction opposed it. Instead,

Prachanda decided to stand for PM once more. BRB and his team insisted that this time Prachanda should not withdraw his candidacy, come what may. However, as feared, he withdrew his name at the last hour to support Jhala Nath Khanal, the president of the UML, as the new PM. Thus, Jhala Nath Khanal became the PM on 20 February 2011. It had taken six months to elect a new PM. Frankly speaking, I felt like I lost my dignity as a member of the Legislature–Parliament, watching and participating in the wrangling and filthy trend of buying votes by any means (a leaked voice-recording of Krishna B. Mahara, a senior Maoist leader, was especially damning)[13] during this six-month-long exercise.

I felt sick to the bone seeing my own party indulging in day-to-day bargaining for power in such a cheap manner.

Prachanda's intention to stop BRB from becoming the PM became obvious to many of us. I remembered the scene at Lawang in Rukum where BRB was politically victimized for his anti-monarchy stance. I felt he was being victimized for the second time for taking a firm position on the CA and the peace process. For the first time, I was shocked to see how insecure and vulnerable Prachanda felt at the prospect of seeing BRB as the PM. It seemed to me that for him, his position mattered more than the fate of the peace process, the fate of the Constitution, and above all, the fate of the country. I was convinced that for him maintaining good relations with the UML mattered more than the CPN (Maoist), especially when it came to safeguarding his authority and position within the party and outside it.

PM Khanal had been harping that his first priority was army integration. However, there were no indications that he was serious about this. Khanal was increasingly facing problems within his own party. He was forced to resign from the PM's chair after just seven months, as he feared being isolated inside his own party. This put Prachanda in a defensive position. He then started drawing closer to Kiran. In Palungtar, where the historic extended meeting had taken place, he had gone to the extent of saying that he always had a relationship of 'unity' with Kiran and 'struggle' with BRB. In the Palungtar meeting, Kiran was insistent on continuing the armed struggle, while BRB had presented his proposal for taking the agenda of the CA and the peace process to its logical conclusion. Prachanda once again took an eclectic position, leaning more towards Kiran's line. He announced that the party would henceforth need to struggle for peace and constitutional agenda and prepare for an armed revolt and patriotic war against India: a typically elusive stand!

Incidentally, by June 2011, Kiran and BRB had come together to check Prachanda's self-seeking, opportunistic tendencies. In an informal meeting organized in Dhobighat, Kiran and BRB managed to rope in more than seventy-five CC members to chart out a new course to fight against Prachanda's high-handed monopolist tendencies. They were united against the centralization of all power in Prachanda. At that time, he was the chairman of the party, the leader of the party in the Parliament, as well as the chief commander of the PLA. As if this consolidation of power was not enough, he also wanted to be the PM. This was against the spirit of 'Development of Democracy in the 21st Century'. Kiran had already worked out the number of votes inside the party required to dislodge Prachanda from the post of chairman. For the first time, perhaps, Prachanda feared that he was in a minority within the party. As a result, in order to save his position, he agreed to back BRB as the PM candidate in the upcoming election.

Now, nobody within the party could stop BRB from fielding his candidacy. BRB won the election, winning a clear majority. He contested against Ram Chandra Paudel of the NC, who was defeated by more than 100 votes. BRB became the fourth prime minister of the federal democratic republic of Nepal on 28 August 2011.

When BRB was elected as the PM, I looked back. I had never dreamt that he would occupy this post. The person who lacked interest in exercising power was now taking up the highest executive post in the country! Since I had an inkling about Prachanda's displeasure regarding BRB's ascension, I wondered how secure his tenure as the PM would be.

30

From Herder to Prime Minister

at the helm of state affairs

Unlike me, who was a daughter of a former minister, someone educated in an urban setting and belonging to a merchant family, BRB was the son of a farmer, who hailed from an uneducated, rural, peasant background. As a young boy and the eldest son, he had to work as a herder to tend cows, buffaloes and goats in his village. It was purely his brilliance in academics and his scientific outlook that enabled him to become the prime minister of Nepal. For instance, even today he tries to stay in touch with his friends who till their lands. However, the journey from a herder to the prime minister was not easy. Because of his strong intellectual abilities, many leaders within his own party harboured insecure feelings. There were often deliberate attempts to keep BRB organizationally weak, so that he would not aspire for a position of leadership. This was clearly visible when he sought to be the prime minister.

He had the required knowledge and experience to be the PM. He had been the convener of the United Revolutionary People's Council (URPC), which was overseeing the parallel revolutionary government during the PW. He was also the coordinator of the people's power consolidation department in the base areas during the PW. His PhD thesis on the underdevelopment of Nepal had given him the required knowledge about the country. Additionally, he had the experience of being a successful finance minister in the democratic republic of Nepal.

Finally, when he became the PM, he displayed his skill of consensus-building by bringing together more than a dozen parties, including the Madhesi-based parties in the coalition government. However, this could not last long. First of all, within the party, Kiran had started mounting an opposition to his government, as he wanted all the major ministries for members of his faction at the cost of isolating Prachanda. When BRB did not yield to his demand, Kiran's faction did not join the government. Later on, the NC and the UML, which had also joined his government for a brief period, walked out over the issue of extension of the tenure of the CA.

Having known about Prachanda's discomfort regarding BRB becoming the PM, I was already apprehensive about BRB's tenure. What made me all the more concerned was the failure to bring Kiran's team into the cabinet. While Kiran started going against BRB offensively, I tried to mend the relationship between Prachanda and BRB. I even invited Prachanda's family twice for dinner to Baluwatar, but both times they turned down our invitation.

At every step, he had to fight people within his party and outside. Within the party, a section of cadres belonging to Kiran's faction were out on the streets demanding his resignation. They were against the promulgation of the Constitution through the CA. They opposed him by displaying black flags, burning his effigy and carrying out a torch rally in the streets for signing the Bilateral Investment Promotion and Protection Agreement (BIPPA) with India.[1] They considered signing the BIPPA as a sell-out of the country's sovereignty to India. Foreign Minister Narayan Kaji Shrestha, from the Maoist party, also opposed the signing of the BIPPA. Moreover, Kiran was against army integration.

The opposition parties, the NC and UML, were probably thoroughly entertained to discover that the project to oppose the government was being generated within the governing party itself.

BRB had to fight tooth and nail to appoint Lilamani Poudel as the chief secretary of his government. For two fiscal years, he was not allowed to present the full budget. This was designed to portray him as a failed PM in contrast to his earlier image as a successful finance minister. President Ram Baran Yadav refused to promulgate the several ordinances passed by the government, thus sabotaging development agendas. He, in fact, made several attempts to unseat the government with the cooperation of the army.[2] Additionally, the judiciary was also not viewed as impartial.

Under such difficult circumstances, BRB tried his best to perform his duties as the PM with conviction. He continued with his developmental and other strategic works.

One of the most unforgettable development projects initiated by BRB was the expansion of roads in Kathmandu by dismantling the illegal structures that encroached on the roadsides.[3] Citing potential earthquakes (which became a reality in 2015), he and his team boldly started expanding the roads despite many protests. I had a tough time fielding SoS calls against the demolition, as I was a sitting CA member from Kathmandu. The expansion of the roads in Kathmandu had been on the agenda of the government for the last three decades, but nobody was willing to take the risk. Similarly, building a new road joining Shahid Gate with Maitighar Mandala, right in the heart of Kathmandu, had been on the agenda for a long time; but neither ministers nor PMs of the past could do it. BRB was able to win the army's confidence, as he was also the defence minister, to get the clearance for the road. The new road cleared major bottlenecks around Maitighar Mandala. From one perspective, it would have been very difficult to carry out these tasks had he had NC and UML ministers in his cabinet. Madhesi parties did not have too much stake in the Kathmandu Valley as their constituencies were mostly in the Terai region. Later on, during his tenure, road expansion projects were taken to other parts of Nepal, particularly the strategic highways.

He had also initiated strict monitoring of drunk driving.[4] He had started twenty-four-hour services for taking complaints of the masses all over the country through the 'Hello Sarkar' desk at the PMO.[5] In the rural areas, he started an initiative called *Janatako Gharma Pradhan Mantri* (prime minister in people's house). It was a monthly programme whereby the PM went to distant rural areas to stay and eat in the homes of Dalits, Musahars, Chepangs, Tharus, Muslims and *mukta kamaiya*'s (bonded labourers), in order to understand and address their problems. He also started the *Janta Sangha Pradhan Mantri* (prime minister with public), a monthly programme in which he directly took complaints from the masses and answered them through national radio and national television.

As a way to encourage national production, he started using a Mustang car instead of the Mercedes that he was entitled to. The Mustang is a domestically assembled car made to withstand rugged mountain terrain, and is far cheaper than the luxurious cars. He also travelled economy class in flights, be it domestic or international.

He had a clear vision for Nepal's economic development. Along those lines, he constituted a powerful board of investment headed by the PM to attract foreign direct investment. He was also instrumental in adding the ministry of urban development and the ministry of cooperatives and poverty alleviation in order to promote planned urban development and to focus on the problems of the larger section of the population below the poverty line (BPL). Similarly, he formed the Karnali Development Commission and the Far-west Development Commission to mitigate regional disparities. To avoid politicization of recruitment and to professionalize the process, he created a public enterprise directorate board to bring all the public corporations under one window. He also launched National Pride Projects[6] in infrastructure development, consisting of seventeen big projects with the aim of finishing mid-hill highways, east–west railway, north–south highways, international airports in Nijgadh and Pokhara, and big hydro and irrigation projects.

He brought in the concept of zero tolerance to corruption. It was under him that one of the sitting cabinet ministers, Jay Prakash Gupta, was put in jail on corruption charges by the order of the Supreme Court. This had never happened before. He was instrumental in making the fund collection in the Pashupatinath temple transparent and accountable.

When he became PM, he had three important agendas he wanted to accomplish: first, complete the army integration process; second, constitute the Truth and Reconciliation Commission (TRC); and third, promulgate the new Constitution through the CA. He was able to integrate the PLA with the NA. He was successful in presenting the TRC Act, which was supposed to be constituted within six months of the promulgation of the CPA. Meanwhile, the deadline given for promulgating the new Constitution through the CA kept getting extended from two to four years. The Supreme Court delivered a judgment in November 2011, ruling that the CA could not be extended beyond 28 May 2012.[7]

I was one of the witnesses to the dissolution of the CA. We were actively engaged in seeking support for an inclusive, identity-based federalism. We managed to get signatures from not only our CA members but also from the CA members belonging to Madhesi, Adivasi Janajati and Dalit women from the NC, the UML and other smaller parties. The non-Maoist Adivasi Janajati leader Pasang Sherpa helped us. On the one hand, Subhash Nembang, the CA's House Speaker, would not start the meeting of the CA; on the other hand, within our own party, Kiran would not cooperate with us. CA members belonging to Kiran's faction would whisper among themselves that a ready-made Constitution from Delhi would be brought in at the last moment. Those in favour of drafting a meaningful Constitution through the CA were working hard to garner consensus. The deadline was around the corner.

On 28 May, the day the term of the CA was to expire, all the members were waiting in the CA hall for directives from either the Speaker or from their respective party leaders. When there was no response, I decided to go to Singha Durbar where the top leaders were meeting. To my surprise, all the leaders were in utter confusion there. They were going from the speaker's hall to the deputy speaker's hall, trying to confirm and reconfirm the various issues that were under discussion. Just when I entered the speaker's chamber, BRB was floating the idea of promulgating a state of emergency as the last legal resort to extend the CA, according to the interim Constitution. Only former PM Sher Bahadur Deupa supported his proposal, while everybody else vehemently opposed it. The NC and UML were against the idea. As time was running out, BRB decided to call law experts to the PMO to avoid a constitutional crisis. According to their advice, it was decided to declare elections for a second CA before the time expired. Because, according to international practice, it was the prerogative of the elected PM to declare a new election when the Parliament remained alive. The CA met its own death as the Supreme Court deadline expired at midnight. Along with the CA, the Legislature–Parliament was also dead.

For BRB, 28 May turned out to be one of the saddest days in his political life. He tried to save the CA by reaching a consensus on major disputed issues in the Constitution, and when it required more time, by postponing the deadline for the promulgation of the new Constitution. However, the judiciary intervened to give an ultimatum. Nobody, at that time, understood the major reason for the expiry of the CA. The fact was that both mainstream internal political forces as well as external actors did not want the new Constitution to be promulgated while the Maoists were in power, lest they take the credit. They also did not want the second round of elections for a new CA to be conducted by a Maoist government, lest they use their power to influence the election outcome.

Meanwhile, criticism started piling up against BRB after the expiry of the CA. He was used to appreciation and being rewarded for his excellent academic performance, but as a PM he was being depicted as a failure. He was blamed for not being able to save the CA, but for failing to bring into place a new Constitution.

However, as the PM, his great achievement was to conclude the historic integration of the PLA and NA on 10 April 2012, after four years of unsuccessful attempts by previous PMs.[8] Before the integration of the army, he had to face many problems in the cantonment. I remember that late one night BRB received frantic calls from the PLA commanders of different divisional HQs. They were desperately requesting him to intervene as the junior PLA cadres had revolted and taken up arms. BRB then had to call the army chief to intervene and avoid a violent uprising in the cantonment.

I felt very embarrassed when I heard the whole episode. Due to the lack of proper political orientation on the one hand, and continuous instigation against the CPA from Kiran's faction on the other, there prevailed great confusion and frustration amongst the PLA members. Also, there was an undue delay in army integration. Slowly, a great divide was being created between the commanders, who were drawing huge salaries and enjoying facilities, and those belonging to the lower ranks of the PLA, whose salaries were low and who didn't get good facilities. Commanders were also discovered to have been taking money from junior cadres in the name of managing logistics, setting up hospitals and building a welfare fund, but these expenditures were not transparent. All these grievances added up until the day they decided to take up weapons against their own commanders.

The same PLA, which had evoked great idealism, a sense of devotion, commitment and sacrifice during the PW, had now been overtaken by frustration, deviation and rebellion against its own commanders! Worse, some of the commanders had become corrupt. I could not believe it.

I was utterly shocked when BRB confided in me and mentioned that Prachanda had asked him to facilitate the sale of hidden arms and ammunition used during the PW to a foreign agency. BRB convinced him to pass on the weapons to the NA, as selling weapons of the PW was a sensitive issue for both the Maoists and the government. Prachanda should be grateful to BRB for saving him from a big embarrassment and an act of treachery. Imagine the consequences of news emerging about a Maoist supremo selling PW weapons to a foreign agency!

Meanwhile, BRB was not able to garner support for holding a second CA election, nor was he allowed to present the annual budget. In the absence of a Legislature–Parliament, he had to request President Yadav to promulgate the ordinances, which were being rejected one after another. The President was posing big hurdles.

It was sad to see the two most educated leaders: President Dr Ram Baran Yadav (a medical doctor by profession) and Prime Minister Dr Baburam Bhattarai (doctorate in regional planning), both with 'Ram' in their names, fighting with each other like Ram and Ravan.

BRB was also apprehensive of Prachanda hobnobbing with the President. The cabinet had announced 22 November 2012 as the date for the election of the second CA, but the NC, the UML and the others rejected it. After that, BRB proposed an election date in December 2013. Again the NC, UML and others rejected it. BRB thus faced insurmountable obstacles as he tried to hold the elections for the CA, for which he had struggled all his life. When he realized that the opposition parties, as well as his own party chief, were not willing to hold new elections under his leadership, he decided to go ahead and form a neutral government, a decision that was agreed on by all the political parties. Thus, Khil Raj Regmi, then the sitting chief justice of the

Supreme Court, was made chairman of the council of ministers.[9] Before leaving the government, BRB was able to promulgate an ordinance to constitute the TRC, which he skilfully tied up with the promulgation of the ordinance to make Regmi the chairman of the council of ministers to lead the interim government.[10]

BRB handed over to Regmi on 13 March 2013. Technically, he did not resign. According to customary parliamentary practice, an elected PM holds the legitimate claim to declare the next election before his/her tenure expires. But, this time, since everyone (including Prachanda) ganged up against BRB, he had no choice but to make way for a neutral government. BRB ultimately gave in because he wanted to ensure that his life-long promise of bringing into place a Constitution through an elected CA would be accomplished.

History will judge whether he did right or wrong.

31

The Cost of Being First Lady

losing my identity

Being the youngest of seven siblings, I was a hyperactive, happy-go-lucky child who had no obligation to do domestic chores. I spent most of my time playing with friends. I remember I used to jump from one wall to another, from one floor to another, in my home in Bhurungkhel. I still have scars on both legs due to incessant injuries. I was good at sports. In India, at the Central School, IIT Kanpur, I used to participate at the local, zonal, regional and national levels in badminton and basketball. I even got the best sportswoman award in SPA, New Delhi, in 1980.

However, years later, when BRB was elected as the prime minister, my hyperactive nature proved to be counterproductive. My extrovert nature was looked upon as intrusive. My educational background was looked upon as a threat. To add to this, my highly educated sisters and brothers were not viewed positively; their positions in government offices were equated with nepotism and favouritism on my part. My indigenous Newari background and my vocal support for identity-based federalism became an irritant to the high-caste Khas Arya community within the party, both in the government and otherwise. Not everybody appreciated it when BRB wore a Jyapu dress (a traditional attire of Newaris) and read out his speech in Nepal bhasa (the language of the Newars) on 'Jyapu Diwas', as a mark of respect for Newari identity.

I never had my nose pierced nor did I wear a *tilhari*, a necklace worn by married Brahmin women, despite being wedded to a Brahmin. I did not wear bangles or rings. I still maintained my short haircut; left my hair grey without dyeing it black. I wore pants, used no make-up and wore no jewellery except small ear studs. I never prayed nor went to a temple. All these unconventional acts antagonized the majority of the mainstream politicians, the middle-class people and the more traditional (orthodox) masses. They saw me as a rebel and not a typical wife. According to traditional Hindu rituals, I would be taken as a widow who cut her hair, who did not wear bangles or a tilhari, who neither put bindi on her forehead nor vermillion in her hair parting.

What made the situation more difficult was that BRB was an introvert, serious and serene, while I was loud, easy-going and impatient. As the wife of a PM, I was expected to be just the opposite of what I was. I was expected to be ladylike. I was expected to be quiet. Similarly, I was expected to be like a socialite. I remember a production manager of a popular daily in Kathmandu sincerely suggested that I work for old-age homes, single-women shelters and orphanages, distributing food and warm clothes. But how could I transform myself into a social worker when I had been elected to work as a legislative member from my constituency? It was even suggested that I host and organize kitty parties! My background of the PW just did not fit in with the etiquette expected from me at Baluwatar.

I was, after all, a former minister who had held several portfolios. I was also an elected legislative member when BRB was voted as the PM. I was, thus, confused as to how to adjust to my new situation as the wife of the PM, the highest executive post in Nepal. I began browsing the Internet, reading up on the status of the first ladies in different countries. I read about Hillary Clinton to find out how she performed her duties as the first lady in the USA. I felt my situation was almost similar to hers, although she had become a member of the senate after being the wife of a US President. Later on, I read a book written by her, *What Happened*, after she lost the presidential election. I realized how state functioning could bring two opposing schools of thought together. The same Hisila Yami, who was in the street demonstrating against Hillary Clinton's Nepal visit in 1995, was now Google-ing Clinton's life as the first lady of the US in 2008!

Besides accompanying BRB for important national and international events, I kept myself busy working on women's issues and making access to various ministries easier for party workers and people who sought to resolve their day-to-day concerns. I also helped entrepreneurs and businessmen get access to respective ministries for their work. I even interacted with women journalists, inviting them for coffee at Baluwatar. I readily gave an interview to a senior woman journalist, Yashoda Timilsina. I told her rather frankly that I was ready to help BRB in his capacity as PM as I had the experience of running three ministries. This statement created a big controversy. I was blamed for running a parallel government, for daring to say that I could 'help' the PM with my past experiences. Similarly, I admitted in the interview that my party had always kept me in a team assigned to collect money from donors after we came to the peace process. This created a bigger uproar, and I was blamed in the media for being corrupt. I had complained to my party asking them to issue an explanation, not only for the media but also for clarity within the party. I did not get any response. I was hurt that my party did not come to my defence. I then remembered Prachanda's followers who would say during inner party struggles that we should be squeezed like lemons and thrown out. It is worth mentioning that senior leaders were asked to donate 10 per cent of their net worth to the party for initiating the PW. Only two had given the full amount, one of them was BRB and the other was C.P. Gajurel. We sold our house for this purpose!

I really felt that my party had unduly used me. I acknowledge that I was the most well-off and the most educated woman who had joined the PW. And this was what I got from my party for joining the movement: being branded as a corrupt person without any evidence, out of sheer jealousy and vendetta!

Despite being an architect, I took greater interest in the tourism sector as I felt Nepal had a comparative advantage vis-à-vis India and China. Although I was no longer the tourism minister, I had tried to get the tourism sector designated as a major industry by coordinating with the private sector, the ministry and the PMO. At that time, the ministry of tourism was under the prime minister. This active intervention was not taken kindly. I was attacked for receiving commission from the private sector. In fact, a magazine called *Crime Today* declared me 'the most corrupt woman in South Asia' without providing any details or proof;[1] I had no idea what 'corrupt' deed I was being accused of! They had my photo on their cover page. It was horrifying. People circulated it on social media and in newspapers when I stood for the elections to the second CA.

I went to the Kathmandu District Court to sue the magazine. I won the case in October 2014, only to be told that the chief editor and publisher of the magazine would be fined Rs 1000 as compensation. I felt disgusted; such a paltry punishment for destroying my political career!

I suffered undue slander. What saved me from breaking down was the memory of my mother. My mother had suffered heavily during my father's ministerial tenure in 1950. She underwent isolation and humiliation from our relatives who instigated my father to remarry. She was criticized for her dark complexion, for being old and not up to his stature. What saved me was my pre-emptive preparation to face criticism when I entered Baluwatar. I knew I, too, would be the target of slander. But I was targeted not for my appearance but because I had a strong political background, because I was vocal, I was educated and I fought for the emancipation of oppressed classes, gender, regions, nationality/ethnicity and religious minority communities. Unlike my mother's suffering, which was of a private, apolitical nature that nearly led to a divorce, my suffering was public and political that nearly led to the demise of my career in politics.

I now realized how in some cases Prachanda, too, had been unfairly criticized when he was the prime minister. The purchase of a bed worth Rs 1 lakh, when he started living in Baluwatar, made big news.[2] In fact, it was the government that had bought the new bed for the PM. When we shifted to Baluwatar, I looked around for that controversial 'expensive' bed and found it stacked in one of the rooms. There was nothing extraordinary about it. Had one not been a Maoist, one wouldn't have been questioned for this at all.

This just indicated how deep-rooted the bias against Maoists was in the minds of people; how non-issues could be raked up to damage the character of a person. Amidst all the slander, I was absolutely shocked and hurt to know that one of the women ambassadors from a 'developed' country commented that she would suggest BRB divorce me![3] Similarly, one of the newspaper writers wrote: If BRB was to remain a successful politician, he would have to cleanse Hisila, just as Ram did with Sita by leading her to (a) burning pyre to prove her purity to the (sic) society.[4]

In due course, I realized that BRB, too, had begun to worry about the negative public perception around me. He would tell me to be careful with my image and to be less visible, quieter. I remember increasingly getting furious with BRB when he would often bypass me during our internal meetings, when it was my turn to speak, or how he would only let me speak at the very end. Once, I remember I shouted and walked out of a meeting when my request to speak was not heeded. At that time, I was the only woman among the ten CC members in the party. I expected that at least one of them, including BRB, would call me back. But nobody did. The meeting concluded as though nothing had happened.

I was deeply hurt. I got a taste of men's attitude towards women as politicians. Till today, I remind BRB how vulnerable women politicians feel, how vulnerable a politician's wife feels before her senior politician husband.

I took some solace from Clinton who, too, was criticized by the press and by the opposition party for her active involvement as the first lady and as the secretary of state for the USA.[5] It was interesting to observe how women politicians had to face the same kind of harassment in all parts of the world, be it in the USA or in Nepal! I also read how Nadezhda Krupskaya, the wife of Lenin, was humiliated by Stalin when the communist party was ruling the country. After Lenin's death, she even joined the political group opposing Stalin but returned to mainstream politics later.

Suddenly, I remembered the fate of the eight Maoist couples who were CA members. One couple had already been divorced. Unlike the PW days, when a combined kitchen mess freed women from domestic duties, during the peace period, women leaders had to again take on the burden of the kitchen and other household tasks besides their political work.

Suddenly, I started becoming nostalgic about how happy we were, and how liberated we felt, even when we were together in a life-and-death situation under harsh conditions in Rolpa during the PW days. How suffocating it was to live in Baluwatar; we were near each other and yet so far! I realized that the period without state power had in fact been a more liberating experience for us despite the harsh physical discomforts. And the period when BRB had executive power had a more constraining effect on our relationship despite the material comfort Baluwatar offered us.

However, there were also interesting moments at Baluwatar. I remember having deliberately re-read the *Communist Manifesto* and other classical Marxist books, just to see what it felt like to read these books at Baluwatar. I asked myself whether the 'withering away of the state' could take place from Baluwatar. We were taught that the bourgeoisie used the state as an instrument of coercion. It used the state for managing the bourgeois class interest. The communist ideal, on the other hand, was supposed to be the withering away of the state. Rather than witnessing any signs of such 'withering away', what I saw was how weak the state was in Nepal. It was so weak that it was not even able to act as an efficient manager for the capitalists. Take the example of the board of investment, which BRB had set up under the leadership of the PM. It was not allowed to function the way he wanted it to due to weak legal provision and the uncooperative attitude of the bureaucracy. One could see the state of lawlessness right at the gates of Baluwatar. The case of Nanda Prasad Adhikari and Ganga Maya Adhikari made me realize how weak our state was.[6] Their son Krishna Prasad Adhikari was killed during the PW. Their younger son, Noor Prasad Adhikari, came to the PM's house's gate and threatened us with consequences if his brother's murderers were not punished. Both the father and mother planned to sleep outside the gate in Baluwatar, threatening to fast until death. And yet the state authority was helpless, unable to address the problem. However, all conflict-related cases were to be addressed by the Truth and Reconciliation Commission.

I also used BRB's tenure as PM to invite as many cadres as possible inside the compound of Baluwatar to demystify the PM's residence. I remember entering Baluwatar during the 1990s when we, as active members of professors' organization, used to be invited for dinner to commemorate Education Day hosted by the PM annually. While participating in protest programmes outside Baluwatar in those days, I used to wonder what went on inside the fortified compound. It was a scary place because it was so unknown.

Since the time we went underground, and even after coming overground, we had changed shelters several times, both in Nepal and in India. I recollected and counted the number of times we had done so; I realized that Baluwatar was my twenty-fifth residence in a span of seventeen years, since the PW started. I remember taking shelter in rooms without electricity most of the time, at times without toilets in Delhi during the underground days. Now I was in the PM's residence in Kathmandu, which had an attached bathroom with each bedroom, ACs in all the rooms, spacious green gardens and many levels of security. So far, the three of us—BRB, Manushi and I—had never had an opportunity to live together; it was Baluwatar which brought us together to stay in one house as a family. Also, I once again began to use my original name, Hisila, after years of adopting different names ranging from Parvati and Saraswati to Sita, Durga, and even Rahul, during the PW period.

Looking back, I started wondering: What if I had not met BRB? Maybe I would have been married to some Newari engineer or doctor and would have been settled in the USA as most professionals had done in Nepal. I would probably have joined the non-resident Nepalese (NRN) associations and held an executive post. And I would have travelled back and forth to Nepal doing some social work on behalf of the NRNs. Or, if I had decided to work within Nepal, I would have joined some INGO or ran my own NGO besides teaching. And what about BRB? I suppose he would have married some educated, urban Brahmin woman, as most Brahmin engineers from rural areas did. If he had not joined politics then maybe he would be working as a development consultant in the UN, coming back to Nepal to share his experience or may become vice-chairman of the Planning Commission of Nepal at most.

While living in Baluwatar, I started realizing that Prachanda and his team were not very happy. I started observing his body language, which was not very pleasing.[7] Some members of the media had told me that a smear campaign against me had also been generated within the Maoist party.[8]

When I look back, the longer BRB held the position of the PM, the more I felt that the relationship between Prachanda and him kept deteriorating. And more and more accusations were being hurled at me. I started feeling isolated within the party, too.

Similarly, relations between Kiran, Prachanda and BRB started deteriorating further, eventually leading to Kiran and his faction breaking away from the UCPN (Maoist). All these developments had an adverse impact on the impending CA elections. And it was bound to have a negative impact on my identity and position within the party and outside it, too.

32

The Cost of Being a Middle-of-the-Roader

electoral defeat

The results of the first CA elections, held in April 2008, had surprised many national and international forces as the Maoists—predicted to be in the third position with about twenty to thirty seats won through FPTP system—had won 120 out of the 240 seats by FPTP and 100 out of the 355 seats through PR.[1] Based on this result, they were able to nominate nine members out of the total twenty-six nominated members. In total, they won 229 out of 601 seats, making it the largest party in the CA. Not only did they emerge as the largest party but also as the most inclusive. The candidates who won belonged to an oppressed gender, region, and ethnic and marginalized communities such as the Dalits. For instance, out of the total of thirty women who won through FPTP, twenty-four belonged to the Maoist party.[2] And out of the twenty-four women, eight belonged to Janajati, two were Dalits and one belonged to the Madhesi community. This had never happened in Nepal's electoral history!

However, this time it was the turn of the UCPN (Maoist) to be shocked when, in the second CA elections held in November 2013, the Maoists came third.[3] The party won only twenty-six out of 240 seats through FPTP. In total, it had only eighty-four seats out of 601. In terms of inclusivity, too, it fared poorly with only one woman winning the election through FPTP. The party was overconfident that it would do better in the second election. The status quo-ists were upbeat after the result.

I, too, lost in the second election from the same constituency in Kathmandu where I had won earlier. Prachanda lost from Kathmandu, but he won with a very slim margin in Siraha district. Similarly, BRB lost in the new constituency in Butwal in the Terai region but won from Gorkha district.

So, what was the reason behind our victory in the first CA election and what reduced us to the third position in the second election? In fact, when we came third, the party alleged there was a conspiracy to keep the Maoist in a marginal position by rigging the election results.[4] However, this allegation was soon dismissed and the party focused on the internal causes and problems within the Maoist party that led to its embarrassing defeat.

The party analysed the defeat as not merely a routine defeat in terms of numbers, but also as a strategic one. There were no doubts that external factors had played a role in the Maoist defeat. But such external factors would have been active during the first CA elections, too. Therefore, it was deduced that these forces would not have been successful in their scheme had it not been for the internal weaknesses in the party. It was thus important to learn from the defeat. If not, then there were greater chances of the Maoist movement disintegrating into oblivion.

The reason why we won in the first CA elections was that the core agendas, such as the formation of a republic, federalism and inclusive democracy were the products of the PW initially and later incorporated into the second people's movement. We all had the zeal of the revolution. People, in general, were yearning for change and the middle class in particular was longing for peace. We promised them both: change and peace. The agenda of an inclusive democracy appealed to the masses. Being a local Newari married to a Brahmin from Gorkha had helped me gain votes from both the communities during the first election. Within the core areas of Kathmandu, where the Newars resided, I received overwhelming support from the Newari community because of my identity as the daughter of Dharma Ratna Yami, a well-known Newari political figure. Outside the Ring Road, where predominantly the Khas Aryas lived, residents, particularly those from Gorkha, trusted me with their invaluable vote because I was married to a Khas Arya from Gorkha.

By signing the peace accord and by placing the PLA in cantonments, we assured people of our commitment to bring peace to Nepal. Since the CPN (Maoist) had been new, untested and known to sacrifice, people had voted for the party. Moreover, the old forces had been discredited and had become weak and rudderless.

Somehow, the zeal for change overshadowed internal debates, thus resulting in electoral victory.

This happened despite the fact that Kiran's faction had been saying that the CA elections would not deliver anything, that it was a bourgeois slogan.

The foremost reason why we lost in the second election was that the first CA had been dissolved before it could draft a new Constitution. First, the status-quoists did not want to give credit to the Maoists for promulgating a new Constitution, which they feared would institutionalize many radical changes. Second, the CA failed because most of the key leaders of the NC and the UML had been defeated in the CA elections and, therefore, were not present in the Constitution-making assembly. For example, Krishna Prasad Sitaula, the general secretary of the NC, who played a key role in the peace process and in drafting the interim Constitution, was defeated by Maoist CC member Dharmashila Chapagain. Mahesh Acharya, a senior NC leader, also lost in the election. Similarly, K.P. Sharma Oli, the current president of the UML and the PM of Nepal, was defeated by Bishwadeep Lingdel Limbu, a relatively junior Maoist leader. Other veteran leaders such as Bhim Rawal and Bamdev Gautam from the UML also lost to very junior Maoist leaders. As a result, they were not able to take ownership of the first CA. Hence, the first reason why we lost in the second CA elections was that we failed to produce the new Constitution through the first CA despite being the largest party.

The second factor was the internal debate that was rocking the party: Kiran's faction stood at one end, ruling out the CA election as rightist reformism, while BRB stood at the other end working hard to help the Constitution materialize through the CA. Prachanda vacillated between Kiran's and BRB's line, thus losing valuable time and initiative. This diverted our attention from running the government effectively.

The third reason was that by the time the elections to the second CA were announced, Kiran's faction had not only split from the party but had also been actively collaborating with other parties to defeat the UCPN (Maoist), although they had announced that they were going to boycott the election. They formally split to form the Communist Party of Nepal-Maoist (CPN-M) on 18 June 2012.[5] They alleged that Prachanda and BRB had discarded and deviated away from the goals of the revolution. They blamed us for following the parliamentary line. The split sent out a confusing message to the masses. Later on, a faction led by Biplab parted ways with Kiran's party over the question of the path of the revolution in 2014.

The fourth reason was that while the party had emerged from the war and was transforming from a rebellious party into a governing party, the whole organizational set-up had not yet changed in accordance with the demands of a new situation. The need to transform its approach from coercion to winning hearts, and its structure from centralized leadership to participatory democracy, had not been fulfilled. The nature of the party was such that it was neither a mass party nor a vanguard party. It had turned into a united front of all tendencies instead of voluntary centralism based on supremacy of ideology.

The fifth reason was that many new leaders and cadres who had quit their old parties to join the Maoist party felt isolated. They were rebuffed for not participating in the PW. They were treated as outsiders; some were even looked down upon as careerists who had come to enjoy the icing off the cake. Their expertise and advice were neither sought nor utilized.

The sixth reason was that by the end of the first CA, anti-federalism forces were misleading the masses by breeding the sentiment that federalism would divide the country. The Maoist party was not able to remove this confusion. Rather, some Maoist leaders started making contradictory remarks on federalism, much to the delight of anti-federalism forces. They started complaining that the party was not paying enough attention to class issues, which had been overshadowed by nationality/ethnicity issues. It was interesting to note that in the second CA elections I lost in the same constituency where I had earlier won because in the Newar-dominated core area I was looked upon suspiciously for having married a Khas Arya. And outside the Ring Road, I became a liability because I did not belong to the Khas Arya community by birth. What a somersault in popular opinion from the first to the second CA elections!

The seventh and most damaging cause behind the defeat was that the Maoist party said one thing and practised something else. For instance, consider identity-based federalism. The party's main political document hardly made space for an inclusive agenda. Also, the party leadership had shown no keenness in implementing the 'Development of Democracy in the 21st Century' document. Similarly, the resolution passed by the party, which heralded socialist-oriented capitalism, was not seriously translated into concrete political and organizational programmes. This resulted in weak management of whole-timer cadres, leaving them dependent on *chanda* (donation). Slowly, the party started becoming alienated from the working class and oppressed communities.

The eighth reason was that the main leader, Prachanda, started centralizing power by holding most of the posts within the party and state machinery. For him, state, power and wealth were everything. Ideological base, organizational structure and mass mobilization started eroding. While on the one hand party leaders at the top started indulging in corruption, on the other some of the commanders of the PLA started getting involved in shoddy deals. Once Maoists entered overground politics, all the central leaders and district-level party leaders started becoming Kathmandu-centric. They became cut off from the masses and started becoming power-centric.

Prachanda, as the leader, was expected to take responsibility for the party's loss in the second CA elections. However, I felt that his eclectic, opportunistic and spontaneous decision-making style, a lack of transparency in his lifestyle and functioning, and his hunger for power had made our party weak.

Since Kiran had split from the party, the person next in line to take responsibility for the party's loss was BRB. He was to be blamed for not taking a firm stand on his line, for his apathy towards organizational matters and his aversion to exercising power. He was to be blamed for being an idealist and for being more concerned about long-term goals without offering solutions to immediate practical problems.

My own experience of defeat in the second CA elections taught me many lessons. I had been one of the few CA members who made regular visits to their constituencies and took initiatives for procuring development funds. But I still lost.

I was surprised at the level of vendetta politics that Kiran's faction practised against me during the second CA elections. His party members threw stones at my car. They had planted many bombs in different parts of my constituency.[6] In fact, one of his cadres even phoned me to say that he had openly campaigned in favour of my electoral opponent who belonged to the UML party. On the day of the election, they threw a bomb inside my mother's house, which was only a few minutes away from the polling booth.[7]

Another factor behind my defeat was the smear campaign that had its origin in a magazine, which depicted me as 'the most corrupt' woman.[8] Photocopies of the magazine article were pasted in different parts of my constituency. People casually made unfounded claims that I possessed land and houses in different parts of Kathmandu. I attempted to defend myself in front of as many people as I could meet by telling them to bring proof of ownership of these properties that allegedly belonged to me, and that I would readily transfer the ownership to them if it was proven correct. Till date, I have no house in my name. I had sold the house I built in Koteshwor, during the PW, as per the party's policy. My Facebook account was hacked when I tried to refute these allegations. Looking back, I feel I should have given more time to my constituency despite the mounting media campaign against me.

Interestingly, during the first CA elections, the Maoists had vigorously pushed for the agenda of state restructuring and inclusive democracy. By the second election, however, Prachanda started deviating from these agendas. Slowly, some other Maoist leaders started backtracking from their original commitments, too. Eventually, those who had been in favour of an inclusive democracy and state restructuring started getting sidelined within the party.

I myself went through a bitter experience. I was shocked to find some of my fellow women CC members criticizing me for taking up nationality/ethnicity, linguistic and regional oppression-based issues. I felt cornered from both sides. On the one hand, my Newari friends were not very happy to see me being deeply involved in women's issues and organizations, because they perceived it as a Khas Arya-dominated agenda and structure. On the other hand, my women comrades were not happy to see me involved in Adivasi Janajati and Madhesi issues, which they considered to be a divisive agenda.

The contradictions and reconciliations between the two leaders, Prachanda and BRB, were worth observing. They were the two principal characters who navigated the PW, peace agenda and the CA to arrive at a new Constitution to institutionalize the agendas of republic, federalism, inclusive democracy and secularism. And yet the relationship between the two nosedived.

33

Prachanda and BRB

two sides of a river

Comrade Post Bahadur Bogati had used a rather amusing allegory to describe the relationship between Prachanda and BRB in one of the CC meetings. He had said, 'Both Prachanda and BRB are like two giant elephants; whether they meet or separate, they disturb the ground either way.' We all had a good laugh then. Indeed, in reality, when these two men fought, they shook the ground; party leaders and cadres would be heavily polarized over their debates. Strangely enough, even when they reconciled, the ground would still quiver. This meant that notwithstanding the agreements reached between Prachanda and BRB, factionalism continued to exist within the party. The reason was that despite their 'unity', there continued to be a contradiction between the ideological line and organizational leadership. Often, when these two men aligned after their 'struggle', it was the political line of BRB that prevailed. However, the onus of implementing that line fell upon Prachanda, the organizational supremo.

Since I was a member of Prachanda's HQ crew for a brief period during the PW, I had the rare opportunity to witness many interactions between Prachanda and BRB. I, therefore, feel obliged to shed some light on the dynamic relationship between the two leaders.

Throughout the movement, whether it was before, during or after the PW, the key players in the Maoist party had been Prachanda and BRB. This was widely acknowledged by people outside the party, too. However, within the party, despite the general acceptance of BRB's significant contributions, it was uncustomary for the party's official documents to mention the role of any leader apart from Prachanda. The one and only time when such a reference was made was after the end of the armed struggle. The combined efforts of Prachanda and BRB were officially recognized during the party's first post-PW congress (the seventh since the formation of the communist party in Nepal) held in February 2013 in Hetauda.[1] This was also to be the last general congress encompassing the whole party. The political document approved by this seventh congress consisted of a review of the past twenty-two years since the formation of CPN (Unity Centre) and the beginning of the preparatory phase of the Maoist movement. It stated that during all these years, the ideological struggle between Prachanda and BRB had ultimately helped the Maoist movement to progress, transform and reach a higher level of ideological synthesis or unity. This acknowledgement was, however, a rare case.

I personally felt that Prachanda and BRB were people with dissimilar qualities, which are sometimes complementary and at times contradictory. Basically, Prachanda was a pragmatist and BRB was an idealist. They were like two banks of the same river.

Let me start with the positive aspects of their relationship. I had been observing how they worked in tandem when they were in unison. Prachanda worked really well on practical and tactical matters, while BRB concentrated on long-term strategic vision. While Prachanda helped in militarizing the masses, BRB helped in politicizing them.[2] Prachanda was good at manoeuvring a united front with different parties, while BRB created political space by

articulating the need for a new sub-stage in their revolutionary
strategy, that of a 'democratic republic'. While BRB charted
a new political course, Prachanda legitimized it by gathering
the numbers required to sanction it in the party's CC. Cadres
identified Prachanda as the movement's heart and saw BRB as its
brain. In short, Prachanda was more of a managerial leader and
BRB was more of an ideological leader. Cadres sincerely wished
and insisted that these two leaders should be united. I felt the
same. In fact, I tried whatever I could within my capacity to make
them collaborate rather than struggle against each other. I made
conscious efforts to develop good relations with Prachanda's wife,
Sita, and provided Prachanda with books that BRB had been
reading.

I thought Prachanda's and BRB's personalities were
complementary. Prachanda was dynamic, an extrovert and had
mass appeal; BRB was an introvert, tenacious and had scholastic
appeal.

Indeed, when these two were in unison, it often yielded
positive results. For instance, the first successful attack on an RNA
camp in Dang in the year 2001 took place after the party's second
national conference.[3] This is when the two were in agreement
with each other on ideological and strategic questions. However,
when these two were at loggerheads with each other, the party
would often experience setbacks. One could cite the example of
the failure of the Khara attack on the RNA barracks in Rukum
in 2005, in which the PLA lost badly.[4] This military assault was
launched when the relationship between BRB and Prachanda was
fraught with trouble. BRB and his team were under house arrest
at that time.

Prachanda recognized the importance of having BRB in the
CPN (Unity Centre) in 1991 for two reasons. First, Prachanda
needed the numbers to ratify the party's resolution to carry out
a protracted PW, as opposed to Nirmal Lama's line of urban
insurrection. Second, Prachanda needed an intellectual public

figure like BRB to uplift the face of CPN (Unity Centre), which was otherwise not known to the public. BRB then had ideological clarity, intellectual appeal and was a face that was agreeable to the middle class. He also had access to both the masses and media. Just like Prachanda needed BRB, BRB needed Prachanda. BRB lacked the organizational strength to implement his ideology. This was something that only Prachanda could provide.

In such a scenario, why did Prachanda have lingering doubts about BRB? This, I could not understand. Perhaps, Prachanda needed BRB more than BRB needed Prachanda. But the dilemma was that he was insecure and scared of BRB. That was the contradiction I observed during the PW. It was clear that Prachanda was using the party as an instrument of power to control BRB. On the other hand, BRB used mass appeal, media, moral strength and his international reach to fight against Prachanda's tendency to monopolize power. Additionally, BRB, from time to time, would write notes of dissent, submit his resignation or demote himself—a kind of *satyagrahi* style of fighting against Prachanda.

I feel it would be easier to comprehend the contradictions between these two men if one were to get an idea of their upbringing, their personal tastes and interests before they became politically active.

Pushpa Kamal Dahal (Prachanda) initially wanted to join the RNA as a teenager. However, he went on to become a teacher in a school. Baburam Bhattarai (Laldhwoj) was interested in cosmology as a young boy. But he ended up studying architecture. BRB had also toyed with the idea of working as a UN volunteer in Africa and then returning to Nepal to work as a development consultant. However, after joining the communist movement, he never took up any professional job. In fact, he became a full-time politician as soon as he finished his studies.

At an early age, Prachanda was exposed to the communist ideology, not just out of choice only but also out of necessity and chance. His father had migrated from the hills to Chitwan; he had to work hard to get his big family (six daughters and two sons) settled. Prachanda had seen his father being roughed up by rich merchants in the city. His father was forced to work in Guwahati in India to earn extra cash. In addition, his house happened to fall on the side of the canal that was predominantly occupied by the left-leaning populace; the other side of the canal was dominated by Nepali Congress (NC) supporters.[5]

Unlike Prachanda, BRB's early life was relatively stable. His father, at one point, had also tried his luck for work in Chitwan but found the place too hostile. So, he returned to Gorkha where he had enough land to support his family. His uncle was an NC supporter. Later on, in school and college, his circle of friends mostly hailed from an NC background even though BRB himself never became a member of NC. Being good in studies and having enough to eat, he had never seen his father being humiliated by others. In contrast to Prachanda, BRB became a communist more through choice than necessity. When BRB became the president of AINSA in India, Prachanda was working in Gorkha as a schoolteacher. Coincidentally, both of them had passed out of school in the same year. But while BRB was the national topper of the SLC board exams, Prachanda had scored a second division. During the days of the PW, Prachanda himself revealed to BRB his inferiority complex and insecurity, which he recounted in later years, too. Before the two political parties, CPN (Bidrohi Masal) and CPN (Mashal), came together in 1991, BRB was a senior CC member of CPN (Bidrohi Masal) and Prachanda was the general secretary of CPN (Mashal). Prachanda ascended in the party's organizational hierarchy from a lower position to the highest rank by climbing the party ladder. BRB, on the other hand, conducted his political journey by combining both non-partisan and party activism. The first step in his political ladder was becoming the president of AINSA, which was not affiliated to any political party. Thereafter, he joined M.B. Singh's Masal party and went on to later become the vice-president of the Maoist party.

As far as ideological capacity is concerned, BRB seemed to have better exposure and an edge over Prachanda. First, his university education provided him a bigger space for acquiring knowledge that was diverse in nature; his interest in science and cosmology additionally allowed him to think holistically and strategically. Second, his enrolment in JNU, which was the bastion of left movement in India, greatly helped him in acquiring a more informed understanding of Marxism, its various trends and practices. Third, his PhD thesis at JNU helped him in analysing the nature of underdevelopment and regional structure of Nepal from a Marxist point of view. Using Marxism as a tool of inquiry, he believed in practising dialectical and historical materialism as a scientific method to unravel and change society. He did not perceive Marxism as an end in itself but rather as a means to transform society. Finally, BRB interacted with leaders of different political parties in India. Therefore, he had a wider exposure to various ideological trends, which made him more tolerant towards differing voices within the party and society.

Prachanda's setting was different from BRB's. Given that Prachanda had been faced with a more difficult economic background, lacked quality education and exposure, I could understand where his attraction for power through organizational supremacy came from. What he lacked in ideology, he sought to make up for in organizational strength. Moreover, when he could not reason politically and ideologically, he sought to rely on conspiracy theories and blame external causes for internal problems. For instance, whenever there were major problems within the party or inside the country, he would often conclude that foreign forces were involved in those incidents. Rather than grapple with the real problem within, he would consider conspiracies to be the cause of failures or problems. He seemed more comfortable with the Stalinist school of thought. For Prachanda, dictatorship of class meant dictatorship of the party, which ultimately translated into the dictatorship of the main leader. The vanguard concept of party formation and mechanism eventually became a rigid and bureaucratic approach to build and lead the party. No wonder when the 'Prachanda Path' was approved as the party's guiding principle, his followers put his photo alongside Marx, Lenin, Stalin and Mao on banners, posters, magazines, pamphlets, and so on. Emphasis was put on quoting Prachanda while delivering speeches, taking political classes and writing articles and books.

On tactical matters, Prachanda was very skilful. He was good at manipulative politics. As a result, he was able to make use of the contradictions between various forces within the old regime, for instance between the NC, UML and the royal forces. However, when he started using the same manipulative means internally within the Maoist party, it became problematic.

Essentially, Prachanda was a 'centrist' who vacillated between BRB's viewpoint and Kiran's beliefs. Prachanda always needed to create two opposing tendencies, so that he could mediate between the two to make himself invincible. To achieve this, he made sure to not let the two conflicting groups align with each other. Therefore, he never made a concerted effort to end factionalism within the party. I could see that he created rifts between his own staunch supporters as well. After all, he had to ward off competitors within his own faction! For example, even before the elections for the first CA, at the fifth extended CC meeting held at Balaju, Kathmandu, in August 2007, Prachanda had compromised with Kiran's line.[6] He had said the current emphasis should be laid on insurrection, whereas the spirit of the Chunwang meeting was to institutionalize the gains of revolution through CA elections. It is to be noted that this was BRB's line, which was endorsed in Chunwang in 2005. At the Kharipati meeting in November 2008,[7] Prachanda again conceded to Kiran's line in order to gain majority support and retain his authority inside the party. Prachanda was, in fact, playing a dual role: he was formally endorsing Kiran's line in the party meetings but practising BRB's line outside. By November 2010, for the first time ever, three documents were separately presented by Prachanda, Kiran and BRB at the Palungtar plenary meeting. Once again, Prachanda came up with an eclectic political document which emphasized Kiran's line.

It also needs to be stated that Prachanda was flexible enough to listen to and adopt new ideological and strategic questions. However, his display of flexibility depended upon whether it would strengthen or weaken his authority. For instance, he would be very agitated if BRB raised questions about ideology, strategy and organization without his approval. BRB would be branded 'bourgeois', 'ambitious' and whatnot. But, if the raised issues could be presented as Prachanda's own, he would eagerly put forth the agenda as a 'revolutionary' one in party forums. One could take the case of the election of a CA for a new Constitution. When BRB initially made this proposal, he was rebuked for being 'rightist'. However, when this agenda became unavoidable in the light of increasing autocratic tendencies of the monarch, Prachanda jumped in to mark this agenda as his own.

Rather than using Marxism as the tool to solve inner party struggle, Prachanda used organizational power to dominate it. Thus, he made sure that the numbers were always in his favour. The way I saw it, for Prachanda, organizational concerns always preceded ideological concerns; he gave priority to tactical questions at the cost of strategic questions. His tactical moves, his vacillations and retention of the general secretary post for a long period had favoured him in holding a firm grip over the organization. Because of his monolithic approach to organization, he tended to gravitate towards Kiran's line. Prachanda loved to be at the helm of all affairs. For him, the organization was the source of power. BRB, on the other hand, did not care enough to exercise power through the organization. BRB would not hesitate to compromise on organizational hierarchy if it meant that his ideological–political stance would be adopted by Prachanda. His lack of interest in exercising power had been his weakest point. This exasperated his followers. They would often complain that BRB could not provide political security to his supporters.

In terms of temperament, Prachanda was more social and approachable. He had the capacity to meet anyone at any time, anywhere and in any way. He had the capacity to carry out multiple moves simultaneously. He had good oratory skills and a charismatic appeal. Prachanda was more emotional, to the extent of displaying a mercurial character. He had an extroverted and dynamic personality.

On the other hand, BRB was reserved, rational and stoic. He was happy with a few friends and content with ideological and theoretical work. It was not in his nature to socialize through personal meetings. He would rather connect with people through Twitter, Facebook and interaction in groups. He was more interested in reading books than in reading people's minds.

At worst, Prachanda could look like an opportunist because of his self-centric and fluctuating stance, and BRB could look idealistic and impractical because of his principled stance.

I could also sense that Prachanda did not hesitate to enjoy consumerism whenever he could. He sported expensive watches and preferred expensive cars. In contrast, BRB was more detached from worldly possessions.

Prachanda could easily get carried away by flattery, but at the same time he could turn vindictive when criticized. BRB could be easily carried away by the intellectual abilities of a person without confirming his or her credibility.

The vigour of war did not allow the contradictions between these two leaders to turn extremely antagonistic, except at one point when Prachanda took political action against us.

However, after having tasted the power of governance, Prachanda seemed to be increasingly hooked on to power politics and numerical games at the cost of sticking to the correct political line.

I personally wished that the relationship between Prachanda and BRB would have been more complementary than contradictory. During the PW, when I had easy access to Prachanda as a member of HQ staff, I tried my best to mitigate their differences. But post the PW my access to Prachanda was reduced. The two families gradually grew apart. I could also sense that Prachanda's personal secretarial staff was becoming more and more hostile towards BRB.

Prachanda and BRB had become like two banks of the same river that could never meet each other.

34

My Relationship with Prachanda

innocence vs conspiracy

My acquaintance and relationship with the top five leaders of
the Maoist movement—Prachanda, Kiran, BRB, Badal and
Diwakar—took different forms under different circumstances.
Between these five leaders, my relationship with Prachanda had
been the longest and closest—except, of course, with BRB.

Prachanda (literally meaning 'the fierce one') was hardly
'Prachanda' when I met him for the first time at my house
in Kathmandu. He was a thin, simple man. He looked like a
schoolteacher, which of course he was for many years. I visited his
den-like rented place at Chyasal in Lalitpur for the first time. It
was a typical Newari mud house in the corner of a small courtyard.
While entering his room, I had to make sure I did not hit my head
against the low ceiling, or trip while climbing up the stairs because
it was so dark even during the day. He made tea for me. His wife
was washing clothes on the ground floor. He had three daughters
and one son. They attended a nearby government school.

We were a class apart when we met.

I had recently built my own house in Koteshwor, Kathmandu.
It was a modern split house that I had designed myself. My parental
home in Bhurungkhel was a mansion-like, five-storey building,

which was inherited by my brother after my parents' demise. After my marriage to BRB, we had rented two rooms at my stepmother's house. I was teaching at the Institute of Engineering, drawing a regular salary. I had a helper to look after Manushi and to help with domestic chores. Manushi was then studying in a private school.

I got to know Prachanda closely only after I became a staff member at the party's HQ with the launch of the PW. I was impressed by his dynamism, his readiness to take initiative, his approachability to cadres and his sociable and warm nature. He was quite charismatic. He had a knack for making people believe in him. During conversation with others, he would often say, '*Maile pani thyakkai tyahi socheko* (Exactly! I am thinking the same, too!).' He was good at reading people's minds. He was a quick learner, too.

Both BRB and I were impressed by the speed with which he learnt to speak in English. This helped him in communicating with the RIM comrades. He was good at disseminating what others had relayed to him. He could articulate ideas as if he were the originator. In fact, he could express them better than the person who originally introduced those ideas. This happened with BRB, too. He would share his ideas with Prachanda, and Prachanda would lace them with his own feelings while presenting them in the party meetings as his own.

We knew that Prachanda lacked the exposure which BRB and I had. And we did not want him to feel insecure because of this. We encouraged him to try out new things when he was in hiding in India. We even asked a Nepali worker to take him to the Centaur Hotel (a five-star hotel near Delhi's international airport). After his first experience inside a deluxe hotel, Prachanda told us of an incident that left all of us laughing to the hilt. After finishing a lavish meal, he was offered a bowl of warm water with lemon on the side. Thinking that it was an after-meal drink, he squeezed the lemon into the bowl of water and drank it. He only came to know something was wrong when the attendant gave him a blank look!

In certain ways, Prachanda's character matched mine. He told me that he used to play the madal, and even dance, when he was teaching at a school in Gorkha. I, too, loved music and dance. He was an extrovert, so was I. Because of these similarities, I felt comfortable communicating with him. I was so impressed with him that I used to complain to BRB for not being approachable like Prachanda, and for not being as proactive as him when it came to organizational matters.

However, I was astonished to discover his drinking habits. It was understood that he should not be contacted after 8 p.m. At a dinner gathering, I recall him saying that drinking alcohol helped in releasing tension and in easing relationships with his comrades by opening up one's heart. I soon discovered that many other leaders drank as well. BRB was the only odd man who did not consume alcohol. For me, drinking was not a problem since it is customary in the Newari community, to which I belong, to serve *aila* (local liquor) at every *bhwe* (traditional feast). Newars, having a large appetite, are accustomed to drinking liquor at the end of a feast—I believe to digest the food. I had been meticulous in taking aila only for digesting heavy food; it was not a habit. Soon, I realized that Sita, too, had taken to drinking to give company to Prachanda. I was worried that it would become a habit for them.

During the time I was working as an HQ staff, what I could not understand was that while Prachanda was so nice to us, his near and dear ones did not treat us well. They used to consider us as intellectuals, opportunists and careerists whose abilities were to be used but not trusted. They particularly treated me lightly and would not give me substantial work. I was mostly given the task of assisting others. Except once, never was I assigned a primary role in organizational matters, not even in a department that looked into foreign relations, which I felt I could lead.

This may not be something that is scientifically proven, but I do feel that women have a better sense of perceiving who is genuine and who is not. Within the Maoist party, I noticed that those who treated BRB and me differently were not trustworthy friends of BRB. They would say one thing in front of him and another behind his back. I also observed that those who hero-worshipped Prachanda were in fact taking Sita for granted. I was also treated somewhat similarly. Often, those who pretended to be near BRB treated me as his wife only, not as a fellow comrade. I had made it a point to relay this to BRB. Especially in Prachanda's case, I often found that his children's body language defied his own good behaviour towards us. From that perspective, I actually came to appreciate Sita's straightforwardness—she was what she was. She was cold, blunt and could not hide what she felt. Prachanda, meanwhile, was not entirely what he portrayed himself to be. What he told us to our face was often very different from what he would say about us to his close circle. For instance, he would tell his close friends that we had shady relations with India, but appreciate our informed relations with external powers when he met us personally.

When the question of the centralization of leadership was discussed in the party, Prachanda told us that he himself was not keen on labelling the new ideological synthesis using his own name. However, those close to him, especially his brother Narayan Dahal, vehemently pleaded for the nomenclature 'Prachanda Thought'. Similarly, his daughter Renu Dahal, who was an active party member, hardly played a positive role in solving factionalism within the party, even as Prachanda formally announced that factionalism should end. His son Prakash was a spoilt brat and not much of a help when it came to addressing tensions between the two leaders. (I'm sorry to mention this here as he met an untimely death at the age of thirty-six, while I was writing this book.) However, rather than being inherently spoilt, I would say that Prakash became a victim of his overprotective parents. In fact, he was a true reflection of what really went on in Prachanda's mind. Most of the time what came from Prachanda's mind was confirmed by Prakash's actions. Thus, I always felt that Prachanda had been double-dealing when it came to us.

Every time we had political–ideological debates with Prachanda, my doubts about him would increase substantially. He would say that he agreed with BRB's thoughts but would generally implement the opposite.

Despite all this, I still considered Prachanda my leader and was hopeful that our relationship could get better. There were good days when our trust level would be high. However, even during those times, I realized that Prachanda behaved differently with the cadres who were close to us. Those who supported us ideologically continued to suffer from subtle biases when it came to work distribution and promotion. I was particularly shattered by his behaviour towards my staff members.

My staff members used to be very badly treated by Prachanda's henchmen in their respective districts, when they were working with me. I relayed this to Prachanda and was hopeful that he would take corrective measures. But that never happened. One of my staff members was accused of financial misconduct by Prachanda's faction. I felt that she had been wrongly accused and had defended her then. However, one day, I myself caught her red-handed as she was making a financial deal behind my back. I immediately sacked her. Soon after, she joined Prachanda's camp. To my big surprise, not only was she welcomed in Prachanda's faction, but they were also actively defending her wrongdoing! I pointed this out to Prachanda, but he seemed totally unconcerned; he did not utter a single word. The same person who was rebuked when she worked with me was embraced with open arms once she left my side. What could this mean?

While we lived in Baluwatar, I was suddenly and increasingly targeted by the media. Without any evidence, I was labelled corrupt.[1] I asked my party to defend me before the media since the only fund collection I ever did was for my party, only because the party had made me a member of the central fund-collecting team.

I always raised money on behalf of the party and handed the funds over to Prachanda. I was thoroughly disappointed that neither the party nor its supremo came forward to defend me. Later, some people in the media confirmed to me that certain accusations against me had been generated and spread from Lazimpat (Prachanda's residence then).[2] Perhaps this was to embarrass BRB, who was then the prime minister. Later, I won a lawsuit against the magazine *Crime Today* for defaming me. It is interesting to note that while I was being charged with corruption by a magazine, Prachanda was silent on the corruption within the cantonment and the party. When intense questions on corruption within and outside the party were raised eventually, the party was forced to set up two commissions, the Bogati Commission (headed by Post B. Bogati, which had the task of probing into financial irregularities of the PLA commanders in the cantonments) and the Sherchan Commission (headed by Amik Sherchan, which had to probe into financial irregularities committed by party leaders). Unfortunately, the findings of both the commissions never saw the light of day.

Whenever the inner party struggle between Prachanda and BRB peaked, I would always refer to Marx's essay 'The Eighteenth Brumaire of Louis Bonaparte'.[3] Increasingly, I would feel that Prachanda's traits matched Bonaparte's character in many ways, especially his mastery in double-talk to suit the situation. Watching his character unfold during the peaceful phase, I often thought that he fit well in the bourgeois world, more specifically in the conventional parliamentary setting where one needed money, muscle and mass to succeed; where you needed the art of mesmerizing the people on tactical, immediate issues; where you needed the art of telling lies or giving false promises. At one time, I even told BRB that it was a pity that Prachanda was the leader of the Maoist party. Had he been the leader of a parliamentary party, he would fit better and be allowed to rule for a longer period.

Today, Prachanda is increasingly criticized, both within and outside his party, for his lavish lifestyle, for living in an expensive and expansive house, and for favouring his near and dear ones in lucrative deals as well as in government appointments.[4]

Having said all this, I have no hesitation in appreciating Prachanda's strong qualities. One has to admit that he is a dynamic, hard-working person. He worked very hard during the armed struggle, he continues to work hard today, and perhaps will work even harder in the days to come. However, his lust for power within the party and in all state affairs is diminishing his 'power' over the genuine masses. How I wish such a hard-working person did not expend all his energy in chasing after power at the cost of losing sight of the common people on the ground!

35

My Relationship with BRB

complementary and contradictory

BRB and I are poles apart in terms of character.

A few days after we got married on 29 March 1981, I had gone to meet Mona Lepcha, a Sikkimese friend, at her hostel in the National School of Drama, Delhi, where she was learning Kathak, a form of classical Indian dance. She immediately exclaimed, 'Can you believe it! Hisila Yami has married Baburam!' She had somehow mistaken me for her uncle who was supposed to visit her that day. Instead, she found me standing in front of her. She then told me that she could never ever imagine that BRB and I could be in a relationship because our personalities were poles apart. She was not the only person to think so.

I remember, a few days after our marriage, I had literally asked BRB whether I got married to a human being or to a wall. Like any other partner, I would want to share my thoughts with my husband. Late at night or the early morning hours were just the appropriate time for that. However, BRB had this habit of staying deep in thought before sleeping at night, as well as after waking up in the morning. Both of us would be busy with our own work during the day. When would I get a chance to speak with him, I wondered?

Even during the PW days, when cadres were eager to meet BRB, he would pay more attention to reading newspapers, magazines and books lying on the table, leaving people to wait around the table, gaping. Instead, I would have to smile more widely and frequently to make up for his lack of response, not to mention repeatedly nudge him to speak to the visiting cadres.

Basically, I am a spontaneous person and BRB is the opposite. I act instinctively without thinking, and BRB thinks a lot before taking action. Once, in Delhi, three of us—BRB, me and a friend called Purushottam Pokharel—were walking back from Katwaria Sarai, a village near JNU, to our married scholars' hostel room after inspecting the printing progress of *Janamanas*, the mouthpiece of the AINSA. It was around 12.30 a.m. and we had taken a shortcut through the forest around JNU. Suddenly, three young men accosted us: they started questioning why we were out so late at night. Before we could grasp what was happening, they started beating up BRB and Purushottam. Soon, we were taken to what looked like a secluded guardroom. They made BRB and Purushottam crouch on the floor with their heads down. When those men insisted that only I should follow them outside, I realized that they were actually after me. Two men were restraining BRB and Purushottam, while the third one was trying to drag me outside. Initially, I pretended I was not well. I told him to do whatever he wanted there and then; there was no way I would go with him alone. Meanwhile, I was looking for an opportunity to escape through the open window facing the road. Somehow, I managed to jump out of the window and started shouting for help. Soon, I started hearing whistles around me; chowkidars were running towards us. Those three men ran away. We were taken to Prof. S.D. Muni's quarters, where we met the police and informed them about what had happened. Later on, I asked BRB why he had not taken action immediately when I was being attacked. He told me he had been thinking about how to handle the situation. I, on the other hand, had started running in the wrong direction, which led towards a more remote area, when I jumped out of the window!

This was so typical of us. BRB had been thinking for too long before deciding to act, and I had acted without thinking. That is how we are. Yet, we complement each other to this day.

In order to systematically unfold our relationship, it is important to see its various aspects.

Politically, BRB's opinions and activism hinged on rationality, reasoning and logic. He had a more holistic approach towards understanding society and politics. He was strategic in his thinking. He would first acquire a general overview and then move towards the particularities. His approach, thus, befits a political, visionary and ideological leader. I, on the other hand, was drawn to political activism because of my strong feelings against the poor condition of Nepali workers in India. I saw them being exploited and oppressed. I also witnessed sexual violence against Nepali women sold to brothels in India. I tend to be more practical, managerial and technical in my approach to politics. I am more attentive towards particularities than towards a holistic overview of society.

Despite this difference in approach, both BRB and I shared similar ideological and political stances when it came to the inner party struggle within the Maoist movement. We consistently fought against monolithic tendencies within the organization. We always sought to make democracy more inclusive and struggled to fuse class issues with extra-class issues, such as the liberation of those oppressed on the basis of caste, gender, nationality/ ethnicity, region, language and religion. We were against personal vendetta and respected debates and differences within the party. We always fought for ideological supremacy over organizational supremacy.

On women's issues, I found BRB to be more of a feminist than me. His gender sensitivity and empathy towards women's movements and leadership are things that I am rather proud of.

Perhaps, Manushi too noticed this from a young age; she had once asked me, '*Ama*, will I be able to get a husband as good as my father?' I was touched by her question and conveyed it to BRB. He let out a silent smile filled with pride.

When it comes to socializing, I love to meet people from diverse backgrounds and converse with them. BRB, on the other hand, is an introvert. He loves to read books and magazines, ranging from those on philosophy, science and cosmology to sports and movies. Of late, he has become very active on Twitter and Facebook; his account on Twitter had the highest number of followers for an individual in Nepal, with 1.2 million followers as of April 2020.[1] I prefer to establish close and personal contact with people rather than be active on social networks. I love to study human behaviour. I am thankful to BRB for instilling in me the habit of reading. But I am also proud that I have managed to make a person as serious as BRB smile occasionally. I also take pride in transforming a man who wanted to remain unmarried into a good father, a good husband and a more practical political leader than he was before. BRB also has contributed towards making me more serious, dignified and hopefully a more responsible political leader.

In terms of education, BRB stands at a much higher pedestal. He was excellent in his studies; always getting the highest marks, emerging as the national topper of both board exams and always obtaining a scholarship. I, on the other hand, was always an average student. While he was doing well in his studies and getting prestigious awards, I was doing well in sports and being awarded for extra-curricular activities.

Since my school days, I had acquired some leadership qualities. I would lead my classmates to complain about teachers who were absent without prior notice, or those who did not come on time to teach. In school, I was the only vocal Buddhist Newar student who would argue with the majority Hindu Newar students. We used to compete on issues such as whose god was superior:

Buddha or Ram? Despite being in a rural setting, BRB had access
to *Encyclopedia Britannica* and magazines such as the *National
Geographic* and *Reader's Digest* through his favourite teacher
Eleanor, an American missionary. While my father was making
my siblings and me listen to Neil Armstrong and Edwin 'Buzz'
Aldrin's landing on the moon on our radio in Kathmandu on 20
July 1969, BRB was listening to the same news on Eleanor's radio
but in a remote village in Gorkha. Like BRB had Eleanor, I, too,
had my favourite teacher, Durga Lal Shrestha (now a well-known
Newar literary figure), who taught us Nepali and Newari in his
beautiful, unforgettable handwriting.

Our family backgrounds were also very different. My parents
came from the business community, but my father switched to
politics. BRB belonged to the Brahmin caste; his ancestors were
priests, but his father had taken to agriculture. My mother was
twenty-four years old when she got married to my thirty-year-old
father. It was a political marriage. They both had had elementary
education at home. My parents gave birth to seven children, all of
whom received high levels of education. Baburam's parents never
received formal education. His father was only nine years old and
his mother was thirteen years old when they got married. They,
too, had seven children, but three of them died at a very young
age. Baburam's elder sister did not get a formal education and
was married off at a young age. His younger brother and sister,
however, are both educated.

I belong to the oppressed Newar indigenous-ethnic
community, while BRB belongs to the upper-caste hill Brahmin
Khas Arya community, which has historically enjoyed the highest
status in society and politics. Coincidentally, BRB hails from
Gorkha, whose ruler (the Shah King) had defeated and captured
the Newar kingdom, while I come from Kathmandu Valley that
was conquered by the Shah king of Gorkha. Ironically, it was
Gajanan Bhattarai, the great-great-grandfather of BRB, who was
one of the influential men responsible for the ascendance of the

Shah dynasty in Gorkha. And it was my great-great-grandfather, Ratna Das Tuladhar, who was a rich merchant who supplied food to the Rana oligarchs.

While BRB was brought up under relatively difficult circumstances, I was brought up in a comfortable environment. His parents would leave BRB with his other siblings while they worked hard in their fields throughout the day. Whereas when I was born, my father had already become a minister. We had a maid to take care of us and a cook to feed us. While BRB was herding cattle in the forest, I was playing in our private stone-paved courtyard. BRB had to walk for three hours through a jungle to reach his school, while my school was only ten minutes away from our home on foot.

Thus, at a young age, he was living in the world of necessity and I was living in the world of freedom.

In terms of physical fitness, too, we are different. BRB takes more care of his brain than his body, that is why he loves reading books. For him, reading is meditation. Even as the prime minister, he would go to sleep only after reading, even if it was way past midnight. In contrast, I take more care of my body. I regularly do yoga besides socializing, singing, dancing, going for walks and playing sports. Usually when he is busy reading, I am already sleeping. I do more walking and talking than reading. For BRB, mental exercise takes precedence over physical exercise.

We have such distinctive personalities that television actors have been impersonating our traits and relationship on TV shows![2] Jyoti Kafle is BRB's impersonator, while Bipana Basnet has made a name for herself as mine.

My relationship with BRB, however, has not always been smooth. At times, I too had to struggle against him. This was especially so when I felt neglected and sidelined within our own internal party circle. Sometimes I felt that BRB deliberately cut my turn to speak during internal meetings. I had to often fight for my space and position not only within the party but also within BRB's ideological faction. I particularly noticed that his position and image within the party, as well as outside, soared after he became PM. It ascended even higher after he won in the second CA election. In stark contrast, I felt my position and image both inside and outside the party suffering after he became the PM. Moreover, I lost in the second CA election. It was a very disturbing period for me.

Both of us were often at loggerheads when it came to asserting power. BRB often ran away from power and organizational nitty-gritties. I, on the other hand, deeply felt that if one was to succeed in politics, one needed both state power and organizational power. You need both *satya* (truth) and *satta* (power). But these two necessities are often contradictory: those who are committed to satya often do not have satta, and those who have satta often compromise on satya. However, one cannot evade the importance of either. One is incomplete without the other.

Occasionally, I have had to remind BRB to be more sensitive towards the difficulties and discriminations I have had to face as a woman politician. If a woman politician asserts her power, she is blamed for either undermining or abusing her husband's authority. And if one maintains a low profile, she is still criticized for being docile and dependent on her husband. Nepali society, in general, still finds it difficult to stomach women who are independent, bold, loud and fearless; it is accustomed to see women in subservient roles.

I have also made it a point to tell BRB that he should take advantage of my ability to discern who his genuine friend is and who is keeping him in the dark. I have warned him against those who are well-mannered in front of him but behave differently with me for no particular reason. I have told him to be aware of those who glorify him and mock me. It is obvious that they are after power and are not concerned about political and social issues.

My struggle with him has always been to get him to respect my extrovert nature. He keeps telling me that I speak too much and that I act too spontaneously. Perhaps this book would not have been possible had I not been spontaneous and extroverted.

36

Manushi, Asmita and Astha

bringing up a daughter

Manushi returned to Nepal after she completed her undergraduate studies from Lady Shri Ram (LSR) College, New Delhi, in 2007. She was ten years old when the PW was launched. She was coming back to her country after having lived underground for ten years in India. She had studied in schools and colleges in different parts of India using the pseudonym Asmita Singh. She had to concoct stories and pretend that she hailed from Darjeeling, Sikkim or Delhi, depending on where she was at that particular moment. Asmita became 'Astha' when she formally became a member of the Maoist party while studying in Delhi.

As a kid, Manushi was brought up in her maternal grandmother's house. Coincidentally, my father, too, had been brought up in his maternal grandmother's house. He had been sent to live with his grandmother because his parents' financial condition was not suitable to ensure proper care. My great-grandfather had stood on the wrong side of the Rana regime and consequently had his business confiscated by the authorities. In Manushi's case, she was staying with her grandmother since we did not own any land or house in Kathmandu; instead, we had rented two rooms in my stepmother's house. Moreover, both of us were

very active in politics during the anti-Panchayat movement, and
we did not have time to look after her. BRB and I were relieved to
know that at least she could be taken care of by my stepmother and
sisters if we were imprisoned.

Having decided to raise only one child, I was very conscious
that a child could easily turn into a spoilt brat if the parents
were too pampering or careless. I used to read articles and books
on parenting an only child. Both BRB and I had a common
understanding regarding our approach to her upbringing. At a
very young age, she had shown signs of emotional maturity. In
Newcastle, UK, she had been more understanding than her age
would allow when I was going through depression. She was a
sensible, responsible girl from a very young age.

Manushi was four years old in 1990, when the people's
movement against the reformed one-party Panchayat system
was ongoing. Night curfew had been imposed in Kathmandu.
Prostitutes would be out on the streets earlier than usual to
solicit customers. One evening, as I was returning from Bir
Hospital with Manushi on my bicycle, I heard a crowd of
boys shouting 'bhalu!'—a derogatory word for prostitutes. I
turned towards them and saw a group of young girls. Among
them, one particular girl who had heavy make-up on stood out.
I immediately recognized her. She was the same thirteen-year-old
child who had inaugurated a seminar on 'Squatter Settlements in
Nepal' three months before the people's movement started. I also
recognized her elder sister (about fifteen years old), who I knew
was practising prostitution. I had met them with their parents in
their squatter settlement on the banks of the Bishnumati. They
had come to Kathmandu from Humla, one of the most remote
districts in the far-western part of Nepal. My colleagues and I
had met them during our research for the seminar. I used to take
Manushi to that squatter settlement, too. I had tried to get that
thirteen-year-old child admitted to a morning school run by an
aid agency. This was to save her from taking up prostitution,

which her elder sister had been forced into. However, she had to wait for the next session to be admitted.

A few months later, in front of Bir Hospital, here was the same girl! I was shocked to see her with her sister. I looked at her with tears in my eyes. She saw me and tried to hide. I came back home and told BRB the entire episode. I did not realize that Manushi was listening. She then pleaded with me to explain what she had heard. We had never told lies to Manushi. I was in a fix, unable to decide how I should handle her query. Nevertheless, I decided to tell her the whole story. I explained what prostitution meant, why it existed and how the girl we were talking about got involved in prostitution. Manushi thought for a while and said, 'Why don't you get her married?' BRB and I were shocked to hear such a response from a four-year-old child. Actually, Manushi had her own sense of intuition. At that age, she was already telling me, 'Ama, you talk too much, you are impatient.' And she would tell her father, 'Ba, you think too much, too ahead of your time; you should have been born in the next generation.'

At an early age, she had been forced to become serious, serene and sensitive because of our busy and difficult lifestyle. I remember that whenever she tried to draw her father's attention, he would always respond with 'hmm, hmm' while nodding. He would be reading all along while pretending to listen to her. She had seen me busy as well. She was used to seeing her parents being taken into police custody periodically. She was also used to not having her father around for several weeks, sometimes months; he would be travelling outside Kathmandu for party activities. No wonder, when we decided to go underground with the launch of the Maoist PW, she took the news quite calmly.

I was ten years old when I lost my mother. Manushi, too, was the same age when she lost her parents—not in terms of death but in the form of psychological, emotional, social, and even physical, absence because we had left her behind to go underground.

During the PW, at one point, I had told her that her father could be killed any day. Soon after, I told her that I could also be killed. When the PW was at its peak, I slowly revealed to her that she, too, could be caught and killed. I made these precautionary announcements, which Manushi took quite calmly, so that she could prepare herself for any eventuality.

During the PW, she had to keep hopping from one place to another and changing schools every year or two. When we left for the PW, we put her under the care of my sister Kayo Yami who lived in Koteshwor, Kathmandu. Manushi was studying in Class five at the Holy Land International School, New Baneshwor. State intelligence investigators were always following her. Soon, things became uncomfortable when her teachers started becoming conscious of her presence as a Maoist's daughter. I was particularly worried when I got to know that one of her teacher's brothers was killed by the Maoists in Gorkha. Moreover, Kayo's house was always under constant vigilance. We all decided that it was no longer safe for her to be in Kathmandu. A year after the PW's launch, Kayo took Manushi to New Delhi. There, a very good college friend of BRB's helped us search for a school for her. Soon, she took admission in St. John's School, Nainital, as Asmita Singh. It was a small, private boarding school. I was supposed to be Nirmala Singh, her Nepali mother married to Suresh Singh from Darjeeling. We rarely visited her. We must have been good at maintaining secrecy because the principal had the impression that she was the daughter of someone working for the Intelligence Bureau of India. Her principal was so impressed with her academic performance that she once told me that Asmita was likely to become an IAS (Indian Administrative Service) officer later in life.

Compared to many other schools of Nainital, this school had relatively low fees. However, it was still beyond our financial capabilities. Moreover, Maoist leaders were being criticized for sending their children to private schools while their own party was demanding an end to the privatization of education. Asmita was

then shifted to a government-aided school, St George's School, in
Pedong (Darjeeling district), which is about an hour away from
Kalimpong by jeep. Much later, I found out that my father had
taken shelter in Pedong around the year 1930 while he was on his
way to Lhasa. He was fifteen years old then. He mentions this
place in his travel epic *Reply from Tibet*.[1] What a coincidence that
his grand-daughter, Manushi (thirteen years old then), had landed
in the same place about seventy years later!

One of the reasons we were keen on sending her to Pedong
was so that she could speak and study Nepali language. Darjeeling,
which falls under the state of West Bengal in India, has a rich
history of promoting Nepali language and other elements of
Nepali nationalism. Before the Sugauli Treaty had been signed,
parts of Darjeeling district were under Nepal.[2] The people of
Nepal and those of the Darjeeling hills share a lot in common—
linguistically, culturally and ethnically. Asmita's Nepali language
skills improved; she even started writing articles for *Janadesh*, the
Maoist weekly newspaper.

After completing her tenth grade, she had to change schools
again due to security reasons. She had to be taken to an entirely
different location. We found a government school in New Delhi
and a Nepali family with whom she could live. I remember one
teacher in Pedong, who pleaded with me not to make her leave
because she had made a very good impression in that school. I knew
the effect of changing schools many times and the consequences
it had on a small child. Moreover, Manushi used to stand first in
all the schools she joined. I had to repeatedly counsel Manushi to
learn to deal with the uncertainties of life, especially with envious
peers due to her excellent academic results. In Delhi, she joined an
NDMC (New Delhi Municipal Council) school, Navyug School,
in Laxmi Bai Nagar.

We could not meet her often. So, I used to make sure that I
wrote letters to her regularly, and I would also make BRB write
to her. I was particularly aware that she needed to be given the

correct perspective of the Maoist movement, and that she should feel responsible for the objectives of the PW. I used to send her letters with drawings showing how girls of her age were living in remote parts of Nepal. I used to write that at her present age (about fifteen), if she had been born in a Nepali village, she would have probably been married already, perhaps even become a mother. And, possibly, by thirty years of age even become a grandmother. I also wrote to her about how many people were watching her critically because she was privileged enough to continue her studies.

While being involved in the PW, I was concerned that our underground life and the vicissitudes of the inner party struggle would cause her to be dejected or alienated from the movement. Thankfully, she did not lose touch with the PW; she would write, translate works for the party, and eventually work with Nepali migrant workers in Delhi and Faridabad.

I remember having met my sister Timila's friend, Jhumur Lahiri, from IIT Kanpur, who was the only child in her family. I had asked her how she was brought up as a single child. She gave me a very important clue: she said that her respect for her parents and a sense of responsibility developed when she lost her father all of a sudden. She was a pampered kid when her father was alive. Both her parents did not find time to exchange thoughts and feelings with her. It was after her father passed away that her mother started sharing all her feelings and responsibilities with Jhumur. She said that adversity and sharing of responsibilities had empowered her even more. The struggle that accompanied the tragic events in her family created a stronger bond between the mother and daughter. I felt that Manushi, too, would learn to grow and become mature if we shared our feelings with her, gave responsibilities and exposed her to all the difficulties and risks of life.

After finishing her school, she joined LSR College in New Delhi to study political science. She really enjoyed the college atmosphere; its academic, as well as cultural and extra-curricular exposure and opportunities, enriched her personality further. Perhaps the kind of facilities I got at IIT, she got at LSR. She had initially wanted to major in economics but changed her mind after consulting Prof. Randhir Singh. At LSR, she had to pretend to be a Sikkimese girl. Because she was a good student, she was well respected amongst the students from the North-east who were proud of a 'North-east' girl achieving highest marks in the class.

I remember I somewhat had an intuition that someday her identity would be exposed and someone from her college would make a documentary film on her. I was pleasantly surprised when Surbhi Dewan, her senior from LSR, came to Nepal in 2008 and made a documentary about Manushi's underground life and her activities and experiences post-PW. This film, which she named *Daughter of Nepal*, was a part of her thesis for her degree in film-making from the USA.[3]

After Manushi graduated from college, we were a bit concerned about what she would decide to do in the future; would she choose to be politically active in Nepal or would she continue her studies in Delhi? We felt relieved when she decided to come back to Nepal and take active part in the students' movement in Tribhuvan University (TU), where she got enrolled for an MA in political science. It was a delightful coincidence that all three of us simultaneously took part in our first electoral tests and emerged victorious with flying colours: BRB got elected into the first CA from Gorkha with the highest votes and margin; I won a seat from Kathmandu; and Manushi won the students' union elections for the post of secretary with the highest votes in her panel. She was the first woman to be elected as a secretary in TU's students' representative body. The three of us were so immersed in politics that we hardly had time to meet or talk to each other on matters other than politics.

It was another proud moment for us when Manushi received a gold medal for being the topper in her university for her subject.

Moreover, she received them from her father when he was the PM of Nepal and the chancellor of TU. It was a rare sight.

In 2014, Manushi decided to take a short break from her full-time activism and pursue an MPhil/PhD at JNU. As I accompanied her to JNU for admission, I told myself: Never had I imagined that one day my daughter, who was conceived in JNU while BRB was doing his PhD, would be at the same place after thirty-four years (1980–2014) for her own PhD. Recently, a journalist working in Delhi showed me a photograph of her protesting in front of the Embassy of Nepal in Delhi in 2015 over the Nepali women's citizenship issue in the Constitution. That reminded me of our own good old student days when we also used to organize demonstrations in front of the Embassy of Nepal. I said to myself: Life has come a full circle!

Manushi also took the initiative to revive *Jhilko*, a Marxist quarterly journal that used to be edited by BRB in the 1980s but was discontinued after we joined the PW. She became the editor–publisher of its new version, *Raato Jhilko*, which was jointly launched by Prachanda, Jhala Nath Khanal—the then chairperson of the UML—and Prof. Maniklal Shrestha.

I hope the fact that I am writing about my daughter is not taken as a boastful exercise. Actually, I deliberately wrote about her to share how we, as parents, had to be sensitive and responsible even while being underground. We wanted to make sure, as far as possible, that she did not feel dejected or feel alienated from politics like many children of Maoist parents were prone to becoming because of the rigours of revolution that their parents faced. I had been witness to such apathy during the PW when some of our dedicated comrades' children revealed their disinterest towards and detachment from the movement through their body language, which I found rather sad and worrisome. I was particularly aware of Stalin's personal life.[4] The tragic suicide of his wife and the apolitical journey of their only daughter, Svetlana, abandoning her father to flee to America had left a deep impression on me. I did not want my daughter to lead that kind of life.

I am immensely thankful to Kayo, Stephen Mikesell, Bal Krishna Mansingh, Sherap, Manu Bhatnagar, Harihar Adhikari, Hari Pant and Sita Pant, who all helped in many ways to keep Manushi spirited, happy and healthy during difficult times. I am particularly thankful to the late Prof. Randhir Singh who convinced her and helped her to take up political science at LSR college. We have never coaxed her to take decisions, whether academic or political, nor have we interfered with her life. We always wanted to leave it up to Manushi (or Asmita or Astha) to be the person she wanted to be.

Apparently, Manushi means 'of the mind or intellect'; Asmita means 'pride or self-respect', and Astha means 'belief'. For us, she represents all these characteristics. I hope she lives up to what her names stand for. We had decided on the name 'Manushi' for our daughter well before she was born. BRB had bought a book, *Daughters of Karl Marx*, and presented it to both of us (while Manushi was still inside my womb) with the text 'for Manushi' written inside. I was very touched by his gesture. Unfortunately, before Manushi could lay her hands on the book, some friend flicked it. We were desperately hunting for the book, but we could not even buy a new copy.

Later, it was Surbhi who found the new edition of *Daughters of Karl Marx* and brought it to us while she was shooting the documentary. She had remembered how we had regretted not being able to find the lost book. BRB was elated to get the book and presented it to Manushi.

This time, she received the book with her own hands because she was out of the womb!

37

Army Integration and State Restructuring

catch-22

The PW in Nepal was unique in the sense that, unlike the Russian Revolution or the Chinese Revolution, the Nepali Maoist revolution did not result in a complete victory. In Nepal, the revolutionaries had to negotiate with the parliamentary forces to topple monarchy, form an interim government and draft a new Constitution. Thus, it was a half-baked revolution in a way. This was in stark contrast to what happened in China in 1945.[1] During the Chinese Revolution, Mao did make an offer for negotiation with Chiang Kai-shek to form an interim government. However, when Chiang-Kai-shek refused the offer, Mao was forced to take up a decisive battle, defeating the opposition completely. In Nepal's case, the two warring forces—the PLA and the RNA—were locked in a stalemate when both sides felt that nobody was winning. Hence, a common agreement was reached between the Maoist party and the SPA to break this deadlock and fight in unison against the monarchy. Accordingly, the twelve-point understanding created an objective background for army integration and state restructuring.

This led to marked transformations in the character, agenda and programmes of both the CPN (Maoist) and the parliamentary parties. As far as the Maoists were concerned, the PW had transmuted into the CPA; ideas of revolutionary transformation had mutated into radical reform; the new democratic revolution had transformed into a quest for an inclusive democracy; the proportional electoral system adopted in the Maoist base areas during the PW had transformed into the mixed electoral system; and federalization based on regional and oppressed nationality functioning under the Maoist parallel state paved the way for federal restructuring based on the five factors of 'identity' and four factors of 'capability'.[2]

Regarding the SPA, particularly the NC and the UML, their pursuit of a second joint people's movement led to the CPA; evolutionary transformation translated into radical reform; neoliberal democracy was forced to accommodate inclusive democracy; the FPTP system was replaced by a mixed electoral system; and, finally, a centralized and unitary state structure under the monarchy was transformed into a federal state under a democratic republic.

The understanding reached regarding the peace process hinged on keeping the two armies, the PLA and the RNA, under the supervision of the UN, or any such reliable international body, during the CA elections to be held after the end of the monarchy. The Maoists insisted that both the agendas—army integration and Constitution-making—must be carried out simultaneously. However, it was in the interest of status-quoists and parliamentary parties to see the army integration happen first so that Maoist armed forces could be nullified as quickly as possible. They were in no hurry to promulgate a new Constitution through the CA. For the Maoist party, state restructuring involving federalism was strategically more important. Therefore, they wanted a new Constitution to be promulgated within a stipulated time, so that they could gain the upper hand politically.

The eight-point agreement[3] reached between the Maoists and the SPA in June 2006 provided the basis for making a formal request to the UN to assist in the management and monitoring of the armies of both parties. Accordingly, a letter jointly signed by the head of the government and the chairperson of the Maoist party was sent to the UN.[4] All these ultimately led to the signing of the historic CPA on 21 November 2006. Seven cantonments were chosen in various parts of Nepal for the PLA. Arms and ammunition were stored inside these cantonments under the supervision of the United Nations Mission in Nepal (UNMIN). Similarly, an equal number of NA personnel and their arms and ammunition were kept inside various barracks of the NA under the UNMIN's supervision.

In the beginning, around 32,250 combatants were camped in various cantonments.[5] The Maoist party had skilfully chosen some senior combatants and political commissars and deployed them in Kathmandu and other districts to lead the party's youth organization, YCL. These senior combatants had not only been replaced by other militia members, but many fake combatants had been enlisted in cantonments. During the time that I was the assistant in-charge of the Newa province, I had seen many members of the industrial workers' front join the combatants in the barracks.[6] When the UNMIN was given the task of verifying PLA members, it registered those combatants who were eligible for army integration. Out of the total number of disqualified PLA members, 4009 were discharged on the ground that they were 'child' combatants, the rest were disqualified as 'new' recruits. Many took compensations ranging from Rs 5 lakh to Rs 8 lakh and left the camp.[7] Many took vocational training like mobile repair and computer training; some decided to take up formal education inside the cantonments. However, the NC and the UML continued to bicker about the number of qualified combatants who had arrived and ultimately consented to integrate only 6050.[8] Ultimately, in the final stage of army integration, only 1422 PLA members got integrated, out of which 104 were women soldiers.

It was disappointing that the number of PLA combatants dropped considerably when it came to army integration. I was particularly disturbed when many women combatants were not integrated. According to Kamla Naharki, a brigade commander, many women combatants, within six years of staying in the cantonment, got married and gave birth to children, leaving them 'unfit' for army integration. Another reason behind the reduced number of combatants was disagreements and objections within the Maoist party regarding the entire peace process. At the same time, instead of dealing with the discontent of PLA members head on and offering them the correct orientation about the changes in Maoist strategy after signing the peace agreement, Prachanda took to cajoling them by saying that army integration was only a sham to hoodwink the reactionaries. In fact, the NA leaked a video of Prachanda's speech made inside a PLA cantonment, where he was declaring that army integration was only a step taken to prepare for another war. This made the whole peace process look questionable and dubious to the rest of the world.[9]

At the same time, many leaders of the parliamentary parties were opposed to the army integration as it was looked down upon as a sell-out to the Maoists.[10] As the minister of physical planning and works, I personally experienced how some NC ministers tried to make the implementation of the CPA difficult by dilly-dallying about providing necessary infrastructure in the cantonments. I found this very strange and contradictory; G.P. Koirala, the then PM, needed the PLA as a guard against the RNA since the monarchy had not been abolished before the CA elections. However, at the same time, the NC and the UML were anxious that the Maoists might win in the upcoming CA elections with the strength of the PLA. Even after the first CA elections, army integration had not taken place. The longer it took to integrate both the armies, the more the PLA were humiliated for having emptied the government's coffer by overstaying in the cantonments, which in reality was not even their fault.

UNMIN, too, was dragged into controversy by former chief of the army Rookmangud Katawal,[11] who alleged that UN representatives were sympathetic to the Maoists.[12] On the other hand, the Maoists were not happy with the UNMIN for not putting enough pressure on the parliamentary parties to implement the CPA. As army integration dragged on, there was fear of increasing external interference from neighbouring countries, particularly India.

Finally, army integration in Nepal took place on 10 April 2012, six years after the initiation of the peace process.[13] Originally, it was supposed to be concluded within six months of confining the PLA and NA in cantonments. Although it got dragged, Nepal's peace process had been exceptional because it was a truly home-made solution.

Federalism turned out to be the most debated issue during the Constitution-making process.[14] The rationale behind the struggle for federalism was to restructure the state in order to empower people belonging to various nationalities, cultural, lingual and regional groups, who had historically been marginalized and oppressed under a feudal, unitary and centralized state structure. This meant effecting fundamental changes in the old political, social, cultural and economic order.

After the first CA elections, a common understanding was reached to ascertain the theoretical basis of formulating a federal structure.[15] Restructuring of the state along federal lines would be based on the five factors of 'identity'—nationality/ ethnicity, language, culture, geographical and regional continuity and history—and four factors of 'capability'— economic interrelationships and capability, status and potential for infrastructure development, availability of natural resources, and administrative feasibility. Based on this understanding, the CA Committee on State Restructuring and Distribution of State Power proposed a fourteen-province model through majority voting. However, contentions regarding the names, number and demarcation of the federal units surfaced alongside complaints that 'capability' factors had been overlooked. This led to the formation of the High-Level State Restructuring Commission mandated by the interim Constitution. The commission recommended the reduction of fourteen provinces into ten units by reallocating the territory of four provinces into proposed neighbouring provinces. However, sharp divisions continued to exist between those who placed an emphasis on identity and those who considered capability as the core factor for federal restructuring. The failure of political parties to reconcile their differences subsequently led to the expiration of the CA's term. Thus, the first CA expired on 28 May 2012 without giving birth to a new Constitution.

The irony is that when the Maoists were struggling to establish identity-based federalism during the Constitution-making process, the allegations from the NC and the UML were that the Maoists had abandoned class issues. Whereas, during the days of armed struggle, when class issues were gaining momentum, the same political forces used to accuse the Maoists of using oppressed women, Adivasi Janajatis and Dalits as mere cannon fodder for winning the war.

The problem was that the parliamentary parties had no sense of ownership as far as federalism was concerned. The agenda of federal restructuring was considered to be a purely Maoist agenda. Thus, it was dragged and prolonged to sap the energy of the Maoist party. Ultimately, federalism was left hanging mid-air while the Maoists were the largest force in the CA.

In the second CA elections, the Maoist party, the chief exponent of progressive change, was placed at third position. The NC and the UML, together with other parties, won more than two-third seats in the CA. They formed a coalition government. The first time that the wings of federalism and progressive agendas were clipped was when the NC and the UML prohibited the formation of caucuses for women and ethnic nationalities.

In the first CA, the caucuses had played a key role in building consensus among CA members belonging to different political parties but similar communities. In addition to this, the NC and the UML reached a nine-point agreement by excluding the Maoists and unilaterally presented their proposal for the restructuring of the state, which was against the spirit of both the restructuring committee and the commission. It advocated the formation of seven administrative divisions, reminiscent of the five development regions adopted by the authoritarian Panchayat system. The essence of inclusion and proportionate representation was heavily diluted with only certain token provisions for women and Dalits in the legislative body. The parliamentary system was reasserted with minor reforms. BRB, in his capacity as the chairperson of the CPDCC (Constitutional-Political Dialogue and Consensus Committee), did not accept the joint proposal of the NC and the UML in his committee, as it went against the Constitutional process and the spirit of consensus. Against the unilateral nine-point proposal presented by the NC and the UML, the Maoists formed an alliance of thirty political parties to protest against superficial restructuring of the state.

The long stalemate finally ended after the devastating earthquake shook many parts of the nation in 2015, leading to a sixteen-point agreement in June 2015. Four political parties— NC, UML, UCPN (Maoist) and Madhesi Janadhikar Forum (Loktantrik)—sat down and signed the agreement on the main contentious topics of the new Constitution. The parties agreed on setting up six provincial units, a bicameral federal Parliament, a unicameral Provincial Assembly, a local government with a mixed electoral system, a parliamentary system of governance with the prime minister as executive head and a Constitutional president.

According to the understanding among the major parties, the formation of the six provinces would be based on multiple identities. The eastern province was to be formed by clubbing two previously proposed regions: Kirat and Limbuwan. The middle province would constitute Newa and Tamsaling regions. The south-eastern province would constitute Mithila and Bhojpura regions. The western and mid-western province would be formed by clubbing Avadh, Tamuwan and a part of the Magarat and Tharu regions. And the far-western province would constitute Seti–Mahakali and Bheri–Karnali regions.

The provisions of this agreement, particularly the formation of the six provinces, were met with intense protests. People of the far-western and middle-western regions, the hotbed of the PW, were the most displeased. People of the Magarat region were unhappy that the region where Magars resided in majority had been divided—one part clubbed with Tamuwan, the other with Tharuwan and another with Khasan.

I felt happiest when the people of the Bheri–Karnali region revolted against their amalgamation with the Seti–Mahakali region.[16] Coming from the oppressed Newar community, I was most excited to watch federalism unfold. During the course of their struggle, they were able to achieve a separate province, leading to the formation of seven provinces. We had supported their demand.

Similarly, the Maoist party fought for incorporating Kailali and Kanchanpur districts, with the oppressed Tharu community in majority, within the Tharuwan province. The party even submitted a note of dissent when it was not heeded in the CA. We felt happy to see all party leaders of the Tharu community coming out on the streets, demanding a separate province. This reinforced the essence and significance of federalism. Now, people from oppressed communities were not only spontaneously accepting this agenda but also rigorously fighting for it. However, it was infuriating that some of the senior Maoist leaders took sides with the *Akhanda Sudur Paschim* (undivided far-west) campaign, going against the spirit of giving political space and power to the Tharus in

Tharu-dominated areas. The Constitution of Nepal was finally promulgated on 16 September 2015 based on this sixteen-point agreement with a few changes. For instance, six provinces were changed to seven. Provinces were given numbers and no names; names would be decided by the elected assembly later. Madhesi and Janajati groups, however, were not satisfied with the numbers, boundaries and the names.

Apart from federal restructuring, we also had to fight for the rights of the oppressed classes, gender, Muslim and Dalit communities during the final days of drafting the Constitution. Our fight for constitutional provisions for women was consistent and yielded some positive outcomes. We had our own share of struggle to attain 33 per cent reservation for women in the legislative body. We also protested against the provision for citizenship, whereby right to citizenship by descent is only through both mother *and* father. As the head of the women's department of the party, I was spearheading the fight for citizenship in the mother's name in coordination with other party leaders and non-partisan campaigners. The ultra-nationalists both inside our party and outside were advocating the provision of 'mother *and* father' as a measure required for protecting Nepali sovereignty.

During the final hours of the Constitution's promulgation, there was a lot of pressure to declare the country a Hindu state. Prachanda had already succumbed to replacing the word 'secularism' with 'religious freedom'. It was through consistent interventions of the Adivasi Janajati CA members and BRB's grit that the final draft of the Constitution proclaimed Nepal to be a secular state.[17] A new Constitution standing on four pillars—republic, federalism, secularism and inclusive democracy—was finally in our hands on 16 September 2015.

However, people of the Tharu and Madhesi communities continued to protest against the new Constitution for diluting the federal agenda. Now that a new Constitution had been sanctioned by the CA with an overwhelming majority, a new phase of political activity was anticipated.

One wondered if the next era would be 'new wine in a new bottle' or 'new wine in an old bottle'.

38

Some Reflections

will the oppressed rise?

During the 1980s, I remember the LTTE's activities in Sri Lanka were increasingly being talked about in the news. I used to think how peaceful Nepal was. Little did I know that one day I myself would be part of an armed struggle, and that I would be tagged as a terrorist with a bounty on my head (according to the media, Rs 25 lakh).[1] Once the PW was initiated, little had I reckoned that the war would end so soon. I had seen similar armed struggles being waged for years and decades in different countries. In India, the armed struggle led by the CPI (Maoist) had been going on for the last forty years.

Time seemed to fly very quickly when I was involved in the PW. When I look back at those ten years, I feel as if it were a three-hour-long movie where the heroes, heroines and villains were portrayed with exaggeration and accelerated actions to convey the message of the PW.

If one were to view all the main characters of the PW in a good light, then Prachanda represented the 'heart' for the cadres; he gave them a sense of security and comfort, mesmerizing them with his hypnotic sermons to bring down the old feudal state. BRB represented the 'head' for them; he gave cadres scientific vision, clarity of thought and imparted a sense of direction to the movement during and after the PW. Kiran represented the 'kidney'; filtering and keeping intact the organizational system with purist classical teachings of Marxism–Leninism–Maoism.

If one were to look at them through critical lenses, then Prachanda, according to me, represented a petty, bourgeois leader who seemed to love being at the helm of activities at all times and in every place. BRB was a bookworm and an idealist leader who loved ideological work more than the nitty-gritties of organizational tasks. And Kiran represented a confused, old rhetorical revolutionary whose actions nearly always brought about opposite effects.

Similarly, if one were to delve into how the PW positively affected the masses, then I had seen with my own eyes how the underdogs, poor marginalized men and women living in remote areas, if given a chance, could become the finest builders, organizers, engineers, leaders, fighters and artists. I also saw a leap in mass mobilization, development of leadership quality and productivity of oppressed communities when they were encouraged to build various mass organizations that addressed extra-class issues.

In terms of the adverse effects of the inner party struggles, I had observed how the tendency to deify Prachanda was produced and propagated in the Maoist movement, and how conspiratorial means were adopted to suppress the voice of dissidents. I had witnessed how the ruling class within the Maoist party resorted to the same method of punishment as that of the old state against those they suspected on the basis of little or no evidence.

From the oppressed ethnicities' and regional perspective, the PW helped raise their consciousness as well as gave them power to claim their autonomous states. However, in the present Constitution, their rights have not been adequately addressed. If one were to look at the PW from the gender perspective, then it is quite evident that it created hell for the feudal, patriarchal family structure. The PW enabled the Khas Arya, Adivasi Janajati,

Dalit, Muslim, Madhesi and Tharu women to emerge from the hearth and be at the heart of the PW. The PW not only expanded their horizon but also expanded their political understanding. The peace process further enabled women's participation in state affairs. However, it is equally true that post the PW, their number and position within the party, state and security forces started dwindling. This was particularly seen during the army integration, when women PLA members were considerably reduced.

And finally, if I were to look at the PW purely in terms of my personal experience, then I must say that it pushed me to understand Nepali society from a holistic perspective. It made me resilient. To some extent, I learnt to shed my original class position in this society. It taught me to be political. However, I also had a tough time adjusting to the vocabulary, lexicon and characteristic style of speech inside the communist party. I had been criticized for not sufficiently quoting Marx, Lenin, Stalin, Mao, and even Prachanda, while delivering a political class or writing articles. I had been told to minimize my own feelings and opinions while speaking or writing.

I must emphasize that the PW was not only about power and politics; it was also about social and cultural transformations. It was a way of solving contradictions between the old and new ways of life. The heroes/heroines and villains were all human beings with merits and demerits. It was just a matter of who played a progressive or regressive role when the actors of history were called forth to do their duties; to lift their society/country from one epoch to the other. Hence, I have no personal grudge against political actors, be it Prachanda, Kiran, BRB or even Gyanendra.

This is because one should not locate the weaknesses of people in their character but in their class background. And class basis in Nepal is predominantly petty peasantry. Hence, many opportunists and counter-revolutionaries in different forms will continue to haunt the communist movement in Nepal. It is a historical fact that in China, it came in the form of Lin Biao who nearly killed

Mao. In the USSR, it came in the form of Fanya Kaplan who tried to assassinate Lenin.

Another important thing to note is that in Nepal, revolutions were always left halfway. The anti-Rana movement was left in the lurch after the Delhi Agreement. It was a tripartite agreement between the NC, the Ranas and King Tribhuvan to do away with the 104-year-old Rana oligarchic rule and to replace it with the coalition government of the three forces to bring in multiparty democracy. The NC's fight for democracy was soon reduced to *melmilap*, a so-called national 'reconciliation' with the king. The Jhapa revolt against the feudal lords could hardly last five years before its leaders became junior partners to the NC. Even the most deep-rooted Maoist PW had to make a political compromise in the form of the CPA. Thus, all transformative movements of Nepal remained unfinished.

Nepal may be materially poor, but it has a rich history of left-wing politics. However, like in many developing countries, in Nepal, too, when one becomes a Marxist it is often not out of choice but out of necessity. It is important to realize that ideological supremacy alone is not enough, it has to be tied with economic development and educational and cultural upliftment. It is only when Marxism is accepted as a product of choice that it becomes creative, dynamic, long-lasting, with new possibilities brought out.

If one were to observe the political chronology of the ten years of the PW, the first five years were devoted to exposing the lacunae of the parliamentary system and its parties. Monarchy was initially lurking behind, while the parliamentary parties were at the forefront in their fight against the Maoists. During this period, it was Kiran's line that generally prevailed in the Maoist party. The next five years of the PW were devoted to strengthening democratic issues. Monarchy came into direct confrontation with the Maoists after the royal massacre in 2001. By then, a triangular struggle between the Maoists, parliamentary parties and the monarchy had transformed into a unique struggle whereby the Maoists and parliamentary parties came together to defeat the monarchy. In this second half of the PW, BRB's line prevailed in the party.

Entering the peace process was more painful for the Maoists than waging a war. From one ideology, one-party system and monolithic thinking, they now had to deal with many ideologies, different parties and diverse ways of thinking. Yet another contradiction we had to face was that on the one hand, the so-called democratic forces had been trying to build a perception that waging the PW was a crime; on the other hand, the dogmatic communists had been creating an impression that nothing had been achieved through the PW.

The challenge today is to seek a new path, build a new force where the spirit of 'Development of Democracy in the 21st Century' can be practised, where the spirit of economic leap is economic growth, as well as inclusive, participatory and sustainable development so that a strong base for moving towards sustainable socialism is built.

Democracy has to be accompanied by the development of productive forces. This is also important because by now a majority of ex-PLA combatants and party cadres have been compelled to leave the country in search of employment in various parts of the world, particularly in the Gulf countries, as labourers.[2] Most of the women whole-timers have been pushed back into household duties. Today, I am deeply disturbed to see women petering out to being confined to their kitchens and maternal tasks. Many are economically dependent on their husbands. Most women at the party's central level are surviving. However, the further we go down the structure, the more women's presence in the party diminishes. Similarly, discrimination against Dalits has surfaced again.[3] Many inter-caste marriages, particularly those involving Dalits, are breaking down. Nationality/ethnicity issues are increasingly being portrayed as divisive agendas undermining class issues.[4] Those fighting against regional oppression in remote parts of Nepal have themselves become Kathmandu-centric, owning houses in Kathmandu. A conflict can arise in the future if ethnic and regional oppression are not addressed. Similarly, TRC, if not effectively implemented in time, may lead to renewed conflict.

This objective condition may lead the three dominant tendencies in the Maoist movement in three separate directions. First, the power-centric tendency represented by Prachanda could align or merge with the old status-quoist forces, such as the UML. Second, the dogmatist tendency represented by Kiran–Biplab may attempt to continue along the path of the old communist movement. And third, the creative, dynamic tendency represented by BRB may attempt to create a new alternative force and move along a new progressive path.

Subjectively, I feel sad to see so many of my comrades-in-arms dead, 'disappeared', or maimed, and to see hard-won achievements petering out on the other hand. I also see that a lot needs to be done to safeguard past achievements and move forward towards inclusive development and democracy.

As I reflect on my life, I consider myself to have lived through diverse experiences. I lived like a free bird; I lived an academic life, an urban life, a rural life, an underground life and am now living an open, political life. I have been a globetrotter, a tunnel-trotter, a night-trotter. I have also been a yoga freak throughout!

I consider myself to have lived a fuller life than BRB. I have gone through depression and failure in the second CA elections, which BRB never experienced. I had high points in my life, too. I was declared best sportswoman at SPA in 1980; I was declared woman of the year (1990) by, *Antarashtriya Manch*; I won the elections to the first CA; I was elected to the Nepal Engineers' Association as its treasurer; and I headed three ministries.

As I flip through my personal diaries, which I had maintained before the PW started, what stands out is that my struggle had always been with BRB—to assert my independent stand, to reclaim my own identity. I had even thought I might divorce BRB at some point because of my gender-sensitive outlook. Never had I expected that my own party would divorce me for six months because of inner party struggle. In fact, that political divorce brought BRB and me closer than before, both ideologically and personally.

One day, Manushi told me, 'Ama, you are so lucky to make history. Your generation has abolished monarchy in this country. I don't think history will ever give our generation a chance to bring another radical change in this country.'

I replied, 'Every revolution is followed by counter-revolution at some point or the other. The point is to check it and move ahead. Your generation has the task of fighting against counter-revolution.'

Lastly, let me share my belief in simple words.

I 'love' capitalists for undermining the poor.

I 'love' communists for underrating the strength of diversity.

I 'love' men for underestimating women.

And I 'love' women for undervaluing themselves.

I truly believe that as long as poverty and oppression exist, patriarchy will prevail. And, as long as patriarchy persists, poverty and oppression will prevail.[5]

Hence, our journey to complete liberation is long and continuous.

I was on the streets before the PW started.

I am back on the streets again.

And I will continue to be on the streets.

This is because at the end of the day, women throughout the world, no matter how powerful they are, are like the Statue of Liberty: liberated with her hand stretched out but chained to the earth just like her feet are, which most people hardly notice.

No matter how many movements come and go, the poor, the oppressed and women are the last to be liberated. Hence, women must strive for continuous revolution till they are completely liberated.

I still remember BRB provoking me with his question in 1977: 'What is your aim in life?' I had replied: 'Why have an aim in life? Let life flow freely.'

Today, my counter-reply would be: 'Can women afford to let their life flow freely?'

It was with this and other such questions in mind that I went to attend the Eurasian Women's Forum on 'Towards Peace, Harmony and Social Well-Being' in St. Petersburg, Russia, in September 2015.

Epilogue

new beginning

I got a call from BRB while I was in Russia on 27 September 2015. I had just landed in Moscow after participating in the Eurasian Women's Forum at St. Petersburg. BRB informed me that he had resigned from the party.

It was sudden news. But I was not surprised.

A day before this phone call, on 26 September 2015, BRB had already announced at a press meet that he had left the UCPN (Maoist) for good.[1] He also stated that he had resigned from the Legislature–Parliament.

This triggered shock waves inside the UCPN (Maoist), which was caught unaware. Prachanda was shocked, too, since BRB was breaking off thirty years of alliance in one stroke. It came as a big surprise to other parties as well. The general public reacted with astonishment. Articles, commentaries, editorials and social-media chats were full of reactions, both for and against his move; some were confused, some bewildered and some hailed it.[2]

Soon after I returned to Nepal, I remember meeting a woman on our way to Gorkha, who approached BRB suddenly and scolded him, 'You silly, Baburam! Why did you leave the party and Parliament when you were going to be the country's next

President!' Such was the concern showed by people on the streets. There were also people who predicted that BRB would henceforth be reduced to a mere Marxist intellectual. From communist parties, particularly the UCPN (Maoist), came the same old predictable allegation that his resignation was the result of external forces.

It was natural for everyone to be shocked because he was one of the chief architects of the Constitution. For this agenda, he not only struggled within his party but also outside. He was the chairperson of the CPDCC. He was also the person instrumental in making the army integration a success. He was an ex-PM as well as the second most senior leader in the UCPN (Maoist). And, besides his political affiliation, he was also looked upon by many as one of the rare visionary leaders of his time.

What also drew attention was the manner in which he chose to resign from both the party and Parliament. He resigned all alone, without taking other friends who supported him during inner party struggles with him. He did not take recourse to the customary way of splitting the party. This was something that very few politicians dare to do. In fact, in communist movements, such resignations have not been taken kindly but with great suspicion.

As for me, I was glad that BRB had finally left Prachanda, who had always allied with or attacked BRB for his own personal motives and political gains. I was also glad that he had left the Maoist party, which had become Prachanda's tool to bargain for power with other political parties. Having seen him cheat on the inclusive democracy agenda, I became all the more convinced that we were doing the right thing. I had no doubt about BRB's vision, but I was sceptical about his capacity to build a new party at this advanced age. Being a woman belonging to an ethnic Newari community, who was against a monolithic way of thinking, I stood with him.

During the last days of finalizing a new Constitution, we were even more disturbed when Prachanda did not support our demand for extension of the deadline, so that the agitating Madhesi and

Tharu communities could be taken into confidence. As a result, the new Constitution did not adequately address the issues of Tharu and Madhesi people, as well as the concerns of women, hill indigenous nationalities and Dalits. In many aspects, the new Constitution had backtracked from the interim Constitution.[3]

On 19 February 2015, Prachanda had also abandoned the agenda of the directly elected executive presidential system with a fully proportionate legislature; a compromise was made to adopt a reformed parliamentary system. This was despite the fact that the proposal for a presidential system was one of the most popular demands that arose when the final Constitution draft was circulated among the people to collect public feedback before its promulgation. This overwhelming support for the presidential system should be seen in the light of the historical context in which a parliamentary system adopted in 1990 had resulted in numerous changes in government—twenty-four within twenty-six years (1990–2016)! To do away with this state of instability, an executive presidential system was long awaited.

Disgusted with Prachanda's opportunism, BRB had confided in me that he would soon resign from the party. But he had not disclosed when.

He decided to resign after the final promulgation of the new Constitution through the CA.[4] After putting his signature on the new Constitution, he declared to the media that it was like a 'half full and half empty glass'.[5]

At the time of his resignation, the UCPN (Maoist) was gearing up to form a government as the junior partner to the K.P. Oli-led government. The Terai region was burning because of protests against the new Constitution.[6] In fact, following the sixteen-point agreement reached between the four major parties after the deadly earthquake, the Madhesi-based parties had taken to the streets to protest the dilution of federalism. Meanwhile, India informally asked the government to take some time to address the Madhesi people's demand before promulgating the Constitution. However, when this was not heeded, India resorted to an indirect economic blockade, leaving the whole country gasping for petroleum products, medicine and other essential goods. The Madhesi movement escalated further.

BRB had warned beforehand that if the soon-to-be-promulgated Constitution did not address the grievances of the oppressed groups, the trouble might escalate. He had additionally cautioned that if the problem in Terai was not solved internally, the Indian establishment might fish in troubled waters, creating further complications. But not only were BRB's words disregarded, he was rebuked for stating the bitter truth. Later, the protests actually took a violent turn and around fifty people, including policemen, lost their lives in Terai.[7] This was more than the number of people who died in the first and second people's movement. The strike lasted for more than three months.

As in the past, the ruling parties were once again trying to play the game of pitting India against China and stirring 'nationalist' sentiments for their political benefit. The struggle between the Madhesi and hill people could have flared up into sectarian violence any time. Already people in Terai had been criticizing people in Kathmandu for being apathetic to their cause.[8] And people in Kathmandu had been condemning the Terai people for blockading essential goods at the Nepal-India border. What began as a struggle between an oppressed region and a centralized state structure took the shape of a nationalist struggle against India, which eventually overpowered the Madhesi agenda and pitted Nepal's own people against one another.

While working as the chairperson of the CPDCC, BRB had found the UML more unaccommodating and intolerant than the NC as far as federalism and inclusive agenda were concerned. He had seen signs of social fascism in K.P. Oli's attitude when he advocated the use of force against the Madhesi movement and indigenous nationalities instead of political dialogue. What shocked BRB more was Prachanda's stance; instead of fighting against Oli's autocratic attitude, he was meekly complying. For BRB, this was the last straw that broke the camel's back. He had been bearing Prachanda's opportunism for too long. On 25 September 2015, BRB had a final dialogue with Prachanda at the latter's residence in Lazimpat, Kathmandu. BRB proposed dissolving the Maoist party, which had completed its mission of institutionalizing the federal democratic republic despite its many flaws. He further proposed to build a New Socialist Party to suit the demands of the twenty-first century. Prachanda did not take this proposal seriously.[9]

After leaving Prachanda and the party, we started campaigning for an alternative socialist party based on inclusive and participatory democracy. Based on this, the Naya Shakti Party, Nepal, was formally launched on 12 June 2016. BRB became the convenor of the party.[10] Then, with a view to acquaint ourselves with the latest developments in human knowledge, science and technology, we undertook a trip to the best universities of Europe (22 July–8 August 2018) and USA (11 September–11 October 2018), interacting with top intellectuals, NRNs, think tanks and the people. Immediately after that we went on a first-hand, one-month-long study tour of rural Nepal along the mid-hill highway from Chiwa Bhanjyang in the far-east to Jhulaghat in the far-west (27 January–28 February 2019), meeting local representatives, leaders of all parties, the teachers, students, bureaucrats, intellectuals and the people. Later, on 6 May 2019, the Naya Shakti Party, Nepal, was united with the Federal Socialist Forum, Nepal, to form a socialist party under the slogan: 'Federalism, good governance, prosperity and socialism'.[11] The party was rechristened as People's Socialist Party, Nepal, after its unification with the Rashtriya Janata Party on 22 April 2020. The socialist polarization process may continue in the coming days. The Kiran–Biplab faction of the Maoist movement is now trying to continue on the old dogmatic path of communist movement.

Meanwhile, the CPN (Maoist) led by Prachanda merged with the UML to form the Nepal Communist Party on 17 May 2018.

It is interesting to note that Prachanda discarded Maoism and the 'Prachanda Path' to embrace 'Xi Jinping Thought'.

We had once again embarked upon a new journey!

It brought back memories of 1977, when I first met BRB. This reminds me of our marriage pledge in 1981, wherein we avowed to act 'as agents of progressive transformation of human society to higher formations with utmost sincerity.'

A new chapter in our relationship has started with a new mission in life.

As for me, another course of struggle has begun.

Acknowledgements

I went through some of the toughest and roughest times when I became the first lady. Attacks on me were mounting. I had been toying with the idea of writing a memoir, but I did not know when and how to start. Knowing my restless nature, BRB encouraged me to write. I found time when I lost in the second CA elections.

I then went to D.B. Gurung (who, unfortunately, has passed away) with my first few pages. He gave me some of his own books and shared his experiences of being a writer. It was finally Shrishti Rana who provided me with many books on memoir-writing and encouraged me to go ahead with writing this book. I am immensely thankful to these people.

I then came across Feizi Ismail who quickly went through my first draft and gave me her inputs. John Mage, too, helped me with this book in its initial phase. Mallika Shakya further encouraged me to add my personal experience of the massive earthquakes that took place while writing this book. Archana Thapa helped me in sharpening the gender perspective in this book. Lok Raj Baral and Aditya Adhikari provided valuable feedback. Anup Chapain fixed my computer issues and helped with my first draft. Dinesh Shrestha provided me with all the photos included in the book.

At the fag end, it was Mahendra Lawati who went through the book, questioned me on some of my generalized views and helped me concretize.

I am very grateful to them all.

I particularly want to thank Prashant Jha for guiding me through the publishing world and helping me find the best publishers for this book.

I am very thankful to the Penguin team of young women, headed by Meru Gokhale, for their patience and help in bringing out this book.

Many thanks to Manushi for her contributions in the final editing of this book.

Special thanks to BRB once again for helping me with fact-checking.

Notes

Preface

1. Rajendra Maharjan, 'Buddha, Marx, and Ambedkar', in Dr B.R. Ambedkar, *Buddha and Karl Marx*, ed. Rajendra Maharjan and Shiva Hari Gyawali, trans. Mahesh Raj Maharjan (Nepal: SAMATA Foundation, 2017), pp. 7–8; Mahapandit Rahul Sankrityayan (1963), *Dharmaratna 'Yami': Aaj ke Nepal ka Rajnitik Sipahi*, Shankar Bahadur K.C., Kathmandu.
2. 'Former Nepal Minister Bogati Dies', *The Hindu*, 15 September 2014, https://www.thehindu.com/news/international/ south-asia/former-nepal-minister-bogati-dies/article6412397.ece
3. For more, visit https://www.cia.gov/library/publications/the-world-factbook/ geos/np.html
4. The per capita GDP in Nepal was recorded at $1025.8 US dollars for 2018. For more, visit https://data.worldbank.org/indicator/ nY.gDP.PCAP.CD?locations=nP
5. Nepal received 699 billion (NPR) in remittances in 2016–17, whereas the annual budget for the fiscal year was Rs 1.049 trillion. For more, see 'Labour Migration for Employment: A Status Report for Nepal: 2015–16' (Kathmandu: Government of Nepal, Ministry of Labour and employment, 2018), p. 35; budget speech of the fiscal year 2016–17 (Government of Nepal,

Ministry of Finance, 28 May 2016, https://thehimalayantimes.
com/business/finance-minister-presents-budget-fy-201617-
parliament).

6. Bhim Rawal, 'The Communist Movement in Nepal: Origin
   and Development' (Kathmandu: Achham-Kathmandu Contact
   Forum, Communist Party of Nepal [UML], 2007), pp. 91–95.

7. For more, visit https://www.ohchr.org/Documents/Countries/
   NP/OHCHR_Nepal_Conflict_Report2012.pdf

8. *Nepal Peace and Development Strategy 2010–2015* (Pulchowk,
   Kathmandu: United Nations Resident and Humanitarian
   Coordinator's Office, January 2011), p. 26.

9. 'Comprehensive Peace Accord Signed between Nepal
   Government and the Communist Party of Nepal (Maoist)', 22
   November 2006, https://peacemaker.un.org/sites/peacemaker.
   un.org/files/NP_061122_Comprehensive%20Peace%20
   Agreement%20between%20the%20Government%20and%20
   the%20CPN%20%28Maoist%29.pdf

10. Hisila Yami, *People's War and Women's Liberation in Nepal*
    (Purvaiya Prakashan, Raipur, 2006).

11. For more, visit http://www.searo.who.int/entity/emergencies/
    documents/ nepal-earthquake-a-vision-for-resilience.pdf

12. The signatory parties were the UCPN (Maoist), Nepali Congress
    (NC), Communist Party of Nepal (Unified Marxist–Leninist)
    [CPN (UML)] and Madhesi Janadhikar Forum–Loktantrik
    (MJF–L). See Joanna Jolly, 'Will Nepal's Earthquake Bring
    Historic Change?', BBC News, 9 June 2015, https://www.bbc.
    com/news/world-asia-33067693

13. The Madhesis are one of the major oppressed nationalities of
    Nepal, who reside in the southern plains.

14. Charles Haviland, 'Why Is Nepal's New Constitution
    Controversial?', BBC news, 19 September 2015, https://www.
    bbc. com/news/world-asia-34280015

15. Ross Adkin, 'Nepal Adopts Constitution Born of Bloodshed,
    Compromise', Reuters, 20 September2015, https://www.reuters.
    com/article/us-nepal-constitution/nepal-adopts-constitution-
    born-of-bloodshed-compromise-idUSKCn0RK0LU20150920

16. Utpal Parashar, 'Former Nepal PM Baburam Bhattarai Launches New Party', *Hindustan Times* (Kathmandu), 12 June 2016, https://www.hindustantimes.com/world/former-nepal-pm-baburam-bhattarai-launches-new-party/story-9UJ2zK4R963gindWQusa2K.html

Part I: The Beginning

Chapter 1: 'Why Have an Aim in Life?'

1. Coomi Kapoor, *The Emergency: A Personal History* (Penguin Viking, 2015).
2. Maninder Dabas, 'Here's the Story of "Double Seven", the Sarkari Cola That Was Launched for "Achhe Din" In 1977', updated 23 May 2017, https://www.indiatimes.com/news/india/here-s-the-story-of-double-seven-the-sarkari-cola-that-was-launched-for-achhe-din-in-1977_-322249.html
3. Sanjoy Hazarika, 'Morarji Desai Dies at 99; Defeated Indira Gandhi to Become Premier of India', *New York Times*, 11 April 1995, https://www.nytimes.com/1995/04/11/obituaries/morarji-desai-dies-at-99-defeated-indira-gandhi-to-become-premier-of-india.html
4. A brief history of *Manushi* is available at http://manushi-india.org/brief-history.htm
5. Published in *Janamanas*, Year 2, Volume 1.2 (1979).
6. Arun Kumar Biswas, 'IIT Kanpur Formative Years: Some Recollections, Residents and Visitors', 2010, https://www.iitk.ac.in/doaa/convocation/data/IIT_KAnPUR_ FORMATIVe_YeARS.pdf
7. S.D. Kapur, 'Nepal: A Country in Crisis', *Outlook*, 2 June 2001, https://www.outlookindia.com/website/story/nepal-a-country-in-crisis/211806
8. BS is Bikram Sambat, a way to mark dates according to the Hindu calendar in Nepal, starting from 1901 AD (or 1958 BS).
9. The Ranas were oligarchic Kunwar Chhetris, one of the courtiers of the Shah kings of Nepal. In 1846, Jung Bahadur Kunwar

staged a violent coup, which eliminated all other courtiers of the palace, introducing hereditary prime ministership under the Shah monarchy. Later on, they changed their titles to Ranas, linking their lineage to the Rajput rulers of Rajasthan. Shah kings were called 'Shree Panch' and the Ranas were called 'Shree Tin'. Later, in 1951, a democratic movement overthrew the Rana regime.

10. Timila Yami Thapa (2046 BS), 'Dharma Ratna "Yami" Smriti Granth', Kathmandu.

Chapter 2: Black Flag, Dharnas, Toy Pistol Revolt

1. Later on, he went on to become chairman of the Nepal Airlines Corporation. At the same time, when I became the minister of tourism and civil aviation, he also became a board member of the Nepal Rastra Bank. For more, visit https://www.nrb.org.np/

2. Durga Subedi (2075 BS), *Biman Bidroha: Euta Rajnitik Apaharan ko Bayan* (Kitab Publishers, Kathmandu).

3. For more, visit https://www.thehindu.com/thehindu/2001/07/29/stories/13290171.htm

4. Please note that he gave a counter statement, but we do not have the copy with us now.

5. Philip Baum, *Violence in the Skies: A History of Aircraft Hijacking and Bombing* (Summersdale Publishers, UK, 2016).

6. Sayami, a medical student from Jabalpur, later became the dean of the Institute of Medicine, Kathmandu, in 2007. See Dr Arun Sayami (2075 BS), *Mero Jeewan–Katha*, editor Bimal Bhaukaji.

Chapter 3: 'Why Do You Come Here?'

1. Mahapandit Rahul Sankrityayan (1963), *Dharmaratna 'Yami': Aaj ke Nepal ka Rajnitik Sipahi*, Shankarbahadur K.C., Kathmandu. Rahul Sankrityayan was an Indian scholar who was also known as 'Mahapandit', meaning greatest scholar. He was known for travelling widely. He taught Buddhism and Marxism to my father when they were in Tibet. My father must have met him in Tibet between 1932 and 1939, the period he was there to work.

Chapter 4: Victim of Underdevelopment

1. Durga Subedi (2075 BS), *Biman Bidroha: Euta Rajnitik Apaharan ko Bayan* (Kitab Publishers Prali, Kathmandu).
2. Harischandra Lal Singh, *Nepal in Records: A Collection of Facts and Principal Events of Nepal in Various Aspects Classified by Subjects in a Chronological Order* (Educational Publishing House, Kathmandu, 2007).
3. Yam Bahadur Kisan, Gopal Nepali (2014 BS), *Badi of Nepal*, published by Central Department of Sociology/Anthropology.
4. The Baadis had been given land by the government for their rehabilitation.
5. Timila Yami Thapa (2064 BS), *Dharma Ratna 'Yami' Smriti Granth* (Kathmandu).
6. In 1985, Nepal's under-five child mortality rate was 176.3 per 1000 live births, which was among the highest in the world according to IndexMundi.
7. Jagadish Sharma, *Nepal: Struggle for Existence*, Communications Inc., Kathmandu, 2006.

Chapter 5: People's Movement against the Panchayat Regime

1. 'Paras Shah', *Nepali Times*, 11 August 2000, http://archive.nepalitimes.com/news.php?id=11290#.YFLZEq8zbIU
2. Kiyoko Ogura (2001), *Kathmandu Spring: The People's Movement of 1990* (Himal Books, Lalitpur).
3. Abortion was illegal in Nepal until 2002.
4. After my mother, Heera Devi Yami, passed away in 1970, my father married Savitri Dahal, a Brahmin from Okhaldhunga district.
5. Ogura, *Kathmandu Spring*.
6. Ibid.
7. Harischandra Lal Singh, *Nepal in Records* (Educational Publishing House, Kathmandu, 2007).
8. Pushpa Kamal Dahal, *Problems & Prospects of Revolution in Nepal: A Collection of Articles by Com. Prachanda and Other Leaders of the CPN (Maoist)* (Janadisha Publications, Nepal, 2004).

9. Ibid.
10. Rosemary Sullivan, *Stalin's Daughter: The Extraordinary and Tumultuous Life of Svetlana Alliluyeva* (4th Estate, London, 2015).

Chapter 6: Bout of Depression in the UK

1. Hisila Yami, dissertation for MSc, 'Gender Issues in Nepal: The Case of Ghalchowk and Madhabalia Rural Resettlement Projects', December 1994.
2. Jon Henley, 'Tories: Mess with Milk at Your Peril', *Guardian*, 9 August 2010, https://www.theguardian.com/society/2010/aug/09/free-milk-schools-tories
3. Yami, 'Gender Issues in Nepal'.
4. Harischandra Lal Singh, *Nepal in Records* (Educational Publishing House, Kathmandu, 2007).
5. Julia Lovell, *Maoism: A Global History* (Bodley Head, London, 2019).

Chapter 7: 'Sorry, We Will Have to Leave This house!'

1. Dr Baburam Bhattarai (2063 BS), *Rajnaitik Arthashashtrako Aankhijhyalbata* (Janadhwani, Kathmandu), p. 76.
2. Julia Lovell, *Maoism: A Global History* (Bodley Head, London, 2019).
3. Pushpa Kamal Dahal, 'Down with Parliamentarism! Long Live New Democracy!' in *Problems & Prospects of Revolution in Nepal: A Collection of Articles by Com. Prachanda and Other Leaders of the CPN (Maoist)* (Janadisha Publications, Nepal, 2004); See also Shuvashankar Kandel (2065 BS), *Maobadi: Bidroha, Bibad ra Rupantaran* (Pairavi Prakashan, Kathmandu).
4. Harischandra Lal Singh, *Nepal in Records* (Educational Publishing House, Kathmandu, 2007).
5. Deepak Thapa with Bandita Sijapati, *A Kingdom Under Siege: Nepal's Maoist Insurgency, 1996 to 2003* (The Printhouse, Kathmandu, 2003).

6. Hisila Yami, *People's War and Women's Liberation in Nepal* (Purvaiya Prakashan, Raipur, 2006).

7. For more, visit https://www.hrw.org/reports/2004/nepal1004/2.htm

8. Kandel, *Maobadi*; *European Bulletin of Himalayan Research*, special double issue, 'Revolutionary Nepal', no. 33–34 (Autumn 2008–Spring 2009), published from Kathmandu in collaboration with Social Science Baha, http://www.digitalhimalaya.com/collections/journals/ebhr/index.php?selection=33; Deepak Thapa (ed.), *Understanding the Maoist Movement of Nepal* (Kathmandu, Martin Chautari, 2003), pp. 391, first published in Dr Baburam Bhattarai, *Barta ra Tatkalin Rajnaitik Nikasko Prashna* (Publication Department, Special Central Command, CPN [Maoist], Kathmandu, Fagun 2059 BS).

9. Dr Bhattarai, *Barta ra Tatkalin Rajnaitik Nikasko Prashna*, https://www.satp.org/satporgtp/countries/nepal/document/papers/40points.htm

Part II: The People's War

Chapter 8: From Free Bird to Fugitive

1. This paper was printed in *Symphony of Freedom: Papers on Nationality Question* (All India People's Resistance Forum, Hyderabad, 1996).

2. Unfortunately, I do not recall the exact names of the papers.

3. *State of Nepal*, Kanak Mani Dixit and Shastri Ramachandaran (eds.) (Himal Books, Lalitpur, 2002).

4. Debates within the communist party on differing ideas are traditionally called 'two-line struggle'.

Chapter 9: Relationship Between Leaders

1. Isaac Deutscher, *Stalin: A Political Biography* (Penguin Books, 1949), p. 368.

2. Rashmi Kandel and Yam Chaulagain, *Nepalese People's War: Biographical Accounts of Its Leaders* (Shabda Satabdee, Kathmandu, 2010).

3. Surendra K.C. (2056 BS), *Nepalma Communist Andolanko Itihas (Pahilo Bhag)* (Vidhyarthi Pustak Bhandar, Kathmandu).

4. Pushpa Lal, *Pushpa Lal: Historical Notes* (Pushpalal Memorial Foundation, Kathmandu, 2010).

5. Surendra K.C., *Nepalma Communist Andolanko Itihas (Pahilo Bhag)*.

6. Anirban Roy, *Prachanda: The Unknown Revolutionary* (Mandala Book Point, Kathmandu, 2008).

7. *Historical Documents of Nepali Communist Movements and People's Revolution*, vol. 1, pp. 393–94.

8. Ibid.

Chapter 10: Centralization of Leadership

1. Dr Baburam Bhattarai (2068 BS), *Maobadibhitra: Baicharik-Rajnaitik Sangharsha* (Jhilko Prakashan Pra. Li., Kathmandu).

2. Jenny Marx Longuet, *The Daughters of Karl Marx: Family Correspondence, 1866–1898* (Houghton Mifflin Harcourt, US, 1982).

3. Dr Bhattarai (2060 BS), *Nepali Krantika Adharharu* (Janadisha Prakashan, Nepal).

4. Netra Panthi, *Divorce Prachanda ra Baburam ko: Rakta Ranjit Yuddha Saathi Ka Antaranga Katha* (Walking Orange, 2016).

5. I had heard this personally.

6. Within the party, Alok's strong tendency towards petty bourgeoisie was known as 'Alok tendency'. He was found extorting money to fulfil his lavish needs, was caught having an illicit affair with a cadre although he was already married, and his bullying and rash decisions led to unnecessary deaths of cadres and civilians.

7. Wagle, an alternate politburo member of the party, was martyred in 2000 in Gorkha.

Chapter 11: 'I Will Fight with a Fuse Attached to My Heart'

1. *Some Important Documents of Communist Party of Nepal (Maoist)*, (Janadisha Publications, Nepal, 2004).

2. Fernando Claudin, 'The Communist Movement: From Comintern to Cominform', *Monthly Review Press* (New York, 1975), https://www.marxists.org/history/etol/writers/birchall/1976/03/claudin.htm

3. Mao Zedong, 'Talks with Responsible Comrades at Various Places during Provincial Tour from the Middle of August to 12 September 1971', https://www.marxists.org/reference/archive/mao/selected-works/volume-9/mswv9_88.htm

4. Explained in the political resolution adopted during the Chunwang meeting of the Maoist party in September 2005. See CPN (Maoist), 'Rajnaitik Evam Sangathanatmak Prastab', *Historical Documents*, vol. 1 (Nepal: UCPNM, Magarat Rajya Samiti, 2069 v.s. [2057 v.s.]), p. 577.

5. A summary of the political document of the second national conference is available in Nepali. See CPN (Maoist), 'Mahan Agragami Chhalang: Itihasko Apariharya Avashyakta', in *Historical Documents*, vol. 1 (Nepal: UCPNM, Magarat Rajya Samiti, 2069 v.s. [2057 v.s.]), pp. 461–503.

6. Mao Zedong, 'Talks at the Chengtu Conference (March 1958)', in *Mao Tse-Tung Unrehearsed: Talks and Letters: 1956– 71*, ed. Stuart R. Schram (Penguin, Harmondsworth, UK, 1974), pp. 96–124.

Chapter 12: Development of Democracy in the Twenty-First Century

1. Prakash A. Raj, *'Kay Gardeko?': The Royal Massacre in Nepal* (Rupa & Co., New Delhi, 2001).

2. Prashant Jha, *Battles of the New Republic: A Contemporary History of Nepal* (Aleph Book Company, 2014).

3. Asmita Singh, 'Ideas and Practices of Democracy: An Analysis of Maoist Politics in Nepal (1996–2015)', dissertation submitted to JNU for MPhil, pp. 81–87.

4. RIM (Revolutionary International Movement) is an international organization of Maoist parties and organizations. It was founded in 1984. The CPN (Maoist) had been one of its active members.
5. Summary of the document. See CPNM, 'Itihaska Anubhav ra ekkaisoun Shatabdima Janabadko Bikasbare', in *Historical Documents*, vol. 1 (Nepal: UCPNM, Magarat Rajya Samiti, 2069 v.s. [2057 v.s.]), pp. 527–31.

Chapter 13: Solidarity, Sabotage and the South Block

1. Surendra K.C. (2056 BS), *Nepalma Communist Andolanko Itihas (Pahilo Bhag)* (Vidhyarthi Pustak Bhandar, Kathmandu).
2. For instance, B.P. Koirala was arrested in Benaras in 1942. To get a brief idea of Koirala's association with the Quit India Movement and the Rana regime's pro-British stance, see Bimal Prasad's 'Jayaprakash Narayan and Nepal', in *Nepal in Transition: A Way Forward*, ed. D.P. Tripathi (Vij Books India, New Delhi, 2012), pp. 133–36.
3. Timila Yami Thapa (2046 BS), 'Dharma Ratna "Yami" Smriti Granth', Kathmandu.
4. AINSA is an all-India organization. We had observed this during our stay there in 1977–81.
5. Dr Baburam Bhattarai, *The Nature of Underdevelopment and Regional Structure of Nepal: A Marxist Analysis* (Adroit Publishers, New Delhi, 2003); Dr Bhattarai, *Nepal: A Marxist View* (Jhilko Publications Pvt. Ltd., Kathmandu, 1990).
6. Dr Baburam Bhattarai (2060 BS), *Nepali Krantika Adharharu* (Janadisha Prakashan, Nepal).
7. Author's conversation with Raju Nepali, one of the presidents of ABNES.
8. Based on the author's conversation with T.B. Pathak.
9. Sudhir Sharma (2070 Bhadra BS), Prayogshala, in *Nepali Sankraman ma Dilli, Darbar ra Maobadi* (FinePrint, Kathmandu).

Chapter 14: 'Workers of All Countries, Unite!'

1. Various issues of *A World to Win* magazine. The magazine is the unofficial magazine of the Committee of RIM (CoRIM), published from 1981 to 2006; *Two-Line Struggle Within RIM (In Context of the Maoist 'Revolution' in Nepal)*, Mohan Bikram Singh (ed.) (Yug Jyoti Publication, Kathmandu, 2009).
2. From various issues of *The Worker* (an organ of the Unified Communist Party of Nepal [Maoist]), atfreespeech@ bannedthought.net.
3. Author's conversation with Suresh Ale Magar, a staff member of the World People's Resistance Movement representing CPN (Maoist) in South Asia.
4. Li Onesto, *Dispatches from the People's War in Nepal* (Pluto Press, London, 2004).
5. See 'Press Statement' in *People's March*, vol. 2, no. 9 (September 2001).
6. Sudhir Sharma (2070 Bhadra BS), Prayogshala, in *Nepali Sankraman ma Dilli, Darbar ra Maobadi* (FinePrint, Kathmandu), p. 153.
7. Ibid.
8. Bhagirathi Yogi, 'Peaceniks on Warpath: Activists Launch Campaign against Military Aid to Nepal', *Nepali Times*, (15–21 November 2002), http://himalaya.socanth.cam.ac.uk/ collections/journals/nepalitimes/pdf/nepali_ Times_119.pdf.
9. Author's conversation with BRB who was in-charge of the international department.
10. *Two-Line Struggle Within RIM*, Mohan Bikram Singh (ed.).

Chapter 15: Tears in Phuntiwang

1. Netra Panthi (2069 BS), *Maobadibhitra Antarsangharsh: Ekta Mahadhiweshan Dekhi Party Bibhazan Sammaka Dastawej Sahit* (Bishwonepali Publication, Kathmandu), p. 92.

2. Dr Baburam Bhattarai, *Monarchy vs Democracy: The Epic Fight in Nepal* (Samkaleen Teesari Duniya, New Delhi, 2005); Manjushree Thapa, *Forget Kathmandu: An Elegy for Democracy* (Penguin Books, New Delhi, 2005).

Chapter 16: Red Flag over Rolpa

1. Author's conversation with Santosh Budha Magar, the head of URPC, Rolpa.
2. *Two-Line Struggle Within RIM (In Context of the Maoist 'Revolution' in Nepal)*, Mohan Bikram Singh (ed.) (Yug Jyoti Publication, Kathmandu, 2009).
3. I received this information from the head of Magarat Autonomous People's Council, Santosh Budhamagar, in Thawang.
4. Author's conversation with Santosh Budha Magar.
5. Li Onesto, *Dispatches from the People's War in Nepal* (Pluto Press, London, 2004).
6. The formation and tasks of the 'militia' are explained in Chapter 24.
7. Lisne encounter, in Pasang, *Red Strides of the History: Significant Military Raids of the People's War,* (Agnipariksha Janaprakashan Griha, Kathmandu, 2008), p. 147.
8. Pasang, *Red Strides of the History.*
9. Based on a conversation with Com. Ganapati, the general secretary of the CPI (ML) PW group.

Chapter 17: Liberation or Death?

1. This book is a collection of the memoirs of five young women of the 1870s. It is edited and translated from the Russian by Barbara Engel and Clifford N. Rosenthal.
2. Shekhar Gupta, P. Jayram, Kavitha Shetty and Anand Vishwanathan, 'Swallow Poison Rather Than be Arrested Is LTTe's Credo', *India Today*, 30 June 1991, https://www.indiatoday.in/magazine/cover-story/story/19910630-swallow-poison-rather-than-be-arrested-is-ltte-credo-815526-1991-06-30

3. *Historical Documents of Nepalese Communist Movement and People's Revolution*, vol. 1, Ekikrit Nepal Cammunist Party (Maobadi), 2069 Magh BS, p. 498.
4. Barbara Nimri Aziz (2001), *Heir to a Silent Song: Two Rebel Women of Nepal* (Centre for Nepal and Asian Studies, Kathmandu).
5. Ludwig F. Stiller (1973), *The Rise of the House of Gorkha: A Study in the Unification of Nepal, 1768–1816* (Manjusri Publication House, Kathmandu).
6. Akhil Nepal Mahila Sangh (Krantikari) Kendriye Samiti (2062 BS), *Mahila Sahid Gatha* (Krantikari Mahila Sahid ko Samman ma).
7. Mandira Sharma and Dinesh Prasain, 'Gender Dimensions of the People's War: Some Reflections on the experiences of Rural Women', in *Himalayan 'People's War': Nepal's Maoist Rebellion*, Michael Hutt (ed.) (Hurst & Company, London, 1988), p. 154.
8. Shuvashankar Kandel (2065 BS), *Maobadi: Bidroha, Bibad ra Rupantaran* (Pairavi Prakashan, Kathmandu), pp. 273–75.
9. Hisila Yami, *People's War and Women's Liberation in Nepal* (Purvaiya Prakashan, Raipur, 2006).
10. Mass fronts are entry points for reaching the party, the PLA and people's council, which explains the presence of women in the central committee in mass fronts.
11. A more detailed and tabulated report of the survey can be found in Yami, *People's War and Women's Liberation in Nepal.*

Chapter 18: Love, Marriage and Children

1. His political status was reduced from that of a general secretary to an ordinary party member.
2. *Historical Documents of Nepalese Communist Movement and People's Revolution*, vol. 1, pp. 393–94.
3. *Historical Documents of Nepalese Communist Movement and People's Revolution*, vol. 1, p. 394
4. Hisila Yami and Baburam Bhattarai (2063 BS), *Marxbaad ra Mahila Mukti* (*Marxism and Women's Liberation: A Collection of Political Essays*) (Twoline Publication Pvt. Ltd, Kathmandu).

5. Baburam Bhattarai, 'Janayuddhalai Prem Garna Sikoun', in *Marxbaad ra Mahila Mukti*, second edition, pp. 99–102.

6. Baburam Bhattarai, 'Naitiktako Prashna ra Janayuddha', in *Marxbaad ra Mahila Mukti*, second edition, pp. 103–06.

7. Shobha Gautam, 'Women and Children in the Periphery of the Maoists' People's War', Institute of Human Rights Communication, Nepal (2001), https://epalconflictreport.ohchr.org/files/docs/2001-12-00_report_ ihricon_eng.pdf

Chapter 19: Rape, Rebellion and Resistance

1. L.S. Chakraborty, 'Gender Bias in South Asia', *Economic & Political Weekly*, vol. 36, Issue no. 42, 20 October 2001.

2. 'Rape and murder of Nirmala Panta', Wikipedia, https://en.wikipedia.org/wiki/Rape_and_murder_of_Nirmala_Panta

3. Author's conversation with an Iranian woman representative of the RIM during the PW period.

4. Khas Arya is the common term used for upper-caste Hindu hill-origin groups, or *pahadi*s, who comprise 31.2 per cent of the total population according to the national census of 2011. Pahadis include hill Dalit, as well as hill indigenous, groups.

5. Hisila Yami, *People's War and Women's Liberation in Nepal* (Purvaiya Prakashan, Raipur, 2006).

6. Akhil Nepal Mahila Sangh (Krantikari) Kendriye Samiti (2062 BS), *Mahila Sahid Gatha* (Krantikari Mahila Sahid ko Samman ma).

7. Ibid.

8. Ibid.

9. Ibid.

10. Ibid.

11. This was revealed to me by one of my Tharu staff members when I was working in Rolpa. According to her, these incidents took place in Banke and Bardia districts.

12. Yami, *People's War and Women's Liberation in Nepal*.

13. Uma Bhujel (2064 BS), *Banda Parkhaldekhi Khula AkashSamma (Aitihasik Gorkha Jailbreak)* (Janadisha Prakashan, Kathmandu).

Chapter 20: 'Are You a Newar or a Nepali?'

1. Author's conversation with Santosh Budha Magar.
2. Ibid.
3. Dhanbahadur Rokka and Karnabahadur Budhamagar, 'Magarjatiko Bhashik Samipyata', in *Magar Jati: Aitihasik, Sanskritik ra Rajnitik Sandarva*', Yambahadur Pun and Jhapendra Ghartimagar (eds.) (Magar Pragik Samuha, Kathmandu, 2014), p. 101.
4. Based on a conversation with Pawanman Shrestha, the founder-president of Newa Khala and Newa Mukti Morcha.
5. Nepalbhasha Sangharsha Samiti (2057 BS Baisakh 23), 'Bhadau 30ya swoniga banda'.
6. Based on a conversation with Pawanman Shrestha.
7. Ekikrit Nepal Communist Party (Maobadi): Magarat Rajya Sammelan Aayojak Samiti (January 2013), *Historical Documents of Nepalese Communist Movement and People's Revolution*, vol. 1.
8. Dr Maheshman Shrestha, 'Newa Adhikar' (Newa Jagaran Manch, Kathmandu, 2014).
9. Prashant Jha, *Battles of the New Republic, A Contemporary History of Nepal*, Aleph Book Company (2014).
10. Rambahadur Thapamagar, *Janayudhhama Adibasi Janajati:Magar Sahabhagitaka Karan ra Parinam* (Bina Rana, Kathmandu, 2014).
11. For more, visit http://www.inseconline.org/victim/candidate_display_user. php?pageno=1
12. Dr Baburam Bhattarai, 'Janayudha ra Newar Jatiya Mukti ko Prashna', *Janadesh*, 1996.
13. For more, visit http://www.inseconline.org/victim/candidate_display_user. php?pageno=1
14. Some of his books include *Hamro Rashtriyata* (Kathmandu: Yami Prakashan); *Nepal Ka Kura* (Kathmandu: Yami Prakashan); *Samajko Euta Jhalak* (Kalimpong: SDPO Upasak).
15. Kesar Lall (translated from Nepal Bhasa), *The Life and Times of Kavi Keshari Chittadhar 'Hridaya'*, 2006.
16. Ibid.
17. People of the merchant caste/clan within the Newar community have traditionally been engaged in trade with Tibet for centuries.

My family belongs to the Newar merchant clan called Udaya, hence the Tibetan influence in these names.

18. The word *tula* means 'weighing scale' and *dhar* connotes 'possessor'.
19. 'Symphony of Freedom: Papers on Nationality Question' (All-India People's Resistance Forum, Hyderabad, 1996).

Chapter 21: The Oppressed of the Oppressed

1. Deepak Limbu, '*Manche MancheYeutai Ho Ni*', YouTube, https://www.youtube.com/watch?v=QPhdo3DOwZU.
2. Anil Thapa (2073, bhadau BS), *Abiram Baburam* (Sangri-La Books, Kathmandu).
3. Rajendra Maharjan, 'Buddha, Marx, and Ambedkar', in Dr B.R. Ambedkar, *Buddha and Karl Marx*, ed. Rajendra Maharjan and Shiva Hari Gyawali, trans. Mahesh Raj Maharjan (Nepal: SAMATA Foundation, 2017), pp. 7–8.
4. 'Nepali Janayodhaka Mahan Amar Shaheedharu', Kendriya Prakashan Bibhag ne Ka Pa (Maobadi).
5. Hisila Yami, *People's War and Women's Liberation in Nepal* (Purvaiya Prakashan, Raipur, 2006).
6. Yam Bahadur Kisan and Devendra Kumar Rasaili, *Kami of Nepal* (Central Department of Sociology/Anthropology, Tribhuvan University, Nepal, 2014).
7. Yam Bahadur Kisan and Gopal Nepali, *Badi of Nepal* (Central Department of Sociology/Anthropology, Tribhuvan University, Nepal 2014); Dilli Ram Dahal and Seema Viswakarma, *Dom of Nepal* (Central Department of Sociology/Anthropology, Tribhuvan University, Nepal, 2014).
8. 'People's War and the Question of Dalits', in Yami, *People's War and Women's Liberation in Nepal*.

Chapter 22: A Twenty-First-Century Political Sati

1. Dr Baburam Bhattarai (2068 BS), *Maobadibhitra: Baicharik-Rajnaitik Sangharsha* (Jhilko Prakashan Pra. Li., Kathmandu), pp. 1–4.

2. Ibid, pp. 5–12.

3. Dr Baburam Bhattarai, *Monarchy vs Democracy: The Epic Fight in Nepal* (Samkaleen Teesari Duniya, New Delhi, 2005).

4. Dr Baburam Bhattarai, 'Princely Tendency and Democracy', in *Monarchy vs. Democracy*, p. 16.

5. Bhattarai, *Maobadibhitra: Baicharik- Rajnaitik Sangharsha*, pp. 13–34.

6. Sati is an ancient custom in which a widowed woman was burnt alive on her husband's funeral pyre.

7. Shuvashankar Kandel (2065 BS), *Maobadi: Bidroha, Bibad ra Rupantaran* (Pairavi Prakashan, Kathmandu), p. 122.

8. Asmita Khadka, 'Maobadi Hirasat Barbartako Kendra', *Himal Khabarpatrika* (16–30 December 2012).

9. Based on a conversation with Kalpana and Devendra Parajuli.

10. Based on a conversation with Biswadeep Pandey.

11. Author's conversation with Om Sharma.

12. Author's conversation with Manarishi.

13. Pasang, *Red Strides of the History: Significant Military Raids of the People's War,* (Agnipariksha Janaprakashan Griha, Kathmandu, 2008.

14. There was only one central HQ, but it was mobile in tandem with the mobility of Prachanda.

15. Conversation with Prachanda after our relations became normal with him.

16. I was unable to locate the tape at the time of writing this. The tape was released by the RNA before the Khara attack.

Chapter 23: When I Saw the Siberian Birds

1. Prashant Jha, *Battles of the New Republic: A Contemporary History of Nepal* (Aleph Book Company, 2014).

2. Dipak Sapkota, *Ten Years of Upheaval: Reportage of the Decade-Long Maoist People's War in Nepal,* Revolutionary Journalist Association (Central Committee, 2010).

3. 'Political and Organizational Proposal' in *Historical Documents of Nepalese Communist Movement and People's Revolution*, vol. 1; Unified Nepal Communist Party (Maoist), pp. 566–80.

4. Ibid.

5. G.V. Plekhanov, 'On the Question of the Individual's Role in History', in *Georgi Plekhanov: Selected Philosophical Works*, vol. II (Progress Publishers, Moscow,1976), https://www.marxists.org/archive/plekhanov/1898/xx/individual.html

6. *Chunwang Opera: Returning from the Battlefield*, available on YouTube.

7. This is available on YouTube at https://youtu.be/ StZD9hrFZkw

8. I got this information through a conversation with him. Comr. Sunil is now martyred.

9. Netra Panthi (2069 BS), *Maobadibhitra Antarsangharsh: Ekta Mahadhiweshan Dekhi Party Bibhazan Sammaka Dastawej Sahit* (Bishwonepali Publication, Kathmandu).

Chapter 24: Dhai-Futte Sena

1. Hisila Yami, 'Ke Mahilaharu Sharirik Roople Nai Kamjor hun Ta? (Are Women Really Physically Weak?)', in Yami and Bhattarai, *Marxbaad ra Mahila Mukti*, second edition (Two-Line Publication, 2007), pp. 8–15.

2. Mao Zedong, *Selected Works*, vol. II (People's Publishing House, Beijing), p. 224.

3. The YCL later converted into a militia, the military wing of the PLA after the PW started. It was revived after the PW ended.

4. Based on my conversation with Bhakta Bahadur Shah, 7th division commissar of the PLA and CC member of the CPN (Maoist).

5. Anand Swaroop Verma, *Maoist Movement in Nepal* (Samkaleen Teesari Duniya, New Delhi, 2001), p. 139.

6. Dipak Sapkota, *Ten Years of Upheaval: Reportage of the Decade-Long Maoist People's War in Nepal*, Revolutionary Journalist Association (Central Committee, 2010).

7. Hisila Yami, *People's War and Women's Liberation in Nepal* (Purvaiya Prakashan, Raipur, 2006).

8. Sapkota, *Ten Years of Upheaval*.

9. Ibid.

10. Bhaskar Gautam, Purna Basnet and Chiran Manandhar (eds.), *Maobadi Bidroha: Sashatra Sangharshako Abadhi*, (Martin Chautari, Kathmandu, 2007), p. 404.

11. Sitaram Baral (2073 BS), *Chacha: Bhakti Prasad Pandeyko Sangharshyatra*' (Sangri-La Books, Kathmandu).

12. Ibid, p. 111.

13. Ibid.

14. Ashok K. Mehta, *The Royal Nepal Army: Meeting the Maoist Challenge* (Rupa & Co., New Delhi, 2003).

15. Gautam, Basnet and Manandhar, *Maobadi Bidroha*, p. 404.

16. Sapkota, *Ten Years of Upheaval, Reportage of the Decade-Long Maoist People's War in Nepal*.

17. For more, visit https://www.hrw.org/world-report/2020/country-chapters/nepal Sapkota, *Ten Years of Upheaval, Reportage of the Decade-Long Maoist People's War in Nepal*.

18. Sapkota, *Ten Years of Upheaval, Reportage of the Decade-Long Maoist People's War in Nepal*.

Chapter 25: Drums, Pen and Rifle

1. Chunnu Gurung, 'Timi sangha gahiro maya basyo Jaljala'. Available at https://www.youtube.com/watch?v=eFBk5nlh0o4

2. Akhil Nepal Mahila Sangh (Krantikari) Kendriye Samiti (2062 BS), *Mahila Sahid Gatha* (Krantikari Mahila Sahid ko Samman ma).

3. Unfortunately, I do not have a copy of the newspaper *Jana Awaj*.

4. Author's conversation with Khushiram Pakhrin, the convener of the Samana Pariwar cultural front.

5. Chaitanya, *Kranti ra Saundarya (Revolution and Aesthetics)* (Pragatishil Adhyan Kendra, Kathmandu, 2007).

6. Author's conversation with Khushiram Pakhrin.

7. Martyrs' Road is a 91-kilometre road from Rolpa to Rukum, constructed by the Maoists with the help of the locals, the PLA and Maoist cadres during the PW.

8. Author's conversation with Khushiram Pakhrin.

9. Dipak Sapkota, *Ten Years of Upheaval: Reportage of the Decade-Long Maoist People's War in Nepal,* Revolutionary Journalist Association (Central Committee, 2010), p. 254.

Part III: A New Beginning

Chapter 26: Maoists in Kathmandu

1. Author's conversation with Bamdev Chhetri.
2. Dinanath Sharma (2063 BS), 'Rabindra Prakaran Awasarbadiharuko Bahirgamanbare', in *Krantikari Bidrohaka Aadharharu* (Janadhwani Prakashan, Kathmandu).
3. For more, visit http://www.inseconline.org/victim/candidate_display_user. php?pageno=1
4. Dipak Sapkota, *Ten Years of Upheaval: Reportage of the Decade-Long Maoist People's War in Nepal,* Revolutionary Journalist Association (Central Committee, 2010).
5. Newa Rastriya Mukti Morcha (2063 BS Chaitra 2–5), 'Nepaya Nikwogu Rashtriya Sammelana Parit: Bidhan wa Pratibedan'.
6. Dr Baburam Bhattarai (2066 BS), *Janayudha ra Newar Jatiya Muktiko Prashna* (Sandhya Times Publication, Kathmandu).

Chapter 27: How Monarchy Was Abolished Inch-by-Inch

1. Hisila Yami, 'Women's Role in the Nepalese Movement: Making a People's Constitution', *Monthly Review*, 21 March 2010, https://monthlyreview.org/commentary/womens- role-in-the-nepalese-movement
2. Grishna Bahadur Devkota, *Nepalko Rajnitik Darpan (Political Mirror of Nepal)* (K.C. Gautam, Kathmandu, 1959).
3. Anil Thapa (2073 Bhadau BS), *Abiram Baburam* (Sangrila Books, Kathmandu).
4. S. D. Muni, *Maoist Insurgency in Nepal: The Challenge and the Response* (Rupa & Co, New Delhi, 2003).
5. Sudhir Sharma (2070 Bhadra BS), *Prayogshala, Nepali Sankraman ma Dilli, Darbar ra Maobadi* (FinePrint, Kathmandu).

6. Julia Lovell, *Maoism: A Global History* (Bodley Head, London, 2019).

7. Ibid.

8. *From Conflict to Peace in Nepal, Peace Agreements 2005–10* (Asian Study Center for Peace and Conflict Transformation, Kathmandu, 2011).

9. Dipak Sapkota, *Ten Years of Upheaval: Reportage of the Decade-Long Maoist People's War in Nepal,* Revolutionary Journalist Association (Central Committee, 2010).

10. Mallika Shakya, *Death of an Industry: The Cultural Politics of Garment Manufacturing during the Maoist Revolution in Nepal* (Cambridge University Press, UK (2018).

11. Sharma, *Prayogshala.*

12. Sapkota, *Ten Years of Upheaval.*

13. Prashant Jha, *Battles of the New Republic: A Contemporary History of Nepal* (Aleph Book Company, 2014); Sharma, *Prayogshala.*

14. *From Conflict to Peace in Nepal, Peace Agreements 2005–10.*

15. Sharma, *Prayogshala.*

16. Author's eyewitness account as a member of the first CA.

17. Sharma, *Prayogshala,* p. 275.

18. *The Oxford India Nehru,* Uma Iyengar (ed.) (Oxford University Press, New Delhi, 2007), p. 207.

19. Sharma, *Prayogshala.*

Chapter 28: Bungee-Jumping My Way to a Republican State:

1. Nepal Sarkar Bhautik Yojana Tatha Nirman Mantralaya, Singha Durbar (2064 BS), 'Naya Nepal ko Aadhar-Naya Bhautik Purwadhar: Soch Patra 2064–84'.

2. Prashant Jha, *Battles of the New Republic: A Contemporary History of Nepal* (Aleph Book Company, 2014).

3. Author's conversation with Ramakant Shah, one of the survivors of the massacre.

4. For more, visit https://www.nationalgeographic.com/adventure/ adventure- blog/2009/11/12/best-new-trips-in-the-world-trekking-nepals- himalayas/

5. Author's conversation with B.K. Mansingh, chairman of Nepal
    Airlines Corporation, while she was the minister of tourism and
    civil aviation.

Chapter 29: Fall of Prachanda

1. Sudhir Sharma (2070 Bhadra BS), *Prayogshala*, in *Nepali
    Sankraman ma Dilli, Darbar ra Maobadi* (FinePrint, Kathmandu).
2. Ibid.
3. General Rookmangud Katawal, *Rookmangud Katawal: An
    Autobiography* (Nepa-laya, Kathmandu, 2014).
4. Cited in *Rookmangud Katawal: An autobiography.*
5. General Katawal's response is reproduced in *Rookmangud
    Katawal.*
6. Sharma, *Prayogshala.*
7. Ibid.
8. Ibid.
9. Sudheer Sharma, *The Nepal Nexus: An inside Account of the
    Maoists, the Durbar and New Delhi* (Penguin Viking, 2019).
10. Sharma, *Prayogshala.*
11. Nepal Sarkar Artha Mantralaya (2065 BS), 'Arthik Barsha
    2065–2066 (BS) ko Budget Baktabya'.
12. More details are available in BRB's 2008–09 budget speech,
    https://mof.gov.np/uploads/document/file/Final%20
    Translation% 20Bud%202008-09%20(1)_20141228082419.pdf
13. Sharma, *Prayogshala.*

Chapter 30: From Herder to Prime Minister

1. BIPPA is an agreement that was signed between the governments
    of Nepal and India. Nepal lacks large-scale investment. BIPPA
    was looked upon as a step to help promote, protect and encourage
    investments in Nepal with all kinds of incentives for the investors
    to stay on. It was signed on 21 October 2011. However, it was
    perceived as a sell-out to foreign investors, thus the tag 'anti-
    national'.

2. Author and BRB's private conversations with certain military personnel.

3. 'Pradhan Mantri Dr. Babu Ram Bhattarai ko Netritoma Gathit Samyukta Sarkar ka Pramukh Kam ra Uplabdhi', Pradhanmantri Tatha Mantri Parishad ko Karyalaya, Nepal Sarkar, Kathmandu (2069 BS).

4. Ibid.

5. 'Hello Sarkar Launched in Pokhara', *Himalayan*, 18 January 2016, https://thehimalayantimes.com/nepal/hello-sarkar-launched-in- pokhara/

6. Government of Nepal's National Planning Commission, National Pride Projects, https://www.npc.gov.np/en/page/74/visualing_development/data/national_pride_projects

7. Anil Thapa (2073 Bhadau BS), *Abiram Baburam* (Sangrila Books, Kathmandu).

8. Ibid.

9. Ibid.

10. Gopal Sharma, 'Chief Justice to Lead Nepal's Interim Government to Elections', Reuters, 14 March 2013, https://www.reuters.com/article/us-nepal-politics-government/chief-justice-to-lead-nepals-interim-government-to-elections-idUSBRe92C1BL20130313

Chapter 31: The Cost of being First Lady

1. *Crime Today: Masik Khabarpatrika*, L.S. Lama (ed.) (Kathmandu, May 2013).

2. 'Baluwatarma Pradhan Mantri ko Bhansabatai Bhadakuda Gayab' (2073 Sawan, 21), Onlinekhabar.com

3. This was conveyed to me by one of BRB's secretaries who later became an adviser to BRB.

4. The senior editor who wrote this article has been postponing sending the article, although he personally came to say that he did not mean to write it in the way the author and others understood it. The writer is Dev Prasad Tripathi, editor-in-chief of the weekly paper *Ghatana ra Bichhar*.

5. Daniel Halper, *Clinton,Inc.: The Audacious Rebuilding of a Political Machine* (HarperCollins Publishers, New York, 2012).
6. For more, visit https://en.wikipedia.org/wiki/nanda_Prasad_Adhikari
7. Author's recollection of an interview on television.
8. Author's private conversations.

Chapter 32: The Cost of Being Middle-of-the-Roader

1. Sudhir Sharma (2070 Bhadra BS), *Prayogshala*, in *Nepali Sankraman ma Dilli, Darbar ra Maobadi* (FinePrint, Kathmandu).
2. Hisila Yami, 'Women's Role in the Nepalese Movement: Making a People's Constitution', *Monthly Review*, 21 March 2010, https://monthlyreview.org/commentary/womens- role-in-the-nepalese-movement
3. Anil Thapa (2073 Bhadau BS), *Abiram Baburam* (Sangrila Books, Kathmandu).
4. As discussed in party meetings attended by the author.
5. Anil Thapa, *Abiram Baburam*.
6. *Sabdhya Times*, 12 November 2013, p. 1.
7. One of those who threw a bomb and lost their hand belonged to Kiran's faction. He had been imprisoned according to a local newspaper I had read then.
8. *Crime Today: Masik Khabarpatrika*, L.S. Lama (ed.) (Kathmandu, May 2013).

Chapter 33: Prachanda and BRB

1. Ekikrit Nepal Communist Party (Maobadi): Magarat Rajya Sammelan Aayojak Samiti (January 2013), *Historical Documents of Nepalese Communist Movement and People's Revolution*, vol. 1.
2. Prachanda, 'Some Ideological and Military Questions Raised by People's War', in *Problems & Prospects of Revolution in Nepal [A Collections of Articles by Com. Prachanda and Other Leaders of the CPN(Maoist)]* (Janadisha Publications, Nepal, 2004).

3. Dipak Sapkota, *Ten Years of Upheaval: Reportage of the Decade-Long Maoist People's War in Nepal,* Revolutionary Journalist Association (Central Committee, 2010).
4. Ibid.
5. Anirban Roy (2065 BS), *Prachanda: Ek Agyat Bidrohi* (Yug Publication, Kathmandu).
6. Shuvashankar Kandel (2065 BS), *Maobadi: Bidroha, Bibad ra Rupantaran* (Pairavi Prakashan, Kathmandu).
7. Ibid.

Chapter 34: My Relationship with Prachanda

1. *Crime Today: Masik Khabarpatrika,* L.S. Lama (ed.) (Kathmandu, May 2013).
2. Author's private conversation with media professionals.
3. For more, visit https://www.marxists.org/archive/marx/works/1852/18th-brumaire/
4. For more, visit https://www.reddit.com/r/nepal/comments/b2ubd3/nepotism_of_prachanda/

Chapter 35: My Relationship with BRB

1. You can follow BRB on Twitter at: @brb1954
2. 'World Cup Dohori Baburam Bhattarai and Hisila Yami', YouTube, RamSar Media Pvt. Ltd, 26 June 2014, https://www.youtube.com/watch?v=D-35I8kvOC0

Chapter 36: Manushi, Asmita and Astha

1. Dharma Ratna Yami, *Reply from Tibet* (Vajra Books, Kathmandu, 2017).
2. The Treaty of Sugauli, which was signed on 2 December 1815 and ratified on 4 March 1816, was signed between the East India Company and the king of Nepal. This followed the Anglo–Nepalese War of 1814–16, which Nepal lost. The present boundary of Nepal is the result of this treaty.

3. Daughter of Nepal, Painted Tree Pictures, Surbhi Dewan (2018).

4. Rosemary Sullivan, *Stalin's Daughter: The Extraordinary and Tumultuous Life of Svetlana Alliluyeva* (4th Estate, London, 2015).

Chapter 37: Army Integration and State Restructuring

1. Mao Zedong, *Selected Works of Mao Tse-Tung*, vol. IV, Foreign Languages Press, 1975.

2. Elaborated on page 176 of the document cited above. See the paragraph beginning with 'After the first CA election, a common understanding was reached...'

3. *From Conflict to Peace in Nepal, Peace Agreements 2005–10* (Asian Study Center for Peace and Conflict Transformation, Kathmandu, 2011).

4. Ibid.

5. Anil Thapa (2073 Bhadau BS), *Abiram Baburam* (Sangrila Books, Kathmandu), p. 237.

6. Rameswar Bohra, 'War-makers to Peace-keeping', *Nepal Times*, 4–10 September 2015.

7. Thapa, *Abiram Baburam*, p. 238.

8. Ibid., p. 237.

9. 'Prachanda Speaking about Combatant Numbers and Verification at Shaktikhor', YouTube, Nepalnews Mercantile, 8 May 2009, https://www.youtube.com/watch?v=6EoQYZ2oa6M.

10. *Nepal in Transition: From People's War to Fragile Peace*, Sebastian Von Winsiedel, David M. Malone and Suman Pradhan (eds.) (Cambridge University Press, New Delhi, 2012), excerpt available at https://assets.cambridge.org/97811070/05679/frontmatter/9781107005679_frontmatter.pdf

11. General Rookmangud Katawal, *Rookmangud Katawal: An Autobiography* (Nepa-laya, Kathmandu, 2014).

12. I read this in a newspaper around the time of the army integration.

13. Thapa, *Abiram Baburam*.

14. Upendra Yadav, *Conspiracy of Nepali Raj against Madhesh* (Madheshee People's Right Forum-Nepal, Biratnagar, 2012).

15. Rajendra Shrestha, *Bishwoka Sanghiya Rajyaharu, Sambidhansabha Ra Nepalko Bato* (Centre for Federal Studies, Nepal, Kathmandu, 2009).
16. This was because the Bheri-Karnali had a culture and language distinct from Seti-Mahakali. During the PW, separate autonomous regions had been designated based on their identities.
17. Thapa, *Abiram Baburam*.

Chapter 38: Some Reflections

1. *Gorkhapatra* (2059 BS Baisakh 12/25 April 2002), a daily newspaper.
2. Author's personal observation.
3. Author was witness to many such complaints by victims coming to the headquarters of the CPN (Maoist).
4. Mahendra Lawoti, *Towards a Democratic Nepal: Inclusive Political Institutions for a Multicultural Society* (Sage Publications India Pvt. Ltd, New Delhi, 2005).
5. Chaitanya Mishra, 'Locating the "Causes" of the Maoist Struggle', in *Essays on the Sociology of Nepal* (FinePrint, Kathmandu, 2007).

Epilogue

1. *Kathmandu Post Daily*, 25 September 2015.
2. Nepalmag.com.np (Bhadra 6, 2074), 'Awaran Katha: Bichara Baburam'.
3. *The Interim Constitution of Nepal, 2063* (2007), SPCBN/UNDP Nepal (2013), revised fifth edition (Lalitpur, Nepal).
4. Sambidhansabha Sachibalaya, 'Nepalko Sambidhan', Singha Durbar, Kathmandu (2015).
5. https://nepaliheadlines.com/new-force-for-ideology-to-change-society-dr-bhattarai/
6. Ram Rijhan Yadav (2073 BS), *Blackout* (Lal Madhesha Masik, Kathmandu).
7. Prashant Jha, *Battles of the New Republic, A Contemporary History of Nepal* (Aleph Book Company, 2014).

8. Author's conversation with some of the leaders of Terai and Kathmandu.

9. Based on the author's conversation with BRB after the author returned from Moscow.

10. Naya Shakti Party, Wikipedia, https://en.wikipedia.org/wiki/ Naya_Shakti_Party,_Nepal#:~:text=Naya%20Shakti%20 Party%2C%20Nepal%20(Nepali,to%20form%20Samajbadi%20 Party%2C%20Nepal.

11. Rohan S., 'Bhattarai, Yadav form new party', the *Himalayan*, 7 May 2019, https://thehimalayantimes.com/nepal/bhattarai-yadav-form-new-party/